Poetic Maneuvers

Hans Magnus Enzensberger
and the Lyric Genre

CHARLOTTE ANN MELIN

Northwestern

University Press

Evanston

Illinois

Northwestern University Press
Evanston, Illinois 60208-4210

ISBN 0-8101-1946-3 (cloth)
ISBN 0-8101-1947-1 (paper)

The following publishers and authors have given permission to
reprint material in this volume:

Bloodaxe Books Limited for "Summer Poem" and "Bill of Fare," in
Hans Magnus Enzensberger, *Selected Poems,* trans. Hans Magnus
Enzensberger and Michael Hamburger (Newcastle upon Tyne:
Bloodaxe Books, 1994).

Hans Magnus Enzensberger for "Eine Lawine," originally published
in *Baemu suti oder das Ibolitische Vermächtnis: Ein literarisches
Gesellschaftsspiel,* ed. Heinz Gültig (Zurich: Diogenes, 1959).

Sheep Meadow Press for "The War, Like" and "Old Medium," from
Hans Magnus Enzensberger, *Kiosk,* trans. Michael Hamburger and
Hans Magnus Enzensberger (Riverdale-on-Hudson, New York:
Sheep Meadow Press, 1999).

Suhrkamp Verlag for "Locklied" and "Küchenzettel," from
Verteidigung der Wölfe © 1957; "Windgriff," from *Blindenschrift*
© 1964; "G. de' D. (1318–1389)," from *Mausoleum* © 1975; "Weitere
Gründe dafür, daß die Dichter lügen," from *Der Untergang der
Titanic* © 1978; and "Altes Medium" from *Kiosk* © 1995; "Further
Reasons Why Poets Do Not Tell the Truth," from Hans Magnus
Enzensberger, *The Sinking of the Titanic,* trans. Hans Magnus
Enzensberger (Boston: Houghton Mifflin, 1980), 50; "G. de' De"
(or "Giovanni de' Dondi of Padua"), in Hans Magnus Enzensberger,
Mausoleum: Thirty-seven Ballads from the History of Progress, trans.
Joachim Neugroschel (New York: Urizen Books, 1976), 1–3.

Library of Congress Cataloging-in-Publication data are available
from the Library of Congress.

Contents

Acknowledgments

At the outset I could not have anticipated how this book would be enriched, complicated, and transformed over time, with the support of family, friends, and colleagues; thus I want to thank sincerely a number of individuals whose encouragement helped me realize this project. It grew from initial research in 1982 to 1983, when I benefited from fellowship support from the German Academic Exchange. I gratefully acknowledge the library access extended to me then by the Deutsches Literaturarchiv in Marbach am Neckar, where I spent nearly a year surrounded by archival resources. Ingo Seidler's suggestion to me at that stage that I should explore postwar German poetry from fresh perspectives set me on a path that I continue to follow. Later, this book took shape as its own entity when I joined the faculty at the University of Minnesota. I would like to thank my colleagues for their support and advice of many kinds, including Ruth-Ellen Joeres, James Parente, Ray Wakefield, Jack Zipes, and especially Arlene Teraoka. As I refined my readings, the comments of Jonathan Monroe, James Rolleston, Rainer Rumold, and others were indispensable to making the book what it has become. I am grateful beyond words for Cecile Zorach, whose friendship, keen scholarly insights, constant contact, and willingness to look at whatever I was working on inspired me to persist. For her very careful work in helping me prepare, proofread, and check the manuscript, I also want to thank R. Blythe Inners, who not only learned to decipher my handwriting but also asked all the right questions about what I was really trying to say because she truly appreciates writing. I want to express my appreciation for the attention given to this project by all the individuals who have been involved with it at Northwestern University Press. Finally, I dedicate this book to my husband, Matthew Rohn, who read the earliest drafts and whose companionship has carried me through all things, along with our children, Eric and Anne, my mother and late father, each of whom in my mind has a connection to the fabric of this book.

Introduction

One of the most influential figures of his literary generation in Germany, Hans Magnus Enzensberger (1929–) has played a prominent role in intellectual debates in and outside his country by stimulating discussions about the relationship between literature and social change. Over the past four decades he has reminded authors and intellectuals of their increasingly peripheral situation, yet he has achieved an unusual status for himself as a public intellectual of international stature. Now past the age of seventy, this author, who first made a reputation for himself as an "angry young man," has long been celebrated in Europe for his prolific and provocative publications—texts that encompass poetry, essays, radio plays, fiction, documentary prose, and translations. Recipient of the prestigious Büchner Prize in 1963 and numerous other literary awards, Enzensberger is one of the few post–World War II German authors to have gained appreciable recognition outside Germany. Translations of his works have been published in Great Britain, Italy, Scandinavia, and the United States, where his journalistic pieces have appeared in such prominent publications as *Harper's*, the *New York Times Book Review*, and *Partisan Review*. Most of his major poetry and essay collections are available in English, including the translation he undertook of his epic poem *Der Untergang der Titanic* (1978a), *The Sinking of the Titanic* (1980b).

The project that has occupied Enzensberger since his early career is the task of resisting the marginalization of literature—especially poetry—by connecting it with ethical imperatives of the post-Holocaust era. Critical attention to date has understandably focused on his political views, particularly their expression in essays and documentaries, with the result that little sustained consideration has been directed toward his poems, their relationship to his other texts, and the international frame of reference the author has adopted for his poetic work.[1] Concentrating on Enzensberger's verse, my interpretations explore the insights his poetical texts offer into how political discourses have intersected with aesthetic change in postwar Europe. These readings are supported by details about postwar cultural controversies, literary connections, and Enzensberger's minor publications that have been overlooked in the scholarship.

In considering why Enzensberger made poetry an instrument for social transformation, and to illustrate the characteristic maneuvering that his poetics display, I have chosen to examine critical categories of genre, signification, rhetoric, literary influence, and cultural politics in connection with strategic readings of individual poems from throughout his career. My analysis elucidates Enzensberger's original contributions to the lyric genre, interrelationships across his poetry and prose, and his influence as a literary mediator. Once established as an intelligent, nonconformist thinker, Enzensberger became a figure emulated by German poets. Since the 1970s, a number of international authors have also defined themselves in connection with or opposition to his work.

With his provocative reasoning and multiple interests, Enzensberger has often perplexed scholars. Beyond the texts he has authored, he founded and worked on the influential leftist journal *Kursbuch* from 1965 to 1975, the respected progressive magazine *TransAtlantik* from 1980 to 1982, and the fine book series *Die Andere Bibliothek* beginning in 1989. He served as editor or commentator for numerous anthologies and reissued historical materials, notably the 1966 volume *Kurzgefaßter Bericht von der Verwüstung der Westindischen Länder* (*The Devastation of the Indies: A Brief Account*) by Bartolomé de las Casas and the 1973 work *Gespräche mit Marx und Engels* (*Conversations with Marx and Engels*), which were internationally disseminated. Meanwhile, his poetic writings stand in dialogue with thinking about social issues among contemporary theorists (including Theodor W. Adorno, Jürgen Habermas, and Michel Foucault). They also display a fruitful response to aesthetic insights articulated by literary critics (such as Hugo Friedrich, Susan Sontag, and Hugh Kenner) and to the work of Edward Lear, Lars Gustafsson, Pablo Neruda, Charles Simic, William Carlos Williams, and many other poets whom Enzensberger has translated. An ardent critic of the media, which he terms the "consciousness industry," Enzensberger has nonetheless embraced arguably postmodern attitudes that allow for a redefinition of culture to admit electronic media.[2]

These copious publications tend by their sheer quantity to obfuscate rather than illuminate the assumptions on which his poetry is based. For this reason, my close readings of poems occur in conjunction with an analysis of Enzensberger's poetic program as it emerges from his prose writings. The overarching topics for this study concern the lyric's status as a genre, the integrity of poetic voice, the role intellectual frameworks play in literary creation, the contributions made by spontaneity, and the defining effects of national and international impulses. The broad question of why the lyric genre remains a vital, if specialized, form of artistic discourse guides this discussion. In considering the unique circumstances that have shaped the lyric genre in German-speaking countries, my findings identify compromising moments in poetry's relationship to postwar history, culture, and society.

To comprehend fully the somewhat hesitant transition from modernism to postmodernism in German literature that affects Enzensberger's poetry, however, we need to draw not only on its sociocultural background but also on the type of theoretical frameworks set out by Anthony Easthope (*Poetry as Discourse* [1983], editor with John O. Thompson, *Contemporary Poetry Meets Modern Theory* [1991]), Julia Kristeva (*Revolution in Poetic Language* [1984]), and other scholars who have sought to account for poetry's conceptual parameters. Marjorie Perloff, one of the most respected authorities on contemporary American verse, contends that the factors necessary but often overlooked in poetry interpretation are "a sense of history and a sense of theory" (1998, 182). We need to sharpen these senses and apply this kind of far-ranging critical approach to Enzensberger's work if we are to discern the multiple levels of meaning embedded in his poems.

The critical historical and theoretical tools suggested by Perloff also prove useful in foregrounding the role of transatlantic cultural exchange. Although German postwar verse has developed in a quite different context from English and American literature, it is not isolated from Anglo-American trends. Contemporary German poets have looked at and learned from the American scene with scant attention to whether a particular author represents the objectivist movement, academic verse, beat generation, Black Mountain school, confessional or deep image strands, surrealist or workshop poetry;[3] what interests them are the possibilities for language innovation realized by individual poets. Given the idiosyncratic character of this reception, the instances I reference in American literary history center around authors whose work had a discernible impact on Enzensberger's development.

My first chapter sets the context for discussion of Enzensberger's work by focusing on how postwar German poetry was redefined through companion discourses about interpretation, translation, and literary taste. Ever since Adorno's famous proclamation that to write poetry after Auschwitz is barbaric (1995a, 31), postwar German authors who choose to make poems have felt themselves to be working in an apparently compromised medium. This construction of poetry as a problematic enterprise made it necessary for the lyric genre to assert its autonomy from competing disciplines significant to Enzensberger's poetics.

The analysis begins with a reappraisal of Emil Staiger's conservative genre study *Grundbegriffe der Poetik* (*Basic Concepts of Poetics* [1946]) and Enzensberger's doctoral dissertation (1961) on the German romantic author Clemens Brentano. The contrast between the restricted notion of lyric poetry posed by Staiger's association of the genre with past time and the expansive, dynamic aesthetic of the present (or *Momementaufnahme*, a capturing of the moment) admired by Enzensberger reflects ideological divisions of the postwar era. Expanding on this reexamination of postwar literary discourse, the chapter turns to discussions about translation. Translators' statements enhanced the status of poetry in the 1950s and 1960s by providing a space in which its claims as an aesthetically autonomous medium received validation. I subsequently delineate Enzensberger's reflections on the status of literary works, electronic media, and challenges to literacy. Examples from his poetry and essay collections provide evidence that continuity exists between his early writings about the "consciousness industry" and later deliberations on literacy.

Focusing on the way in which Enzensberger's construction of a naturalized poetic voice responds to the representational crisis after 1945, my second chapter explores connections between his poetry and speculations about literature in contemporaneous essays. This reading takes into account the convergence of two lines of development often considered to be diametrically opposed in German letters. One follows from the synthesis of Marxist analysis and modernism achieved by the Frankfurt school (especially in the work of Adorno, with whom Enzensberger was in close contact). The other displays the influence exerted throughout the 1950s by poet Gottfried Benn and literary historian Hugo Friedrich.

This second chapter moreover supplies an overview of Enzensberger's early career, the period from 1957 to 1965, when he published three poetry collections, an international verse anthology (*Museum der modernen Poesie* [*Museum of Modern Poetry,* first published in 1960]), and two major essay volumes. My discussion traces how Enzensberger's progressive efforts to define a modern literary canon for German readers and to mediate American poetry to a European audience transformed his own verse and distinguished him from his contemporaries. The change from an obtrusively rhetorical mode to plain style in his work reflects an absorption of international influences that supported his efforts to create a revalidated discursive language in German poetry. For Enzensberger, translation played an important role in this process as a heuristic practice that allowed him to grapple with critical issues of content, register, and the handling of poetic line.

The third chapter then examines what is generally regarded as Enzensberger's political phase, 1965 to 1975. Critics and scholars alike have assumed that during the late 1960s Enzensberger abandoned poetry in favor of political activism and essay writing because his widely known publications from this time were documentary prose and drama. Enzensberger did, however, continue to create poetry, in effect concealing this endeavor from German audiences by placing his verse in literary magazines in the United States—a remarkable situation given his critical views on U.S. foreign policy at the time. I delineate the poetic development that occurred in these sheltered publications, connecting this tangential evolution with the author's central efforts to redefine literature.

His project during this period, I contend, was directed toward achieving a speculative, more public capacity for the lyric genre that would allow it to reengage with social questions of the kind considered to belong to the domain of theory. This poetic response resonates with the social analyses proposed by Jürgen Habermas and Michel Foucault, whose discussions of system crisis and historically determined epistemologies are formative to Enzensberger's ballad collection *Mausoleum* (1975). *Mausoleum* attempts a complex fusion of analytic frameworks with the representational capacities of poetic language. Here Enzensberger employs an approach that involves documentary modes, heteroglossic discourse, translative writing, proselike diction, and active engagement of readership. Several studies of prose poems have concluded that their appearance often coincides with moments of social and aesthetic turmoil.[4] In Enzensberger's case, interrelated experimentation with long poem forms, documentary verse, and prose poems should be viewed as related to a protracted crisis in German literary representation.

Although a sense of cataclysmical change in social, epistemological, and literary order characterizes Enzensberger's publications throughout the 1970s, the fourth chapter demonstrates that *Der Untergang der Titanic* (1978a) seeks to claim a positive space in which an artist can surmount crisis. Looking at Enzensberger's interest in contemporary science and poetry, I propose that he takes up the paradigm of chaos theory in the epic because it accounts for the coexistence of superficial randomness and underlying order. Spontaneity and constraint—fundamental constitutive elements to the lyric genre—help Enzensberger redefine a position for poetry in the contemporary world. His ambitious project leads to questions about the sources of poetry (in nature, experience, or the textual medium itself), the role of the author (as original creator, appropriator, self-editor, or contingent figure), and the purposes of literature (as a didactic enterprise, forum for shared values, or mode of resistance to the status quo). My analysis identifies systematic representations of chaos phenomena in Enzensberger's work. I suggest, then, that by attending to how the author explores applications of chaos theory, we find a mechanism for appreciating crucial relationships among his poems, self-translations, experimental texts, didactic pieces, and critiques of literary criticism.

The fifth and final chapter considers the question of artistic identity, which for Enzensberger is fundamentally related to how his writings construct his position as part German and part transnational. As a poet, a sometimes expatriate writer, and an author whose stature exceeds national boundaries, Enzensberger has cultivated the tension between the very local origins of art and global culture. The lyric genre can articulate this condition because poetry's flexible capacities as an intimate, private form of expression, on the one hand, and as a performative, international, public medium, on the other, bind individual and collective identity. Enzensberger claims the position of the nomadic intellectual in his poems as he employs a repertoire of techniques that geographically map points of reference, make insinuations about national character, and introduce protagonists identified as transients. To complement this analysis, I consider the reception accorded Enzensberger's work internationally, with special reference to the attention given him by the American poet Carolyn Forché, who makes use of his concept of engaged literature to define a "poetry of witness." The chapter concludes with a consideration of late style in Enzensberger's recent poetry, where we find a blending of individual memory, collective history, and self-consciously acknowledged Eurocentric perspective that responds to the globalization of culture.

In the afterword to the international verse anthology he edited, *Museum der modernen Poesie,* Enzensberger describes poetry as a dynamic substance: a source of materials for practicing authors, a body of texts that changes as works are created or forgotten, and an inherently subversive process of creation (1980, 767). Given the volume and diversity of Enzensberger's oeuvre, rather than striving for a comprehensive overview, my study locates key artistic problems addressed in his poetry and proposes interpretive strategies to disclose the context in which his poems need to be read. Enzensberger redefines the lyric genre, varies poetic voice, salvages reflective frameworks, experiments playfully with spontaneity, and broaches provocative questions about national character. By recognizing these acts as purposeful poetic maneuvers, readers can understand his work in the lyric genre as a complex yet coherent project that plumbs fundamental issues of representation, contingency, and ethical commitment.

Except where noted otherwise, English translations of German source materials are my own.

Poetic Maneuvers

1. The Politics of Genre

"The Old Masters—believe me, there is no such thing," the poet disguised as a painter muses in the epic poem *Der Untergang der Titanic* (*The Sinking of the Titanic*). "I ought to know. For thirty years now / I have been a preserver of all good things: / half an alchemist and half a joiner. / I was unsurpassed as a restorer" (1980b, 68–69). These lines sketch the work of the artist as part magical creation and part practical handicraft—a symmetrical formulation complicated by acts of erudite conservation, which the text elsewhere labels "forgery." Although Enzensberger frequently employs such triadic examples to outline a problem rapidly or assumes a persona to voice positions with rhetorical strength, here the poet's retrospective candor focuses attention on how he crafts his art.[1] That Enzensberger has succeeded, more than his contemporaries, in expanding the boundaries of what is considered lyric speaks to the synergy of his disparate labors as a metaphoric alchemist, carpenter, and restorer. Drawing on theoretical discussions, political debates, and parallel writing projects for the sake of verse, he has revived a public role for the lyric genre and blended this communal function with poetry's today perhaps more familiar capacities for marking how individual experience becomes language.

An old art operating in a rapidly changing world, poetry exists in relationship to discourses emanating from academic, literary, and public culture—venues for collective expression that have aggressively competed in the German postwar context with the space occupied by the lyric genre. Enzensberger frequently dramatizes this predicament in poems by casting the struggles of postwar writers as encounters with foes, imperious schol-

3

ars, and fellow authors who quarrel about literature.[2] Their theatrical wrestlings and gloomy sermonizing on the future of art mirror the situation of German literature, which after 1945 existed in a climate shaped to a great extent by the ethical assumption that it could serve as an educating force to counteract the effects of fascism, wartime atrocities, and repressive values (Saunders 1999). The cultural disequilibrium that ensued from this political upheaval was richly productive. Self-reflection about the legacy of the Nazi period, openness to international trends, and experimentation with language stimulated the evolution of postwar German poetry. My aim in this chapter is to read such complex conceptual strands in the work of one of the most significant authors of the period as part of the canvas of the lyric genre.

While the ethical dilemmas that needed to be faced after the war created a precondition for Enzensberger's revisioning of literature, they do not in themselves explain how lyric poetry became one of the more powerful components in this project or why internationally the lyric genre proved so tenacious in the late twentieth century. Indeed, as Martha C. Nussbaum (1995, 4) rightly observes in advocating a role for literature in public life, many obstacles hamper the acceptance of art as a tool for commentary in the civic sphere:

> The contest between the literary imagination and its rivals can best be focused by starting from three objections commonly made against "fancy" when public policy-making is in question. . . . First, it will be said that the literary imagination is unscientific and subversive of scientific social thought. Second, it will be said that it is irrational in its commitment to the emotions. Third, it will be charged that it has nothing to do with the impartiality and universality that we associate with law and public judgement.

For poetry, often regarded as subjective and esoteric, these objections have particular salience; in Enzensberger's texts it is precisely that uncanny interface between subversive, poetic elements and cold, public judgment that becomes potent. Employing the evocative capacities of verse, the *poeta doctus* Enzensberger redirects attention to critical social issues, invariably challenging assumptions from competing disciplines about the limits of the lyric genre's capacity to bring imagination, emotions, and subjective perceptions to bear on public dilemmas. The main body of this chapter focuses on three aesthetic discourses spanning the post-1945 period that facilitate this redirection of poetry—situations in which Enzensberger seizes upon a conservative constraint to artistic autonomy and proposes a radical alternative.[3] These aesthetic discourses, which have to do with time, translation, and literacy, overlapped with one another in the latter half of the twentieth century and have continued into the twenty-first century.

Although recent history commanded much attention among younger German writers after 1945, fascism was a topic assiduously avoided in one of the most influential studies about the genre of lyric poetry to appear immediately after the war, Emil Staiger's *Grundbegriffe der Poetik* (1946), later translated as *Basic Concepts of Poetry* (1991). Staiger eschews the obvious problem of how to express the process of *Vergangenheitsbewältigung* (mastery of the past) in poetry by defining the lyric genre as associated with *Erinnerung* (individual memory). Against this background, Enzensberger's rejection of Staiger and cultivation instead of an aesthetics of *Momentaufnahme* (capturing the moment) constitutes a response to the ostensible neutrality of academic discourses, for the *Momentaufnahme* style links the temporal character of individual experience with representation of historical context. A second, related discourse about aesthetic autonomy gains momentum slightly later in statements by translators and poet-translators such as Enzensberger about their craft. Sentiments voiced by this group of writers mark a gradual evolution that continued through the 1970s, freeing poetry from prescriptive definitions of its utility as the mere tool of postwar reeducation efforts. Displacement of discussions about artistic autonomy from the lyric genre to a companion field, literary translation, amplifies arguments about the independence of writers. After considering why Enzensberger promotes creativity as a trait to be especially valued in translations (at times more openly than in his writings about poetry itself), I turn to recent remarks by the author concerning literacy. Amid dire predictions about the marginalization of poems and calls for aesthetic quality that suggest a narrowing of audience, Enzensberger's assertion that poetry serves an essential human function can be read as an effort to expand again the purview of the lyric genre. His impassioned remarks anticipate the stunning revival of the lyric genre in the 1990s, a development marked by the fashionability of certain verse types and poetry events.[4]

Poetry and Memory

The frequency with which postwar social, aesthetic, and academic discourses erected limits to poetry in German-speaking areas is startling, even in studies purporting to define the lyric genre in terms that cut across national boundaries.[5] Those forces brought to bear on poetry as an institution involved its mechanical production, consumption, and eventual academic evaluation, and they grew out of the painful changes set in motion by the German collapse. Discomfort with aberrant values often seems to lurk behind the fatherly advice dispensed by literary historians in the first postwar publications of the late 1940s. Studies of poetry by Wolfgang Kayser and Emil Staiger, which exerted an enduring influence, thus invite reappraisal of their authors' concern with justifying their integrity as scholars.[6]

In prefatory remarks to his concise handbook of meter, stanzaic forms, and rhyme, *Kleine deutsche Versschule* (*Little German Verse School* [1946]), Kayser prescriptively tells readers, "Finally, the booklet is directed toward the young poets. For that time is surely past when one believed that the poet creates in complete freedom and should not permit himself to be constrained by anything" (Kayser 1946, 6–7). "Lyric poetry is unhistorical," Emil Staiger observed that same year in *Grundbegriffe der Poetik* (*Basic Concepts of Poetry*), "has no foundation and no consequences. It speaks only to those who can empathize; its effects are of a fortuitous nature and pass, as a mood passes" (Staiger 1991, 130). The most famous imperative of the time, Theodor W. Adorno's "To write poetry after Auschwitz is barbaric" (1967a, 34), was penned a short time later, in 1949. The normative sentiments that guide these comments are quite the opposite of what one might imagine Bertolt Brecht hoped would result from his famous plea "An die Nachgeborenen" ("To Those Born Later") from *Svendborger Gedichte* (*Svendborg Poems,* 1933–38), which beseeched future generations to think tolerantly about those who struggled through times that were dark for literature: "Ihr, die ihr auftauchen werdet aus der Flut . . . Gedenkt unsrer / Mit Nachsicht" (Brecht 1967a, 724–25).

For *Grundbegriffe der Poetik,* Staiger was intent on defining the genres of lyric, epic, and dramatic poetry in terms of categories of time.[7] Lyric poetry he associated with the past and with processes of individual memory, *Erinnerung.* Epic style, by contrast, he considered grounded in the present and a mode of representation, *Vorstellung* (a word that can also be translated as "presentation" or "performance"), which involved the showing of details through the eyes of a narrator who experiences events alongside the described protagonists. Finally, dramatic style corresponded (according to Staiger) to the future, for it relies on *Spannung,* a gradually unfolding tension about what will occur next. Staiger's examples for this genre configuration included lyric poetry by Goethe, Mörike, Eichendorff, and Hölderlin, the epics of Homer and Schiller, and dramatic passages from Sophocles,

Corneille, Schiller, and Lessing. Pressing the terms "present," "past," and "future" into service as analytical categories, Staiger acknowledged that his choice entailed a certain kind of assumption (*Vorurteil*).[8] He also conceded a natural fluidity among the genres, especially in the case of lyric poetry, which, he noted, has elastic capacities because, in his estimation, "a lyric poem, precisely because it is a poem, cannot be just lyric. It participates to varying degrees and in different ways in all genre concepts and only a *predominance* of the lyric in them causes us to call the verses lyric" (Staiger 1991, 178).

But despite these modest correctives, when Staiger insisted that lyric poetry inhabits a past time frame, he offered a discussion of poems that follows from the theoretical assumption that poetry must be grasped rather than explained, a bias that Arthur Zimmermann aptly identifies as intrinsic to Staiger's interpretive work in general (Zimmerman 1977, 396). This insistence on a temporal categorization of genre definitions even ran counter to his most important example, the poetry of Goethe, who, Staiger concluded, conceived of poetry as a medium that conveys a sense of active presence. Emphasizing the artistic illusion of process, Staiger enthused, "the person who is immersed in the lyric mood does not take a stand. He glides along in the flow of life" (1991, 78). The appearance of presentness, under this analysis, is a simple illusion of immediacy. To salvage his definition of poetry as a medium of the past, Staiger (1946) determined that poetry must subjectively represent the inner world (*Innenwelt*) of the poet through its lack of distance from its subject matter (*Fehlen des Abstands*). Staiger further characterized *subjektive* lyric poetry as distinct from the epic, which he marked with terms diametrically opposed to those chosen for lyric: *objektive Poesie* and *Außenwelt*. To the epic he accorded the capacity to narrate history via *Gedächtnis,* intellectualized capacities of memory: "The past as the object of a narrative is stored in that part of the mind from which memories can be recalled at will. The past as a theme of the lyric is stored, as something very precious, in that part of the mind from which memories arise spontaneously" (Staiger 1991, 77).

The conspicuous difficulty Staiger encounters in reconciling Goethe's poetics with his own categories of analysis begs the question of why he insists on definitions that rigidly correspond to temporal frames. When Staiger handles a text so violently, as Benjamin Bennett (1993) trenchantly concludes in his analysis of the famous debate over Mörike's poem "Auf eine Lampe" ("To a Lamp"), another agenda can be assumed. Bennett's appraisal of the Mörike controversy among Staiger, Martin Heidegger, and

Leo Spitzer deduces that beyond preserving the notion of lyric poetry as a symbolic rather than allegorical form (1993, 62), the three participants manipulate their readings of the text to vest interpretive authority collectively "in a specific type of naturally gifted and appropriately trained individual consciousness" (67), the literary scholar. Staiger's discussion of lyric poetry, *Grundbegriffe der Poetik*, has a similar result, for it authorizes the interpreter always to reread the poet—even when the poet is Goethe.

This asserted prerogative raises thorny questions about the hierarchical relationship of critic and poet that Staiger promoted. Zimmer points out that antifascist criticism in exile rejected arbitrary, ideologically motivated interpretation and turned attention toward the poet, a move that at least superficially resembled a nostalgia for the sympathetic readings in which criticism became the servant of poetry (1988, 376).[9] Staiger seems to counter that trend by reasserting the authority of the critic, yet in so doing, he in effect bars the lyric genre from access to recent history and individual experience of the present. At first blush, Staiger charts purely literary categories, but in fact he chooses loaded terms that undermine academic objectivity. The afterword later appended to the study (a guest lecture delivered in Oxford in 1948) cryptically admits that peculiar historical circumstances lie behind it. "If I am to say, in a contemporary poetics written in German, what is lyric," Staiger comments, "then I must honor contemporary German usage" (1991, 201). The situation of contemporary German poetry, however, receives scant attention here, even less than in Kayser's *Kleine deutsche Versschule*. Skimming over the specifics of the aesthetic hiatus represented by 1933 to 1945, Kayser admitted a historically justified didactic motivation for proposing that young poets needed to learn *Handwerkliches,* the nuts and bolts of poetic craft.[10] Staiger, by contrast, excludes this history from the domain of lyric poetry. His promising conception of lyric poetry as a genre that broadly directs attention to the past leads instead to a narrowing prescription of what poets and their texts can accomplish. This gambit favors the expansion of conservative, academic authority.

Enzensberger differs sharply with Staiger concerning temporal categories when he cites *Grundbegriffe der Poetik* in the section of his 1961 dissertation on Clemens Brentano devoted to distinguishing between poetic and empirical consciousness.[11] Noting that Staiger characterized Brentano's work as a project dominated by a passive absence of planning, "in which the random spontaneity of the poet is radically negated," Enzensberger calls that disparagement of Brentano a biased misreading of the German romantic poet's work and reminds his readers that Brentano termed himself the "größte[r] Dichter des Augenblicks," hence intentionally the greatest poet of the momentary (1961, 122). After reasserting the authority of the poet over the scholar, Enzensberger further emphasizes the importance of the present for lyric poetry. While Enzensberger is primarily concerned with calling attention to the ways Brentano distances himself from his subject matter and manipulates language (with *Entstellung*), his comments about time intersect with academic and writerly discussions of contemporary poetry that in Germany were delimiting its boundaries as a genre.[12]

By contrast, Staiger had sought to separate the terms *Erinnerung* (which he associated with lyric poetry) and *Gedächtnis* (a term attached to narrative)—a fine distinction that identifies differences between private and public spheres. The reminiscences, memories, and animated associations of *Erinnerung* are evocative in character, but they are private treasures. Good recall abilities, the faculty of memory, and acts of remembrance—in other words, *Gedächtnis*—organize and institutionalize the past. Even when this process does not take the form of a systematic recovery of past events, it implies abstraction, permanence, ritual, and mimetic representation (or re-presentation) of elements.[13] Enzensberger elicits the private/public distinction of these terms but for his part emphasizes that Brentano works selectively with vocabulary from the *Innenwelt* and contrasts these operations with language linked to elements from the *Außenwelt*. In reality, for postwar German poetry, the separate categories of *Erinnerung* and *Gedächtnis* insisted upon by Staiger appear exceptionally porous. Private memories become indistinguishable from a collective *Vergangenheitsbewältigung* (mastery of the past); poets conjoin the historical context of the lyric genre and the ability of lyric poetry to capture the present—in blatant contradiction to Staiger's theory. "For a poem does not stand outside time," Paul Celan observed in a 1958 speech (1999b, 34), a comment enlarged upon in his 1960 Büchner Prize lecture with his remark that the poem "is mindful of its dates, but it speaks" (1999a, 48).

For Enzensberger, the temporal capacities of the lyric genre relate ultimately to the inseparability of *Poesie* (poetry) from *Politik* (politics), for their unity requires a new understanding of how a writer transposes and recasts transient events in poetic time. Rejecting all artificially imposed political content, Enzensberger in his 1962 essay "Poesie und Politik" ("Poetry and Politics") recovered a notion of artistic autonomy in part by claiming a separate temporal domain for the lyric genre. "Poetry and politics," he deduced, "are not 'specialized fields' but historical processes, one in the medium of speech, the other in the medium of power" (Enzensberger 1974a, 79). This logic leads him to spurn dichotomizations of the two as "on the one hand . . . the party calendar, on the other timelessness" (1974a, 79). Convinced with Adorno that the apparently least political works can in fact be the most political, Enzensberger defends the timelessness of poetry but refuses to abandon its time-bound aspects. In this he agrees with Adorno, who with reference to the special capacities of poetry remarked, "The paradox specific to the lyric work, a subjectivity that turns into objectivity, is tied to the priority of linguistic form in the lyric; it is that priority from which the primacy of language in literature in general (even in prose forms) is derived" (Adorno 1991b, 43). The passage into objectivity from subjectivity is signaled by temporal positioning, accompanied by condensation of language and artistic choices concerning metaphoric register, performative mode, and textual presentation.

Many of Enzensberger's poems, to be sure, pointedly use temporal references to call attention to their own historical position. References to the past abound in their titles: "Erinnerung an die Schrecken der Jugend" ("Remembrance of the Horrors of Youth"), "Erinnerung an den Tod" ("Remembrance of Death"), "Prähistorie" ("Prehistory"), "Historischer Prozeß" ("Historical Process"), "Erinnerung an die sechziger Jahre" ("Remembrance of the Sixties"), "Eine schwache Erinnerung" ("A Faint Remembrance"), "Ich bin, was du vergessen hast" ("I am what you have forgotten"), "Andenken" ("Souvenir"), or "Zum Ewigen Frieden" ("In Eternal Peace"). The present and future are more sparsely represented: "Anwesenheit" ("Presence"), "Spur der Zukunft" ("Trace of the Future"), "Gedicht über die Zukunft, November 1964" ("Poem about the Future, November 1964"), "Aufbruch in die siebziger Jahre" ("Departure for the Seventies"), and "Zukunftsmusik" ("Music of the Future"). Time elements are also subtly incorporated into the metaphorical language of his poems, employed in the contrastive patterns of texts and even implied by the subtitles within volumes, such as the headings "Augenblicke" ("Blinks of an Eye") and "Zeitläufe" ("Passages of Time") from Enzensberger's international verse anthology *Museum der modernen Poesie* (*Museum of Modern Poetry*). Further, development of a new poetic aesthetic of *Momentaufnahme* in the 1960s is supported by Enzensberger's discussion of poetry written by William Carlos Williams, an analysis focused on the capacity of lyric poetry to capture a sense of the present associated with the visual image of the snapshot.[14]

Gleaning terms from modernist work by Ezra Pound, Williams, and James Joyce, and especially from imagist poetry, Enzensberger in *William Carlos Williams* (1962b [trans.]) describes the American's verse in terms of its ability to convey "glimpses" and "epiphanies."[15] His notion of the *Momentaufnahme* enlarges the lyric genre by reintroducing a sense of the present. This aesthetic program was readily accepted by German poets and exerted considerable influence throughout the 1960s, often in connection with techniques of linguistic montage or cinematic splicing.[16] The approach is a significant correction to Staiger that brought German poetry into line with international, and especially American, verse that built on the accomplishments of modernist imagist poetry. The "rapid and fleeting insights," as Enzensberger described them, involved a formidable exercise of memory and mental capacities. "Their transformation into poetry not only assumes a keen eye, but also an extraordinary gift of recall," Enzensberger commented (1962b [trans.], 185). This formulation blends a concern with presentness with a desire for timeless memory.

In the assessment of Marjorie Perloff, whose scholarship has compellingly analyzed artistic discourses that have shaped the recent American poetic landscape, "claims for timelessness and universality were characteristic of the mid-fifties moment" (1998, 87). Perloff's observations concerning the strong relationship of American verse to photography during these years emphasizes values associated with an aesthetic of the present that German poets who emulated American style found intriguing. Perloff persuasively demonstrates that the "one world vision" promoted by such expensive photographic exhibitions as *The Family of Man* was consonant with much contemporary poetry production in that both constructed an idealized, harmonious present that repressed underlying power relations and intractable social problems.[17] In American poetry, this repression also led to the counterpoetics of John Ashbery and Frank O'Hara. For German poets belatedly absorbing that aesthetic, the "capturing of the moment" undergoes another transformation and gains association with the enhanced aura of authenticity that is used to validate expression of individual, quotidian experience. This photographic mode breaks the rigid temporal dichotomy of *Erinnerung* and *Gedächtnis*.

Enzensberger's formulation of this visually conceived literary aesthetic celebrates the capacity of language to capture images, hence challenging the postwar triumph of visual media. Biographer Jörg Lau, who notes that one hobby of Enzensberger's father was photography (1999, 14), characterizes the author's media criticism from the late 1950s as an attempt to reassert the primacy of text-based culture. Lau summarizes, "Here no disappointed admirer of the media speaks wanting to better his condition, but instead a slightly disgusted snob looking for a way to bring the corrupt picture apparatus under the control of writing culture" (1999, 72–73). This writerly approach to photograph-like images became more sharply delineated around 1962 to 1964, when Enzensberger published his translations of poems by William Carlos Williams and his own poetry collection *Blindenschrift* (*Braille*). After Enzensberger's publications, the *Momentaufnahme* approach grew yet more concretely linked to photography through the work of Rolf Dieter Brinkmann, whose conviction that poetry approximates "snapshots" led him to experiment with formats combining texts and images.[18]

By the time Brinkmann and other younger writers began to appropriate the *Momentaufnahme* aesthetic in the 1970s, however, Enzensberger's poetry had turned from a focus on presentness, everyday elements, and the individual experience of time to a palpable marking of historical chronology in *Mausoleum* (1975). The collection confronts the reader with reminders of mortality at every turn, beginning with the title. Later a quotation from Tennyson ("Every minute dies a man. / Every minute one is born") clocks the cycle of life and death (Enzensberger 1975, 71). The demise of the American efficiency expert Frederick Winslow Taylor leads the text to comment that in his last moments, he wound his pocket watch (Enzensberger 1975, 111). Throughout the collection, Enzensberger compares past and present. This comparison underscores the persistence of lethal, repressive structures and the inescapable limit of time:

> Andere Raubtiere. Andere
> Wörter und Räder. Aber
> derselbe Himmel.
> In diesem Mittelalter
> leben wir immer noch.
>
> (1975, 9)

> *Different predators. Different*
> *words and wheels. But*
> *the same sky.*
> *That's the Dark Age we still*
> *live in today.*
>
> (1976c, 3)

Here no progress occurs. Mortal participants are condemned to a Sisyphean repetition of private missteps, historical blunders, and perpetual human agonies. An insistent background noise mounts as clockworks, elaborate gears, and models of the universe tick off the seconds, minutes, years, and centuries in a pattern that continues throughout the collection. Through these auditory devices in *Mausoleum,* the individual memories or *Erinnerungen* of the figures depicted are subsumed by historical consciousness or *Gedächtnis*—a reiteration of the two ways of apprehending time fundamental to Enzensberger's poetry.

Between Staiger's *Grundbegriffe der Poetik* and Enzensberger's *Mausoleum* lie three decades of literary debate over the fate of poetry, debates that changed the way in which poetry operated as an institution in Germany. The exchanges about the lyric genre and time suggest that these discussions of content, autonomy, and social value deeply impacted postwar literature. By defining genre in relation to only one temporal category—the past—and narrowing it yet again to private memory, Staiger elides references to recent German history, conservatively restricts poetry, and sets up a problematic niche for the lyric genre within the academy. Enzensberger's fascination with time produces a bold and systematic redefinition of the lyric genre, first by scholarly counterargument to Staiger and then by poetic example. The new content areas and poetic techniques he explores later become attractive to other poets. Through the aesthetic of the present he pursues, the past becomes visible again, for the "momentary" (*Augenblick*) aesthetics of the present allow poets rather than the academy to define the lyric genre. This act finally dislodges powerful conservative forces exerted by the older academy and celebrates the forward-looking dynamism advocated by younger postwar authors who found validation in explicitly confronting the past.

Translation and the Lyric Genre

A second clash between conservative and progressive values, one that commences slightly later than the genre discussion initiated by Staiger, emerges in writings about literary translation from the postwar period. These statements about translation practices form a companion discourse about poetry that is less coherently developed than academic studies of genre by single individuals. In aggregate, such statements view literary translation as a forward-looking activity that promotes cultural reconstruction and a reorientation toward an international context.[19] Those proponents who comment on translation—and I focus here primarily on translators, writers, and publishers rather than scholars—present the merit of their own contributions in understandably partisan terms. While initial considerations in literary journals and monographs tend to emphasize prescriptively the didactic utility of international literature, subsequent ones, especially those by younger writers, stress the creativity of translators, the aesthetic autonomy of translations, and the potential aesthetic impact of the works in translation. During the late 1960s and early 1970s, statements about translation display a shift in focus as they begin to center on questions of fidelity to original works and the value of scholarly editions.[20] This evolution in translation culture parallels related trends in contemporaneous debates about artistic freedom, public versus private expression, and moral responsibility.

For the purpose of marking the starting point of these shifts, Staiger's *Grundbegriffe* is again instructive because it so openly expresses hierarchical and hieratic notions concerning the respective functions of interpretation and literary works. The afterword confidently draws an analogy between the science of poetry (*Wissenschaft von der Dichtung*) and ethics. Staiger asserts that "[j]ust as, according to the ethics of antiquity, virtuous behavior presupposes knowledge of the nature of virtue, so the ancient doctrine of poetic creation and of all poetics . . . presupposes knowledge of the nature of poetic creation in as general a sense as possible" (1991, 195). Explaining next the veneration of creative genius, Staiger remarks that prior to Gottsched, poetics consisted of samples from the formal repertoire considered available to poets. After Gottsched, poetry is no longer regarded as an imitation of nature created in existing patterns but becomes creative achievement (*schöpferische Leistung*). Staiger then asserts the need for theory, because "[w]hen poetic creation no longer imitates nature and the available models, as it did for Gottsched, but is a creative achievement . . . , only the most fundamental thought can accommodate it" (1991, 195) Freed from a system in which it simply models itself on existing tradition, poetry is nonetheless subordinated by Staiger to theoretical interpretation, which for him supplies the intellectual apparatus that justifies and ethically grounds any literature that is not merely mimetic. This altered balance between poetry and theory expresses a diminished appreciation of writerly craft that, as will be seen, postwar discussions of translation mightily assail.

A proliferation of theory existed in the twentieth century once the indeterminacy of poetic language became obvious, Eric Williams contends in his discussion of Freud, Wittgenstein, Lévi-Strauss, Derrida, and Barthes in connection with the work of Georg Trakl. Williams further proposes that theory especially informs the position Enzensberger takes in describing modern poetry in *Museum der modernen Poesie* (E. Williams 1993, 95–114). Although this is true, Enzensberger also yokes his analysis of modernism to an appreciation of poetic technique that celebrates the practical acumen of working writers.[21] This linkage to craft privileges the value of creativity over the conservation of traditions (the position it occupies in Staiger's account of literature before Gottsched), but it also threatens to unseat theory. Enzensberger's remarks endorsing writerly experimentation obliquely equate progressive social attitudes with the individualism that is expressed through the ingenuity of the translator. That equation suggests the necessity of reading the discourse about translation in the postwar era in relation to ideological debates.[22] Situated in a literary field where academic standards were by no means systematically applied, these statements on literary translation overthrow the authority of the scholar as interpreter and confirm the importance of authors and translators. Moreover, the emergence of rhetoric about literary translation as a transgressive practice differentiates descriptions that valorize artistic freedom circa 1970 from early postwar comments about the burdensome duties of translators.

Texts about translation from the initial postwar years absorb the vocabulary of public political rhetoric to define their position, a practice that wanes as translators search for new metaphors to describe translation craft. One of the more openly programmatic tracts of this kind is a 1947 essay by Karl Schwedhelm that considers the distinctions among *Übersetzung* (translation), *Übertragung* (rendering), and *Nachdichtung* (imitation).[23] Schwedhelm, who subsequently translated work by Louis Aragon and Jean Cocteau, considers the educative capacity of translations, which he contends should serve to reintroduce European culture to German audiences, tellingly referred to as *ein Volk*.[24] Schwedhelm continues with a description of the translator's work that incorporates bureaucratic terminology of service and duty:

> Thereby a responsible office arises again for the translator, a high tradition is taken up again: a mediating work that the best have always experienced as creative service to the spirit of one's own people (*Dienst am Geiste des eigenen Volkes*), as gratefully received commission from the foreign spirit, begins anew. (1947, 14)

By citing a fundamental need for intellectual and ethical reorientation that can be satisfied by translations, Schwedhelm assigns translation the role of politicized expression. His discussion of the various translation modes acknowledges the possibility that variable relationships exist between authors and canonical works, ranging from obedient conservation to poetic apprenticeship and unconstrained adaptation. The essay's concluding call for translations that are artistically viable, rather than merely literal, effectively liberates writing from the burden of institutional constraints, despite the fact that this plea clashes with the text's own rhetoric of duty.

In the 1950s and 1960s, similar statements emphasize artistic creativity and translator identity. Poet Karl Krolow, whose position represents the apogee of this evolution, describes translation as an exhilarating chance to enrich one's own work. "In this manner," he writes in 1963, "one's own work can be neutralised for a certain time, and things reach that peculiar situation that, in translation, one practices the ability to forget one's own person and simultaneously cannot get rid of it" (Krolow 1963, 119).

A similar exuberance infuses a 1965 statement by Hans Erich Nossack, an author and literary translator who terms himself a *Liebhaber* (admirer) rather than a translator of literature.[25] Confessing that as a youth, foreign works of literature attracted him more than German ones, he outlines in pragmatic terms how translation can serve as a form of apprenticeship:

> One learns thereby not so much to know the other language better as to handle one's own language more precisely. In order to find the equivalent in one's own language for the foreign metaphor or to convey a foreign linguistic gesture through an approximately equivalent idiom, one is forced to use words that originally did not belong to one's own vocabulary. (Nossack 1965, 13)

Nossack deduces that writing itself is a form of translation, thus completing his elevation of translation to the status of an original literary work.

Comparable endorsements of the aesthetic value of translations were used by prominent publishers to justify the disproportionate publication of foreign over German works throughout the 1950s. And the influx of works in translation was enormous. One article investigating the state of the German publishing industry in 1953, for example, notes that in the area of belletrism, a full 50.7 percent of book production consisted of works in translation (Er 1955). Ernst Rowohlt, responding in 1950 to the concern that too many foreign works were flooding the German market, asserted the interest of his firm in seeking out good books rather than merely calculating profitability. Although conceding that the economic realities of the situation disadvantaged young German authors, Rowohlt (1950) voiced the sentiment that a commitment to quality would remain the primary factor influencing his decision to publish works from Germany or abroad. Peter Suhrkamp, when considering the topic of publishers and translations in the prominent literary journal *Akzente* in 1956, seconded the opinion that translations of poetry must themselves be poetic.

The emphasis placed on creativity in the preceding statements carves out a position for translations vis-à-vis original writing that blurs the boundaries between the craft of translator and of poet. In fact, many post-war writers worked in both media. These functional circumstances impacted the character and relative stature of translations and connect to dynamics affecting the generic matrix that shaped the German poetic canon.

Recent translation studies take such operations of cultural systems into account by considering problems of linguistic equivalence or specific problems of literary translation as historical formations (Bassnett-McGuire 1980, 73–75). Thus James McFarlane's 1953 discussion of how differences in the handling of a particular work reflect aesthetic choices made by a translator marks out an area later explored by George Steiner in *After Babel*, his far-ranging account of the history and significance of translation. Steiner emphasizes that writers who import new forms of expression via translation have ideological influence, for as they enrich their own literature, that process significantly transforms the literary culture that receives it (1981, 352). The conditions under which significant translation influence occurs have been more precisely defined from a structuralist perspective by Itamar Even-Zohar, who proposed that "not only is the socio-literary status of translation dependent upon its position within the literary system or polysystem, but the very practice of translation is strongly subordinated to it" (1978, 125). Even-Zohar further reasons that during periods when a literature is young or weakened, translation enjoys greater importance than at other times. Such a circumstance clearly existed in Germany after World War II.[26]

During the reconstruction period, as the statement by Schwedhelm suggests, literary translation was regarded as a didactically justified, ideological tool—a means to import desired cultural material, yet it ultimately became, as Krolow's observations indicate, a vehicle for developing individual expression. I find it useful to read this ideational spectrum as evidence of change in the institution of literature. As more poets engaged in translation projects, the status of literary translations rose, and discussions of translation more frequently included inquiry into matters of taste and quality. That opening of the literary system generated peripheral discourses that relate to Enzensberger's activities as a translator of American modernist verse. One such discourse concentrated on perceptions of cultural difference, especially the disparities between German and American English. A second propounded the hypothesis that the quality of translations can surpass that of the original. Enzensberger, a poet-translator whose work has ranged from scrupulously exact to wildly parodic, fused these two lines of reasoning.

Already by the late 1950s, statements about translation register the degree to which German literature was open to international influences by noticing cultural differences. Statements to this effect appeared with regularity in the leading German literary journals and in various monographs. In a 1956 article for *Akzente,* a literary journal whose coeditor Walter Höllerer was a poet and an influential mediator of American literature, Walter Schürenberg enumerated syntactic differences between languages. His essay "Über einige Verschiedenheiten des Englischen und Deutschen" ("On Some Differences Between English and German") commented by way of introduction that translation brings an awareness of the "subjectivity of one's own feeling for the language" (Schürenberg 1956, 420). The following year, the exceptionally prolific poet and translator Erich Fried published a piece in *Texte und Zeichen* (a literary journal that promoted experimental work) that attributed the difficulties encountered in translating poetry by E. E. Cummings to the idiosyncrasies of his style and the unique properties of American colloquial language (Fried 1957). Along these same lines, Karl Krolow's 1958 review of Cummings translations by Eva Hesse extolled her success in finding adequate language because, according to Krolow, "[o]ur language cannot be made so 'palatable' and used in the way that the American original often prescribes" (Krolow 1958, 742).

Mediators of mid-twentieth-century avant-garde American authors to German audiences restate this perception about colloquial texture many times. Höllerer advised in an important article about American verse that appeared in *Akzente* in 1959 that "American English has a quick repartee of monosyllabic words, of precise, cool sentence formulations, that can hardly be brought into German without ambient noise" (Höllerer 1959, 39–40). In the 1962 *Jahrbuch für Amerikastudien,* scholar Wolfgang B. Fleischmann confirmed this conclusion from an academic vantage by identifying the jazzlike, loosely grammatical flow of American poetic language as unique with the observation that "[n]either the lexical nor the syntactic pliability of the German language will allow the creation of the super-regional, anonymous medium the translator requires here" (Fleischmann

1962, 181). These perspectives on American poetry's discursive style were shared by Kurt Heinrich Hansen (1979), a prominent anthologist of the period, and Klaus Reichert (1967), translator of works by Charles Olson. Reichert cast this new language as an opportunity: "This then is the obligation [*Pflicht*] and opportunity [*Chance*] of German translation: either to press out from the ground up or to construct gradually a colloquial language as literary language which adequately translates the original text and at the same time little by little makes available [to that literary language] an artlessness of spoken language that poets can then use" (1967, 4).

A conservative critique of foreign works and their dissemination ran parallel to such affirmations of translation as a desirable stylistic influence, however. Poet and literary scholar Hans Egon Holthusen in a 1955 essay on Eva Hesse's exemplary translations of Ezra Pound's work voiced skepticism about the influx of foreign literature. Although he praised the translations in unequivocal terms, Holthusen questioned the benefit of these texts for German literature, asking what can be decided (*entschieden*) by a translation:

> It is certainly above all the question of whether a foreign poet, when he is introduced into the hospitality of the German language, can get through with his idiosyncrasies and mannerisms and gain the upper hand, or whether he must be more or less transformed according to laws and customs of the dominant linguistic moment. (1980b, 133)

Holthusen extended this analysis by asserting that the classic and modern works in German and English differ so much that translations enjoy sporadic success at best. Pound's esoteric language, in his view, posed almost insurmountable difficulties for the translator. Holthusen's doubts foreshadow perceptions voiced by Ingeborg Bachmann in her 1959–60 University of Frankfurt lectures, when she attributed the delayed reception of international trends in German to the inherent difficulty of transferring the language of poetry into a new context (1980, 24).

Though literary internationalism in postwar Germany was tempered by such cautions from scholars and more established writers, creativity displaces aesthetic tradition as a measure of worth by the time Enzensberger begins publishing his series of influential translations—*Museum der modernen Poesie* in 1960, *William Carlos Williams* in 1962, and *César Vallejo* and *Franco Fortini*, both in 1963. The motto adopted by Austrian novelist Adelbert Muhr for a 1960 essay, "Die Übersetzung soll besser sein als das Original" ("The Translation Should Be Better than the Original"), expresses this shift in emphasis (Muhr 1960). Muhr dismissed fluency in two languages as a prerequisite for credentialing interpreters, a radical comment that positions this work outside the domain of professional translators and welcomes a proliferation of free translations.[27] Countering one major objection to amateur translations, Muhr praised the frequent consultation of dictionaries. When he dispenses with linguistic proficiency as an essential qualification for translators, he asserts the uniqueness of poetry in this respect, claiming that "[o]ne can easily dispense with a command of the original language, especially in the lyric genre" (Muhr 1960, 40). The steady growth in numbers of published translations (hence an unmet demand for qualified translators), the forays German writers themselves made into translation work (in part for financial reasons), and the renewed confidence which authors were beginning to exhibit about their accomplishments become factors in this progressive aesthetic revaluation. Nearly every important poet of the postwar era, including Enzensberger, translated.[28]

By the late 1960s, statements endorsing creative translations outnumbered those against it. A formulation by literary translator Curt Meyer-Clason sums up the situation by calling for the *Übersetzer aus Berufung* (translator by calling) to replace the less esteemed *Berufsübersetzer* (professional translator). His analogy of dialogic exchange is reminiscent of Hans Georg Gadamer's model of hermeneutic interpretation, which depicts translation as a process of creating a reflection of the original, a *Spiegelbild:* "Insight into the whole, the undivided—the starting point of the writer, his vision into the unborn work—is for me likewise the prerequisite for a genuine dialogue with each sentence of the book that lies untranslated before me" (Meyer-Clason 1966, 170). Meyer-Clason asserts that it is distance and primal detachment (*Urdistanz*) rather than the proximity of language that forms the basis of the translator's relationship to the text. And indeed, his choice of sexually charged imagery of disrobement and embrace to describe the encounter with the original heightened the association of the art of translation with intimacy and private acts.[29] More vividly than most descriptions, his account releases the translator from the role of mere public pedant and validates personal creativity. Poet Max Hölzer in a 1967 article for the progressive literary journal *Sprache im Technischen Zeitalter* goes even further. Admitting that he himself had long preferred literal translations, Hölzer now rejects prose paraphrase and interlinear versions as unacceptable and confesses a new allegiance to renderings that mystically grasp the meaning of words, sentences, and images (Hölzer 1967, 59–64). Hölzer, who cites Paul Celan's work on poetry by Fernando Pessoa as exemplary translation, praises the poet's creation of new language.

The tone of these statements reverberates in writings about translation from the 1970s. Author Zenta Maurina foregrounds creative practices by objecting to the categorization of translation as a second-class activity in a 1973 essay entitled "Übersetzung als Umdichtung" ("Translation as Re-Poeticizing"). In 1976, a whole series of publications endorsed the independent aesthetic significance of translations. Hans Wollschläger terms Erich Fried's translation of Dylan Thomas's "Under Milkwood" better than the original. The innovative, experimental poet Oskar Pastior lauds the ability of translation to enlighten, while East German poet Rainer Kirsch devotes an entire monograph, *Das Wort und seine Strahlung* (*The Word and Its Radiance*), to the expressive qualities of translation.[30]

As had previously been the case, this drift toward explicitly poetic translations was viewed with reserve by the pre–World War II generation of authors and by scholars. Sounding a note of caution about current trends, poet and anthologist Hilde Domin in 1968 questions the tendency of some translators to choose extreme equivalents over familiar terms, a predilection she attributed to the aesthetic influence of Hugo Friedrich's theories of modern poetry.[31] Likewise, although terming translation a creative act, the classicist Wolfgang Schadewaldt insists that translations have no status independent of their originals. Rather, he proposes, they should rely on the linguistic repertoire of their times. Schadewaldt thus advocates the sort of transparency that allows the original to remain visible through the translation, which Walter Benjamin famously articulated in 1921 in "Die Aufgabe des Übersetzers" ("The Task of the Translator"). According to Benjamin, interlinear versions constitute the ideal mode of translation because "[a] real translation is transparent; it does not cover the original, does not block its light, but allows the pure language, as though reinforced by its own medium, to shine upon the original all the more fully" (1968, 79).

By around 1970, statements about literary translation that value fidelity over creativity are heard from individuals who came to translation through academic paths (such as Walter Jens [1974], Annemarie Schimmel [1980], and Barbara Frischmuth [1969]) or who engaged in extensive, scholarly translation projects (Janheinz Jahn [1970], Erich Fried [1969], and Peter Urban [1972; 1981]). Eva Hesse (1968), one of the most important professional literary translators of the postwar period, speaks of translations as needing to be faceless. Prolific translator, anthologist, and poet Michael Hamburger (1976) describes himself as a mediator of culture. In the 1980s, the question of whether translations should be undertaken with didactic intent, creative verve, or scholarly meticulousness becomes a function of translator choice (cf. also R. Grimm 1998b). German poetry in the 1990s, which embraced linguistic experimentation and self-conscious reflection about the text medium, saw a resurgence of internationalism. And once again, this rethinking of the aesthetic values in poetry emerged hand in hand with a wave of poetry translations, international anthologies, and programmatic statements about the lyric genre and translation, including the print and audio CD *Mutmassungen über die Poesie* (*Conjectures about Poetry* [Enzensberger and Schrott 1999]), a set of readings and a conversation between Hans Magnus Enzensberger and Raoul Schrott.[32]

With respect to Enzensberger, whose translation approaches vary greatly according to his writerly purposes, poetic creativity and progressive ideology converge in his deliberations about the field of translation. Translating poetry by American modernists, Enzensberger handles the texts in a scrupulous manner that subordinates his own style to that of the original. Yet these translations do creatively import new content and vernacular language. By contrast, other translations he undertakes are creative to the point of being transgressive.[33] Over time, a complex, intertextual relationship develops between Enzensberger's translations and texts as his translation projects coincide with periods when his own writing seems to have been in flux. Often the character of the translations stands in inverse relationship to his literary work. Thus, his daring rhymed verse translations of *Edward Lear's Complete Nonsense* (*Edward Lears kompletter Nonsens* [1977 (trans.)], ironically subtitled as "smuggled into German by Hans Magnus Enzensberger") and his exuberant rendering of *The Misanthrope* (*Der Menschenfeind* [1979 (trans.)]) cap a phase in his work dominated by the production of documentary literature (especially prose), while his convincing and meticulous translations of poetry by William Carlos Williams overlap with a formative early phase, a period of high productivity for him in the lyric genre.

A sheer linguistic playfulness, an eye for audience responses, and a sense of didactic potential all color Enzensberger's statements about translation, which steadily reflect on the creative potential of this activity. One of his earliest publications deals with translation. The text, a piece that appeared in a self-proclaimed literary parlor game, *Baemu suti oder Das ibolithische Vermächtnis* (*Baemu suti or the Ibolithian Legacy*), edited by Hans Gültig (1959), finds a place next to contributions by Hans Arp, Günter Eich, Wolfgang Hildesheimer, and Christine Lavant. Each writer renders into German an essentially untranslatable sound poem. Their commentaries and translations predictably reveal more about each author than about the text. Enzensberger parodies academic translation conventions by meticulously parsing the "text" and proposing both a stilted interlinear version of the work and a polished translation. Piously citing the limitations he confronted in using German to convey the spirit of the original, he delivers the lines in a sort of chant:

> Eine Lawine von Tauben gehängt
> reglos über der Piazza.
> Huste nicht! Beim ersten Laut
> begräbt sie uns donnernd.
>
> (Gültig 1959, 43)

> *An avalanche hung with doves*
> *motionless over the piazza.*
> *Cough not! At the first sound*
> *it buries us thunderously.*

Decades later, *Baemu suti* finds its place again in Enzensberger's own intellectual game, *Das Wasserzeichen der Poesie* (*The Watermark of Poetry*, 1985). There, in the context of a purported handbook of poetic terms and styles, *Baemu suti* illustrates one of some twelve modes of translation that range from parsing and interlinear versions to free renderings, machine translations, and parodies.[34]

The translation styles cataloged in *Das Wasserzeichen* mirror Enzensberger's prodigious accomplishments as a translator of French, English, Italian, Russian, and Spanish texts into German—and of his own work, chiefly *Der Untergang der Titanic* (1978a), which he rendered into English as *The Sinking of the Titanic* (1980b).[35] For Enzensberger, trenchant interpretation and a gestural approach to language need not exclude each other in translation, as indicated in the essay accompanying his documentary theater piece *Das Verhör in Habana* (*The Interrogation in Havana*):

> Translation, for example, cannot content itself with literal rendering. It must, seen formally, unfold the scenic possibilities of the text, i.e., it has

to be gestural. With respect to content, translation always means taking sides, and indeed to the extent of working out the social character of the person speaking. (Enzensberger 1979a, 20)

Discernment of the multiple possibilities of a text hence depends on a nuanced understanding of how semantic intricacies, technical considerations, performative aspects, and intellectual perspective concurrently inform a translation.

Enzensberger has on occasion been taken to task by critics for projecting himself into the translated text or adapting with abandon, but his inventiveness as a translator is as brilliant as his work as a poet. His controversial version of *Der Menschenfeind* casts Molière's work in iambic pentameter peppered with contemporary verbage and foreign phrases. The clashing language underscores the chic, shallow artificiality of the play's characters through outlandish rhyme pairs (such as *unfair/mon cher, hier zu lande/Gangsterbande,* and *Western/gestern*), combining a freehanded approach with a high degree of reflection about translation.[36]

"The poetry translator is no martyr, but a brotherly egoist," Enzensberger (1999c, 391) comments in his recent retrospective collection of translations and imitations, *Geisterstimmen* (*Phantom Voices*). This admission of bold opportunism forcefully elevates translation from an office of derivative service to one of artistic independence. Elaborating on this point, Enzensberger describes the echoes and overtones of other writers in the mind of the poet as a "radio play inside one's head" (1999c, 391). Full of these sounds, translation exists as the most intensive form of criticism, and as a sort of creative writing course (1999c, 392). *Der Untergang der Titanic* represents translation thematically as an act that creates, restores, and reconstructs texts. Content is manipulated, every available writerly technique employed as the writer-translator engages in an endless process of creation. "I restore my images," the poet comments, "I fake my own work" (Enzensberger 1980b, 18). And the more he writes, the more this poet questions what he is doing. "What was it like / in actual fact?" he asks, "And in my poem? Was it in my poem / at all? . . . I'm not prepared to take an oath on it. And in ten years from now / I shall not be sure that these very words are my own" (1980b, 18). Enzensberger's protagonist is a figure who in his past life was "involved / in disputes metaphors, endless love affairs" (1980b, 18). He recognizes himself less and less with each line. Sheer translation into words leads to infinite digressive linguistic metamorphosis and to a poetry that operates evocatively rather than mimetically. The canto concludes majestically with an image of a sublime spectacle that restores the sovereignty of the poet-painter's imagination: "I am overcome by an enormous calm. I don't know why. / I gaze outside like a god. There is no iceberg in sight" (1980b, 18).

Literacy and the Poetic Imagination

Poetic imagination and literacy, Enzensberger has often reminded his audiences, are necessary to society. "Literacy is not an individual hobby. It is an essential feature of human ecology, and therefore it has to be safe-guarded against the blind forces threatening it from all sides," he proposed in a talk presented at the Swedish Academy Nobel Jubilee Symposium (1993b, 45). The literacy that concerns him is not merely the ability to read but a heightened, thorough commitment to reading and thinking. The vigor attributed to poetry expresses Enzensberger's confidence in the powers of the poetic medium to promote this project. "One line of a new poem may defy all literary science," he summarizes (1993b, 34). This revel-ing in poetry's subversive capacity matches stances Enzensberger has taken throughout his career: poems are useful commodities (*Gebrauchsgegen-stände*); poems resist all attempts to subordinate them to external impera-tives; poems are, above all, communication (cf. "Gebrauchsanweisung" ["Instructions for Use"] in Enzensberger 1960d).

The traffic around the twin issues of literacy and poetry in the 1990s has to do with the compromised status of texts, yet it also returns us to questions about the civic function of literature that I had raised in citing Nussbaum's observations at the outset of this chapter. Enzensberger's af-firmation of the value of poetry runs counter to others' descriptions of the lyric genre in the late twentieth century as an anachronistic, perhaps mori-bund medium—and if not that, then certainly a field of esoteric, effete spe-cialization. The particulars of his argument, however, overlap with debates that have preoccupied German writers since 1945. Each of these quarrels, whether about the proper foundational material for poetry or the merits of high versus low culture or the sanctity of book art, has led back to the conundrum of literature's collective function.

In *The Marginalization of Poetry,* Bob Perelman (1996) explores the rifts between poetry and the disciplines with which it interfaces (criticism, writ-ing, and theory). Although Perelman is specifically concerned with lan-guage poetry, his insights into how active writing strives to reconfigure critical categories, why verbal textures have significance, and where poems express identity politics apply broadly to late-twentieth-century American poetry. I want to take up one assertion he makes about the formal link-age of poetry and politics, both because resonances exist between recent German and American verse and for what his argument can tell us about the space Enzensberger and other German poets have claimed by talking about the marginalization of the lyric genre. Perelman observes:

> But the very weakness of the links between poetry, community, and state makes the issues of power and place in society vital for the poet. The fact that poets are hardly on the map adds an intense twist to the questions, what kinds of maps are poems? What authority does the poet have as a mapmaker? (1996, 110)

Perelman concludes that asking such questions can serve to map the way different corners of the poetry world connect (1996, 110). My task in this part of the chapter is to look at various linkages that have occurred in the German context that elucidate Enzensberger's intense, programmatic con-cern with literary and the lyric genre in the 1990s.

The bleak prognosis for German poetry after about 1980 contrasted sharply with the arguably naive optimism that grounded discussions about poetry and translation around 1945; for the last decade of the twentieth century, doubt seemed to set the tone. Immediate postwar traditions of na-ture poetry, hermetic verse, and experimental work had once before been overshadowed by pessimism about the lyric genre as German poetry under-went the paradigmatic shift of the tumultuous 1960s that subordinated it to instrumental purpose (as *Agitprop* [agitation-propaganda]) and a crude discovery of reality (*Entdeckung der Wirklichkeit;* Korte 1989, 100).[37] But the mood of resignation that ensued in the 1970s—which witnessed the development of *Neue Subjektivität* (New Subjectivity)—represented, if not an actual contraction of literature, then at the very least an unraveling of the coherent trends chronicled by Hermann Korte in his definitive survey of postwar German poetry. Korte concluded that "the lyric genre at the end of the 1980s no longer places any confidence in a binding goal-oriented perspective" (1989, 206), an assessment shared by most scholars of poetry from the last decade of the twentieth century.

Since conclusions about this recent poetry have necessarily remained tentative, historical dates have often been used to achieve a formal peri-odization or the necessary unifying perspective about the profusion of trends. Thus, James Rolleston eloquently asserted that in the post-Wende era after 1989, "German poetry can never be divorced from German history and the perpetual socio-linguistic unease that accompanies consciousness of that history" (1997, 8). Karen Leeder's definitive study *Breaking Boundaries* (1996) made productive use of history as a foundational concept in recent GDR poetry. Indeed, this sense of history has weight all across German verse, where, as Judith Ryan has noted, "[m]any postreunification poets regard the world as a kind of palimpsest in which past texts co-exist with present experience" (1997, 47). The explicit postwar sense of history evident in the work of Volker Braun, Wolfgang Hilbig, Karin Kiwus, Uwe Kolbe, Sarah Kirsch, Ursula Krechel, Günter Kunert, and Thomas Rosenlöcher meshes with the layered linguistic references to the past that Ryan discerns in the work of younger authors such as Kurt Drawert, Rainer Schedlinski, Bert Papenfuß-Gorek, and Durs Grünbein.

Despite the confidence of scholars and poets in historical dates as an index for poetry, recent articles by critics and poets in German literary journals have increasingly pointed to the ways in which the lyric genre per se distances itself from social entanglements and political imperatives. The perceived disengagement has given rise to some poetry criticism written for a broad, educated audience that operates at cross-purposes to tracts for academic scholars in the exclusive discipline of *Literaturwissenschaft* (literary science). These appeals ask readers to appreciate literacy and the autonomous, artistic imagination. Whether or not an audience of sophisticated readers for poetry exists (or should exist) and how literary taste corresponds to quality have become hotly debated topics. Enzensberger's essays and poetry generally anticipate the attention other authors have given this subject, as a survey of literary journals indicates. In fact, most writers who lament the palpable eclipse of the lyric genre reiterate the controversy about the so-called death of literature that Enzensberger started in the late 1960s.[38] New to the current discussion is the drastic pressure that mass culture, electronic media, and esoteric theory apply to poetry.

In observations from 1995 in a journal for intellectual debate, *Merkur*, Ulrich Schödlbauer asks, "Why, under conditions of modernism, does poetry and not only prose exist?" (1995, 171). Schödlbauer concludes that poetry is a marginalized art form, a medium stabilized only by the praxis of criticism. "Poetry," he comments, "distances itself in every possible way from communicative aspects that dominate in the prose of everyday commerce and the scientific formation of theory" (1995, 174).[39] This distance marks the raw edge where poetry seems to end. Wholesale abandonment of the lyric genre is often linked by writers to the failure of the 1960s culture to synthesize literature, life, and theory. With a recent, autobiographical article, "Was ist Lyrik heute?" ("What Is Poetry Today?"), Michael Rutschky (1998) confesses to not having read poetry for a long time. The beginnings of this avoidance he dates to the era of student protests:

> It must have been about 1966, before the student protests really took off. Hans Magnus Enzensberger, acclaimed as a poet, first declared one year later, if I remember correctly, that literature was at an end. To escape from an unhappy romance, I changed my place of study and stopped my lyric production. (1998, 170)[40]

Harald Hartung, responding to Rutschky, contradicts his views in a 1999 special issue of *Merkur* devoted to poetry.[41] Citing Enzensberger for support, Hartung concludes, "The lyric genre is dead, but the poem lives" (Hartung 1999, 330). His aphoristic rebuttal announces that although lyric poetry may have lost its former status, poems continue to be written, and indeed prolifically.

Hartung's authoritative reference in this matter is Enzensberger's 1989 essay "Meldungen vom lyrischen Betrieb" ("Reports from the Poetry Business"). Here Enzensberger hypothesized with characteristic tongue-in-cheek wit that readership numbers for the lyric genre operate according to what he termed the "Enzensbergerian Constant." This factor, according to the author, guarantees an audience of ±1,354 individuals for works of lyric poetry (1997c, 184). Reprinted in the 1997 collection *Zickzack* (*Zig Zag*), where it becomes part of 1990s discussions of poetry, the essay provocatively claims, "A good poet can count on exactly as many readers in Iceland . . . as in the United States" (1997c, 184).[42] An obviously rhetorical ploy, the "Enzensbergian Constant" dramatically labels the paradoxical status of poetry as an obscure, anachronistic enterprise in the public domain. Poetry exists as a tenacious private endeavor, yet is practiced by hundreds of thousands of aspiring writers, as Enzensberger recognized in *Wasserzeichen* (1985), where he commented, "If it were a matter of the number of producers, poetry would be a mass medium" (V).[43] The lyric genre has all the hallmarks of a failing business: a limited audience of consumers combined with rampant overproduction. Nonetheless, Enzensberger optimistically concludes that the lyric genre has undergone surprising reversals throughout history (1997c, 199).[44]

Enzensberger's tract boldly sketches a plethora of interrelated problems that challenge the viability of the lyric genre. Other recent essays about contemporary verse also diagnose the symptoms: German literature occupies a marginal status in relation to international trends; poets worry that aesthetic quality is declining in part because poems have been subordinated to heavy-handed theorizing or mere communication; poetry has apparently become socially irrelevant. These challenges are by no means unique to poetry written in German, or to this time.[45] Remarking that German literature has shrunk to a fraction of the publishing trade, Martin Hielscher in "Literatur in Deutschland—Avantgarde und pädagogischer Purismus" ("Literature in Germany—Avant-garde and Pedagogical Purism") reminds readers that "today contemporary German literature is a vanishing dimension not only in Europe but also in America, and American literature is considered exaggeratedly as a synonym for everything that is missing in German literature" (1995, 53). Of course, in the United States the lyric genre fares no better, for poetry itself captures only a tiny percentage of the U.S. literary market (Perloff 1998, 188–89). Indications of its further marginalization and specialization in the German literary context surface in essays that emphasize the ineffable ability of the *Kenner* (knowledgeable reader or perhaps connoisseur) to comprehend poems while rejecting externally imposed, rationalizing interpretations.

This recent focus on aesthetic quality in discussions of contemporary poetry has been accompanied by a burgeoning of companion discourses about writing that has similarities to the proliferation of texts about translation in the 1950s and 1960s. While literary journals have seen a resurgence of essays and statements authored by poets concerning the unique character of the lyric genre and the effects of technical innovations, poetry anthologists have chosen to emphasize matters of literary taste and the value of importing an international canon. Rather than casting poetry as either a vehicle for reconciliation or a tool for political communication as in earlier decades, current discussions focus on the very materiality of poetic texts. The poem's irreducibility to signifying operations, its appeal to all the senses, and its appropriation of presentational means from nonliterary sources figure prominently as issues. These formulations challenge both fixed academic canon and abstract theorizing about literature.

Gerhard Falkner's influential tract on poetry, *Über den Unwert des Gedichts* (*On the Worthlessness of the Poem*), drew attention to poetry's fundamental capacities as a medium of language in a manner that met with broad resonance (1993, 50). Thus Jörg Drews, referring with obvious admiration to Falkner's position in his afterword to *Das bleibt: Deutsche Gedichte 1945–1995* (*That Remains: German Poetry 1945–1995*), similarly argues against an "anything goes" attitude and in favor of a craft-oriented focus on language (1995, 264). Drews further uses his anthology to appeal to a specialized audience of connoisseurs or discerning readers:

> The foregoing selection of poems is dedicated to a reader of German poetry who has a quite different conception of it, whose seriousness and commitments in putting together his "Eternal Stock of German Poetry" I nonetheless cherish and revere. (1995, 265)

The program Drews propagates in *Das bleibt,* one that draws attention to the materiality of poem texts, accordingly insists "that poetry complexly has something to do with knowledge [*Erkenntnis*], with knowledge in the medium of the aesthetic" (1995, 264). His elevation of the poetic medium as a cultural and intellectual commodity is echoed in the attention the lyric genre has recently received as an international art form, of which two massive anthology projects, *Atlas der neuen Poesie* (*Atlas of New Poetry*), edited by Joachim Sartorius (1996), and *Die Erfindung der Poesie: Gedichte aus den ersten viertausend Jahren* (*The Invention of Poetry: Poems from the First Four Thousand Years*), compiled by Raoul Schrott (1998), give evidence.[46]

This new trend toward literary internationalism, the third since 1945, is more nuanced than its predecessors, for rather than clumsily articulating a naive universalism or espousing general philosophies, contemporary poets seem by and large to be distancing themselves from both theory and rationalizing interpretations of texts that claim to speak for poetry itself.[47] Much like Falkner, then, poet Brigitte Oleschinski cautions in her recent essay "Sturmzwitter" ("Storm-cross") that poems should under no circumstances be forced into a prescriptive mold.

> You should not force any poem, to anything. You should not mislead it into fitting into your intellectual inclination. You should neither burden it with your diagnoses of the time nor with your aesthetics, nor your politics. You should not place it on a stage. (1999, 390)[48]

Oleschinski reacts in particular against the constraints theory and politics place on poetry, but hers and other statements share a common distaste for literary criticism. This stand against external constraints is anticipated in Enzensberger's "Bescheidener Vorschlag zum Schutze der Jugend vor den Erzeugnissen der Poesie" ("Modest Proposal for the Protection of Youth from the Products of Poetry"; 1976a), which itself referenced American author Susan Sontag's iconoclastic essay "Against Interpretation" (1976).[49]

A tacit undercurrent in contemporary discussions is the contest between the poem and mass culture. This relationship is fraught with ambivalence, but an ambivalence that gives evidence of contemporary German poetry's debt to modernism even as it edges toward postmodernism. The culture of modernity, as Andreas Huyssen has persuasively contended, entails "a volatile relationship between high art and mass culture" within which a dialectic exists between the avant-garde and technology (1986, 9). Productions of poem texts have with ever increasing frequency employed electronic terminology, digital imagery, and even computer-based formats; yet these technical means, which promise new modes of expression, challenge the lyric genre's traditional textual strengths.[50]

The symbiosis between new media and the lyric genre problematizes the question of where poets choose to situate poetry within the continuum of high to low cultural artifacts. An established tradition of experimentation within literature exists in German-speaking countries (particularly Austria). This is currently represented in poetry by textually innovative authors including Friederike Mayröcker, Ernst Jandl, Elke Erb, and Oskar Pastior. Younger writers, including Gerhard Falkner, Durs Grünbein, Thomas Kling, Barbara Köhler, and Albert Ostermaier have more openly explored dynamic tensions between public and private language by exploiting intersections growing among poetry, the electronic media, film, and the visual arts, even though new media unquestionably challenge the integrity of old genres.[51] Indeed, Dirk von Petersdorff in a discussion of this problem reminds readers of Adorno's aversion to movies. Before describing the effect of new media on literature, von Petersdorff observes, "new media endanger the mechanisms of distinction. They call into battle the relevant orthodox intellectual type" (1997, 170). Enzensberger, for his part, has remained characteristically skeptical of electronic media, although fascinated by its potential for poetry. A strong advocate of the printed book, he invokes Gutenberg when he muses in a recent poem "Altes Medium" ("Old Medium") from *Kiosk* that those who are truly interested in virtual reality work minimally with words (1995b, 96), a somewhat paradoxical comment for an author for whom dozens of Web sites exist on the Internet.[52] What is at stake for him is the social relevance of the poem as a collective enterprise exhibited through an exchange between poets and readers over texts.

Amid so much flux in the lyric genre, Enzensberger appears to have come full circle in his late poetry, returning to Adorno, whose writings on the culture industry so uncannily forecasted the challenges posed to poetry by declining literacy, shifting values, and burgeoning competition from new media. "The lyric work hopes to attain universality through unrestrained individuation," the philosopher observed in "Rede über Lyrik und Gesellschaft" ("On Lyric Poetry and Society," 1991b, 38). "A second immediacy," he proposed, "is promised: what is human, language itself, seems to become creation again, while everything external dies away in the ends of the soul" (1991b, 41). It is this sense of the generative capacities of pure language—an essential kind of literacy—that infuses some of Enzensberger's most powerful late verse.

"Empfänger unbekannt—Retour à l'expéditeur," in English "Addressee Unknown," from *Kiosk* (1995) takes its title from a section of Adorno's *Minima Moralia* (1974a). Written in a style reminiscent of the final poems of Benn and Brecht, Enzensberger's text reflects, "Many thanks for the clouds, / Many thanks for the Well-tempered Clavichord / and, why not, for the warm winter boots" (1995, 124). Of the items cataloged, many are elements from earlier poems. The cloud mentioned here occurs in "Die Frösche von Bikini" ("The Frogs of Bikini") and the strawberries in "Sommergedicht" ("Summer Poem"). Other items belong to common experience—a lighter, caffeine, wine, and sleep. Finally, and in what Ziebritzski (1997) labels a liturgical tone, Enzensberger gives thanks for fleeting time:

> für den Anfang und das Ende
> und die paar Minuten dazwischen
> inständigen Dank,
> meinetwegen für die Wühlmäuse draußen im Garten auch.
> (Enzensberger 1995, 124)

> *for the beginning and the end*
> *and the few minutes in between*
> *fervent thanks,*
> *even, if you like, for the voles out there in the garden.*
> (Enzensberger 1999d, 84)

This touching, eschatological gesture of gratitude ends the poem on a note of self-effacing reflection.

In his own "Retour à l'expéditeur" ("Addressee Unknown"), Adorno cautioned against imposing inappropriate exploitative demands on art. "Cultivated philistines are in the habit of requiring that a work of art 'give' them something" (1974a, 216), an excuse, he continued, for dismissing works that do not comply with this demand. And here the reader must sense the irony of the gestures Enzensberger's poem performs by way of thanks, for in this the text places itself out of the reach of untoward demands that art serve a particular politic, follow a certain style, or exclude a marginalized genre like lyric poetry. Already in *Der Untergang der Titanic,* one of the main protagonists, the painter, rejected the notion that art should serve ideological purposes, declaring "There is no art without pleasure" (1980b, 24). Adorno's "Retour à l'expéditeur" pursues this point by looking for what is essential, concluding that art must always be predicated on an undemanding reciprocity of give-and-take that is found in the best human relations.

One of the chief paradoxes Enzensberger has addressed through his poetic work is how to reconcile contradictory demands on the lyric genre—its capacity to express intimate perceptions and its status as a public medium. For this purpose, dichotomies, such as tradition versus the avant-garde or poetry and politics, have often served him well because they efficiently sketch out contested terrain. And although the private and public are not necessarily congenial elements within the lyric genre, they are perhaps less incompatible than they initially appear. Adorno noted in his 1957 talk "On Lyric Poetry and Society" that poetry offers the possibility of moving beyond purely personal utterance:

> Today, when individual expression, which is the precondition for the conception of lyric poetry that is my point of departure, seems shaken to its very core in the crisis of the individual, the collective undercurrent in the lyric surfaces in the most diverse places: first merely as the ferment of individual expressions and then perhaps also as an anticipation of a situation that transcends mere individuality in a positive way. (1991b, 46)

While Enzensberger from the start of his career has harbored a perception of crisis akin to this sentiment, he quite famously departed from Adorno's position—especially the latter's statement concerning poetry after Auschwitz—by insisting that it is necessary to continue writing.[53] Mapping the collective spaces available to the lyric genre, Enzensberger has enlarged poetry through his work in translation and his defense of literature against incursions on literacy. He has practiced poetry writing as a matter of choice. Such poetry does not simply rely on unexpected sporadic, private inspiration. The poems Enzensberger has self-consciously crafted systematically mine the given—existing canons, related discourses, and ephemeral conversations—using a highly varied set of strategies. He has resisted genre constraints, mediated international literary currents, absorbed new language, oscillated from critical theory to an exploration of long and prose-like poems, engaged with scientific theory, and looked to the local to explain the global. Beyond these subjects, of course, there are many other ways in which Enzensberger's poetry can be read. The poetic maneuvers I have chosen to trace in his work are unified by their role in sustaining the lyric genre's collective ends as part of larger purposes—a gesture of resistance that keeps the poem itself from being overwhelmed by the cacophony of mere individual voices.

2. Righting and Rewriting Poetry

What remains striking about the poems in Hans Magnus Enzensberger's first three collections of verse is the virtuosic poetic talent they display. Few authors writing in any language ply such a broad repertoire of techniques or have so quickly thoroughly transformed their poetic idiom as Enzensberger did from *Verteidigung der Wölfe* (*Defense of the Wolves;* 1957b), through *Landessprache* (*Language of the Country;* 1960d), to *Blindenschrift* (1964d). The poems in these collections move from a magniloquent and highly rhetorical register toward an unembellished plain style. They also progress from narrative to discursive mode while testing language's mimetic capacities from multiple vantage points. Read in terms of their poetic strategies, the texts in these collections explore subtle relationships between poetry and its context in a way that redefines the lyric genre. They interrogate the capacity of verse to speak with moral authority about political concerns, reflect self-consciously on the construction of poetic discourse, and traverse the distance between individual, provincial origins and what Enzensberger termed the *Weltsprache,* or universal world language, of modern verse.

These and other protean changes have since continued to characterize Enzensberger's writings. During his early career, they vexed even sympathetic readers of his work. "He abandons one position after another," the novelist Martin Walser (who was acquainted with Enzensberger) observed in 1961, continuing wryly, "no wonder that he is hit on the open field by every storm" (1999, 18). Still, coherent transformations did in fact characterize his initial verse collections. Enzensberger's project to rethink writerly concerns unfolded not only in his poems but also in journalistic pieces, literary essays, and translations. Its salient features included both deliberations about the social, historical, and literary position of texts (in other words, the ways in which contemporary poetry situates itself externally) and progressive experimentation with content, voice, and formal devices (that is, aspects internal to poetry texts). Enzensberger's insistence on the capacity of the poetic medium to deliberate theoretical issues elevated the lyric genre to a unique position within his oeuvre that it maintained throughout the 1950s and early 1960s. Close reading of his verse in conjunction with prose pieces and translations from this period identifies intertextual connections among his publishing activities that are more extensive and nuanced than has generally been recognized in interpretations of his work. In particular, American and other international models that interested Enzensberger during the first two decades after World War II played a pivotal role in his efforts to argue against a dichotomous view of the lyric genre as either *poésie pure* or *poésie engagée*. In the ostensibly objective yet culturally fluid space of essays, anthologies, and translations, Enzensberger began to connect poetic technique with theoretical reflections about how authors or intellectuals should reshape literature, address social issues, and position texts with respect to readers.

Enzensberger's concern with a broad array of writerly matters shapes the voice that characterizes his poetry up to 1965. While his essays vigorously advocated a poetry legitimated by political integrity, connection to a canon of world literature, and technical innovation, his verse and translations give evidence that the working out of this agenda followed several paths, some of which proved more productive than others. Tracing the continuities between Enzensberger's early poetry and that of the American modernists he translated, I shall argue that in absorbing their aesthetic of plain style and discursive mode,[1] Enzensberger sought both a new language and a validation of poetry as a genre. His realization of these values, however, followed a very gradual process, one that raised issues of poetic representation that eventually had a destabilizing impact on German lyric poetry.[2] A preliminary sketch of the postwar literary scene will precede discussion of Enzensberger's views of the poetic canon, for my analysis of his translations from the English (the problems encountered and solutions devised) leads to the conclusion that his response to foreign texts formed one stage in the progressive articulation of poetic voice that was played out against that background of intellectual flux after 1945.[3] This incremental reception helps explain two unresolved issues in the history of postwar German literature: where to locate continuities in discussions about poetic authority that occurred in Germany between the end of the Second World War and the early 1960s, and how to discern the oblique yet powerful influence of American verse on German poetry.

The shift in Enzensberger's lyric poetry from an approach that relied to a conspicuous extent on self-conscious rhetoric to one that cultivated unpretentiousness constitutes an initiative to draw the abstract medium of language into a closer relation to reality. The effect of these two poetic modes is quite different. Rhetorical poetry, which is often associated with didactic verse, is characterized by an antagonistic stance toward precursors and a preference for poetic structures driven by lexicon and logic. Poetry written in plain style, which tends to emphasize individual insight, is marked by naturalized voice, poetic line used as the unit of meaning, and informal verse forms. The reality evoked by plain style represents a world of quotidian experience and everyday speech in which the poet assumes the role of a reliable participant-observer. But this notion of verisimilitude—which Enzensberger takes up in his essay on William Carlos Williams where he favors *Evidenz* (evidence) over *Deutung* (interpretation) as an aesthetic value—raises fundamental questions about how literary representations can be constructed and how poems need to be interpreted. Quotidian subject matter within a poem ostensibly invites readers to understand a text on its own terms rather than as an expression of generic conventions, yet this representational mode does little to resolve the tension of sometimes conflicting discourses foregrounded in Enzensberger's writing. Indeed, not long after his account of Williams's work was published, Enzensberger began to question the notions of artistic illusion, literary convention, stable dichotomization of perspectives, and political autonomy toward which he had been working. The reservations he subsequently voiced about the situation of contemporary literature, most notably in his 1968 essay "Gemeinplätze, die Neueste Literatur betreffend" ("Commonplaces on the Newest Literature") in *Kursbuch* 15 (1968a), were mistakenly interpreted as proclaiming a "death of literature" (*Tod der Literatur*). This apparently radical challenge to literature, however, mirrored again an earlier postwar sense of rupture that had originally prompted Enzensberger's efforts to address questions of political engagement, literary canon, and the nature of poetry.

World and Provincial Literatures

Somewhat younger than the authors and intellectuals who had initiated the immediate postwar discussions about the relationship between politics and literature, Enzensberger established himself in the late 1950s and early 1960s as an insightful commentator on the literary scene, in part by persuasively evoking and summarizing debates that had been under way for a decade about German literature in the post-Holocaust era. Drawing conclusions that could be substantiated retrospectively, his accounts of the reconstruction epoch, expressed chiefly in literary essays published around 1960, focused on the break signified by 1945 and on the drive on the part of younger authors to reshape poetic language in the wake of dramatic political and social change. Enzensberger, who presumed an abrupt rupture with the past, advocated a program of aesthetic and cultural renewal in which poetry figured prominently. Yet as Frank Trommler (1977), Hermann Korte (1989), Ralf Schnell (1993), and other scholars have confirmed, the lyric genre immediately after the end of the war was characterized more by continuity with existing stylistic traditions than by radical transformation.[4] In contrast to the findings of literary histories, Enzensberger's labor to recapitulate and consolidate the persuasive narrative of the *Stunde Null* (zero hour) has an ideological function, identifying poetry as a site for public discourse about historical change rather than as a medium reserved exclusively for the expression of private, affective impressions.

The immediate postwar years had witnessed repeated calls on the part of German intellectuals for fundamental social change, as in the appeal crafted by Alfred Andersch (with whom Enzensberger came into contact while employed as a radio editor in Stuttgart) for *Deutsche Literatur in der Entscheidung* (*German Literature at the Decision Point* [1948]), which admonished intellectuals to take a leading role in advocating democratic practices. The terms coined to characterize the situation, like *Kahlschlag* (a clear-cutting), originally used by Wolfgang Weyrauch to describe Günter Eich's famous poem "Inventur" ("Inventory"; Weyrauch 1949, 214), *Nullpunkt* (zero point), and the phrase *Stunde Null,* had the salutary effect of countering "unprogressive" restoration tendencies in the first postwar decade. Vivid metaphors, these rubrics, along with *Trümmerlyrik* (*Rubble Poetry*), allowed progressive authors to distance themselves effectively from conservative trends by envisioning an open space for new literature to claim.

Efforts to achieve cultural transformation after 1945 were also enhanced by the policies of the occupation forces and changes in the structure of the German publishing industry (Schnell 1993, 1–65, 82–88). After an initial period when works determined to be inappropriate faced removal from circulation, a constructive phase followed, during which licensed translations became one tool for reeducation (Schnell 1993, 87). The massive influx of books by international or previously banned authors was regulated under the strict licensing procedures established by the Allies. Subsequent critical analysis from the late 1970s, such as Hansjörg Gehring's "Literatur im Dienst der Politik: Zum Re-education Programm der amerikanischen Militärregierung in Deutschland" ("Literature in the Service of Politics: Concerning the Re-education Program of the American Military Government in Germany" [1977]), recognized the ideological intent of these initiatives, largely unacknowledged at the time. As Schnell observes, "the intention of the American re-education program was to change fundamentally the German national character, which was seen as the primary cause for the rise of Fascism, through schooling, upbringing, culture" (1993, 83). In essence, this dichotomization of art and politics worked for two decades to obscure the power dynamics of these cultural alliances.

Remarks by John R. Frey, a contemporary American university professor, attest to the impact these policies had by the mid-1950s. "It is not uncommon," Frey commented about European critics, "to find them suggesting that the adoption of some things American might well be beneficial to Europe" (1953–54, 4). Reporting on the fascination with American literature, Frey cited the astonishing fact that between 1945 and 1950, some seven hundred American books were published in German translation (1954–55, 9).[5] And yet, Frey explained, "American lyric poetry is not offered abundantly in German," to which he added that despite the availability of works by Eliot, MacLeish, and Auden, "they come nowhere near filling the demand for lyric poetry" (1954–55, 11). Frey sees the supply problem from a monolingual perspective that overlooks the fact that many Germans knew or quickly learned English after the war.[6] The apparent quantitative discrepancy between the availability of German poetry and the paucity of translated verse becomes qualitatively less significant when we consider that exposure to American poetry did not depend on a poem being mediated via translation.[7] Writing about events after the German capitulation, Enzensberger recalled the paperbacks he had obtained through contact with an American officer. Among books that he was allowed to take was an anthology by Louis Untermeyer. "His anthology of modern American poetry opened new perspectives to my malleable understanding," Enzensberger comments (1999f, 100). Such testimony is evidence of ephemeral, unmediated encounters with international literature that have become difficult to piece together. Even direct contacts between American authors and writers on the continent left only faint traces of important literary exchanges, such as the letters among Rainer M. Gerhardt, Charles Olson, and Robert Creeley.[8]

By the mid-1950s, the steady influx of foreign literature had provoked a wary ambivalence that led many to reconsider the meaning of the cultural transformations that had occurred. Frey commented in 1954 that "for the past two years there have been increasing signs among the intelligentsia of a definite weariness and wariness toward American literature" (1954–55, 11). Christian Ferber's short statement "Die Legende vom Kahlschlag" ("The Legend of the Clear Cut") in the literary magazine *Die Literatur* (1952) signals the emergence of this reaction; later comments by the influential anthologist Hans Bender in "Letter from Germany: The Myth of Kahlschlag" (1972) verify that much dissension developed over the concept of the *Stunde Null*. This shift in attitudes about international influences is especially noticeable within the writings of Karl Krolow, who in the 1950s described the influx of foreign literature as "the most important event with which above all the younger poets had to deal after the war" (1954, 475). By the 1960s, however, Krolow cautioned against misguided, uncritical adoption of foreign poetry (1961, 13).[9]

Taking up the optimistic narrative of rupture, progressive change, and a new beginning represented by the *Stunde Null,* Enzensberger's own accounts of the literary scene selectively reiterate salient points of postwar history. In essays from around 1960, Enzensberger pointedly invokes *Stunde Null* to mark ideological and aesthetic boundaries between his vision of literature and the literature of the recent past. His afterword to *Museum der modernen Poesie* links the closing date of the anthology, 1945, and by extension the fate of the lyric genre, with political events when it asserts, "Is it superfluous to say that the Second World War, that Auschwitz and Hiroshima also marked epochs for poetry? Many don't want to admit it" (1980 [ed.], 774–75).[10] A swift refutation of those who would dismiss claims that Auschwitz changed poetry forever follows this rhetorical question. For Enzensberger, this matter does not require debate. His subsequent 1963 essay "In Search of the Lost Language," which offered an overview of German postwar poetry for a British audience, similarly emphasizes the discontinuities of the two epochs. "In Germany 1933 and 1945 are not merely dates of political history. These years are total, like the regime whose domination they mark. During these twelve years German literature of more than parochial significance existed only outside the frontiers of Germany: among the émigrés" (1963d, 44).

This stark rendering of the interplay between literature and history introduces Enzensberger's description of how poetry evolved after the war. The evocation of historical dates foregrounds the capacity of poetry to speak to highly emotional issues (fascism and the Holocaust) and maps out a social framework that reminds readers of literature's function in representing national culture. In its general outlines, the depiction corresponds to a view of events already formed by other, more established poets, but here it models an intellectual attitude of coming to terms with the past.

Around 1960, the concept of paradigmatic change became strongly equated with a commitment to creating a new German poetry; at this point the concept of a literary ground zero gathered affective force. Paul Celan, the author of some of the most significant poetry against the Holocaust, had, for instance, in a 1958 speech upon his receipt of the Bremen Literary Prize, poignantly described the sense that everything had been lost in the war except for the language, out of which a new poetry needed to be painstakingly shaped (1968, 127). In 1961, Karl Krolow, known for his lyric poetry about nature, also cited the war's end as significant for literature. Employing a somewhat more reserved formulation than Celan, Krolow nonetheless passionately defended his view that "[t]he often-enough-cited and thereby worn-out 'Zero Hour' of the year 1945 was also an unparalleled opportunity for the poem to establish itself anew" (1961, 11). Enzensberger's writings, by contrast, utilized concrete evocations of history (the names and dates Auschwitz, Hiroshima, 1933, and 1945), which he wielded as factual evidence to support his contention that German poetry should resituate itself in an international context. Only doing so, he deduced, would allow the lyric genre to surmount the provinciality to which fascist cultural policies had previously constrained it. His is an appeal directed to several audiences, especially the international reading public and practicing poets.

The synopsis of postwar trends supplied in Enzensberger's "In Search of the Lost Language" (1963d) affords a broad celebration of German verse that embraces progressive (though not exclusively avant-garde) literary currents. The language of this essay commingles portrayal and critique of its subject even as it represents German verse traditions, a design that advantages Enzensberger's own carefully reasoned priorities. Nature poetry, which initially dominated the German postwar literary scene and only gradually gave way to more innovative forms, is depicted as exceedingly popular but insidiously precious in its focus on an unrealistically constructed "kleine heile Welt" (safe little world). As one of the initial challenges to this trend, "In Search of the Lost Language" acknowledges Gottfried Benn as the figure who paved the way for the development of hermetic verse through the emphasis on the formal aspects of poetry advocated in his influential address *Probleme der Lyrik* (*Problems of the Lyric* [1951]). Yet Enzensberger also quite explicitly sounds a cautionary note about *l'art pour l'art* attitudes by mentioning Benn's initial fascination with Nazism and the earnest consequences morally detached aestheticism had after Hitler's ascent to power. This coalescence of the aesthetic with the political is the characteristic thrust of Enzensberger's poetry and essays during this period, the manner in which he insistently defines the parameters of a postwar debate about the position of literature in contemporary society.[11]

The disparate impulses Enzensberger cites in "In Search of the Lost Language" as contributing to the diversity of German poetry resist comfortable synthesis, but he describes at length trends to which he himself was unambivalently drawn: Brecht's work, political verse, expressionism, dadaism, and concrete poetry (see Werner 1968). Enzensberger's account of hermetic poetry—a trend that dominated literary attention until 1970 when Celan, whom many regarded as its leading representative, committed suicide—is predictably mixed. Hermetic verse is hailed by Enzensberger as one of several developments that allowed German literature to aspire once again to international stature. His assessment of it, however, introduced by an extensive quotation from Celan's famous poem "Todesfuge" ("Death Fugue") dwells not on literary nuances but rather on its potentially effete aspects. Describing Celan as "the first [postwar poet] to recognize that in poetry as little could be achieved by opinions as by the current flight into the herbarium" (1963d, 48), Enzensberger predicts a trajectory from the poet's recently published *Sprachgitter* (*Speech-grille*) into a space of linguistic rarefication. In this respect, hermetic verse shared with Enzensberger's quite different work a preoccupation with one highly intractable problem of the postwar era: how to counter its own marginalization. Hermetic poetry thematized this marginalization by mirroring the effects of a progressive silencing of the human voice; Enzensberger's poems vociferously railed against the world, refusing to accept politely a lesser, marginal role.

Enzensberger's pessimistically tinged prediction of an ominous silence reminds readers that at this time, and indeed well into the 1960s, the conservative literary climate was unwelcoming for poets like himself, who pursued a literature that unabashedly reveled in the pragmatic and quotidian. Resistance to the outspokenness of his work colored the reaction of critics who wavered in their assessments of his talent. Sometimes pigeonholed as merely political or rebellious and at other times regarded as an anomaly, Enzensberger's suitability for the Georg Büchner Prize in 1963, which he received precociously early in his career, was challenged by conservative critics.[12] For Enzensberger's part, an acerbic critique of prevailing literary tastes motivated poems such as "Goldener Schnittmusterbogen zur poetischen Wiederaufrüstung" ("Golden Paper Pattern Chart for Poetic Rearmament"), a parody of Hölderlin, Benn, Celan, and nature poetry that quips "Stiftet lieber, was bleibet: Die Dummheit. / Balsamierter Lorbeer der Anthologien / Das Unvergängliche: Teerosen und Kartoffeln" ("Endow rather that which will remaineth: Stupidity. / Embalmed laurel of the anthologies / The immortal: Tea roses and potatoes") (1957b, 87).[13] In these lines, Enzensberger attacks a literary parochialism with which his essays contrast an enlightened, cosmopolitan concept of a *Weltsprache der modernen Poesie* (world language of modern poetry) (1980 [ed.], 773). As an aesthetic program, this internationalization had much to offer younger German poets, but it also complicated the construction of individual poetic identity.

By calling up notions of a poetic lingua franca and of *Weltliteratur* (world literature), Enzensberger advocated a rigorous coming to terms with modern tradition instead of a passive reception of foreign models. This project endorsed world literature as a collective intellectual discourse venerated in German letters since Goethe. Engaging with that progressive ethos by invoking a world canon as the standard against which German writing must be measured, the *Museum* essay employed terminology that subtly co-opted elements of fascist rhetoric that had vilified cosmopolitanism. Here admiration of the international stands in blunt contradiction to the deprecation of cosmopolitanism that can be found, for example, in the writings of Oswald Spengler.[14] Enzensberger's language positions his statements about poetry in a framework of public debate about national identity, yet allows for self-presentation of Germany to the world community through culture, thereby avoiding overtones of nationalism.[15]

In some respects Enzensberger's literary program resembled projects begun by the poet Rainer Maria Gerhardt (who committed suicide in 1954 and with whom Enzensberger had come into contact in Freiburg), but it also displayed several distinctive features.[16] Central to Enzensberger's writings are the assertions that translation could serve as a heuristic device for transforming contemporary, original poetry, that American authors were an integral part of the canon of modernism, and that neither the gratuitously new nor the hidebound old should be endorsed (1980 [ed.], 765–66). Three key texts delineated Enzensberger's position: "Die babylonische Bibliothek" ("The Babylonian Library" [1960b]), "Die Weltsprache der modernen Poesie" ("The World Language of Modern Poetry" [1960c]; originally the afterword to *Museum,* revised in 1962 for inclusion in *Einzelheiten II* [1964f]), and "Die Aporien der Avantgarde" ("The Aporias of the Avant-Garde" [1976b]; written in 1962 and later reprinted in *Einzelheiten II* [1964f]). Although literary internationalism figures in his other writings as well, these essays contain the most fully articulated expressions of his position, for in them the author rejects both epochal and national boundaries for literature. He attributes instead an eclectic spirit to modern poetry. This assertion of universal aesthetic principles, which occurs via general, programmatic statements about modernist literature, elides potential questions about the extent to which the author's assumptions reflect generational, class, or gender values. Enzensberger's description of literary culture likewise equivocates about where high modernism and mass culture divide.

The first of the essays to be published, "Die babylonische Bibliothek," raises issues of canon formation and eclecticism by means of evocative vignettes and hyperbole.[17] This brief feuilleton begins with the fictive "nightmare" of a world where everything is reproducible and where the author finds himself in the role of a librarian barred from discarding a single book (1960b, 37). Reading much like a thinly veiled account of what happened in Germany with the postwar influx of foreign literature, the text muses that such a drive for completeness could result in an utter loss of perspective. "Nothing may remain untranslated, everything is dated, edited, immortalized and thereby made present. In the process, the following paradox arises: The more this historical treatment of everything that was near its completion, the more the consciousness of the historical distance from which this process derives vanishes" (38). Enzensberger resolves this dilemma not by endorsing more vigorous historical contextualization but rather by urging rigorous selectivity because, as he continues, "Where everything (from synthetic fiber to the bomb) is potentially a 'classic' there is no Classic anymore. It is only imaginable where strict selection, but that also means limitation, indeed limitedness, is practiced" (38). While conjuring up a vision that borders on postmodernism in its prediction of jumbled aesthetics, Enzensberger reaffirms essentially modernist cultural values, which are to be preserved through discerning connoisseurship that will dispel this nightmare.

The imaginary library, where the critical reader "wants to advance his work or find his pleasure" (Enzensberger 1960b, 38), bears a strong resemblance to the Nuremberg library, where Enzensberger reports having found refuge from detested wartime military drills by immersing himself in holdings "from polar exploration to sexuality research, and from trash novels to Catullus and Marcus Aurelius" (1999a, 120). It also resembles *Museum der modernen Poesie*, which Enzensberger declared a hands-on collection and thus by no means a permanently defined exhibit (1980 [ed.], 767). A highly influential anthology, *Museum* contained poetry translated from sixteen languages by some of the most prominent German poets of the postwar era (Bachmann, Celan, Fried, Heissenbüttel, Hermlin, Kaschnitz, Krolow, and Sachs) and accomplished translators (Ernst Robert Curtius, Eva Hesse, and Kurt Heinrich Hansen).[18] While a number of its authors were familiar to German audiences (Eliot, Benn, Brecht, and Rilke, for instance), others were virtually unknown. Its inclusions reflected the postwar rediscovery of surrealism, dadaism, and German expressionism, combined with a broadening of the canon to include American poets and also a few authors residing in South America, the Middle East, and Africa whose works were unique to what Enzensberger collected.[19] Further, Enzensberger divided the anthology into genre-oriented sections, many of which correspond closely to approaches to poetry adopted in his own work—*Momentaufnahme*, poems that are the snapshots of a moment, portraits, and apocalyptic visions.

The selections in *Museum* respond to, but also diverge from, the poetic canon formed by the work of two unacknowledged predecessors, Hugo Friedrich and Gottfried Benn.[20] In addition, as indicated in the essay that accompanied this volume, the poems themselves employed construction techniques common to Enzensberger's own lyric poetry, especially montage (detailed by Reinhold Grimm in "Montierte Lyrik" ["Montaged Poetry"; 1984, 21–43]) and polyvalent language (identified by Wulf Koepke in "Mehrdeutigkeit in Hans Magnus Enzensbergers 'Bösen Gedichten'" ["Ambiguity in Hans Magnus Enzensberger's 'Angry Poems'"; 1971]). Together the anthology and its original afterword propose a poet's canon of poetry. A dense web of allusions to progressive and conservative writers offers a richly textured account of poetry as the product of individual authors, writerly style, national character, and an elusive poetic essence. This subtle blending of the perspectives of poet, scholar, and critic produces a highly relational description of the lyric genre that casts it as a medium shaped by tenacious internal forces and the influence of its context.

Friedrich's study of modern poetry, *Die Struktur der modernen Lyrik* (*The Structure of Modern Poetry* [1958]), originally written in 1956, had supplied an influential set of interpretations based on close readings of texts, an approach eminently suited to the nascent trend toward hermetic poetry but also reflective of the historical context in which modernism developed.[21] For Friedrich—who contended that "[t]he type of poetry that dominates the twentieth century was born in France during the second half of the nineteenth century" (1958, 107)—the modern lyric followed a lineage that extended from Baudelaire, Rimbaud, Mallarmé, and their followers. Novalis and Poe received brief mention in this genealogy; Whitman appears unimportant. Enzensberger in *Museum,* on the other hand, began his canon quite differently: "Modern poetry here means: poetry after Whitman and Baudelaire, after Rimbaud and Mallarmé" (1980 [ed.], 765). His remark accorded a prominence to the American poet that registers a postwar shift in cultural center from Europe toward the United States. A more detailed list of major protagonists (especially Poe, Dickinson, Hopkins, Alexander Blok, and Yeats) maps a further expansion beyond Friedrich's Continental bounds (Enzensberger 1980 [ed.], 771–72). In an examination of the individual poems *Museum* included, Christoph Rodiek in "Lyrische Weltsprache als Intertext" ("Lyrical World Poetry as Intertext"; 1990) has demonstrated that Enzensberger displayed a highly complex understanding of intertextuality in his selection. Concerning how Enzensberger's ideological preferences shape the afterword, Karla Lydia Schultz observes, "Enzensberger conceives of modern poetry in a way that is more limited in time and defined more precisely in political terms than Friedrich, but takes it much further in spatial terms" (1993, 431). Enzensberger's categories of poetic technique also diverge from Friedrich's. While Friedrich applies to modern poetry descriptions such as "disorientation," "depersonalization," "the aesthetics of ugliness," "language magic," "monologue poetry," "the nearness of silence," and "obscurity," Enzensberger interrogates these typologies by calling attention to the prescriptively formative nature of critical labels. As an alternative, he proposes deferring to the text itself as the arbiter of meaning:

> About the rules of modern poetry certainly very little has been determined. It is tempting to read its production in a direction we believe we

can recognize: montage and ambiguity, fracturing and refunctioning of rhyme, dissonance and absurdity. . . . To what extent these and other catchwords and categories that one has mustered up for the theoretical understanding of modern poetry are valid and useful, that the texts themselves will determine. (1980 [ed.], 770)

The notion of textual authority evoked here, reminiscent of the author's objections to Staiger's account of poetry, accords a higher priority to creative production than to criticism of literature. Enzensberger's evaluative scheme invites comparison with at least three different discussions of literature operative in the German postwar context. Two were approaches to literary interpretation: the American New Criticism and the Continental *werkimmanent* (work immanent) interpretation, especially as articulated by Hans Georg Gadamer.[22] The third and most immediate antecedent to Enzensberger's afterword to *Museum* existed in the work of Gottfried Benn.

Enzensberger's interest in and suspicion of Benn's aestheticism hinges on the intersection of political and aesthetic questions. Like Friedrich, Enzensberger considers *Destruktion und Rückgriff* (destruction of and recourse to the past) fundamental traits of the modern lyric. Moreover, of the authors included in Friedrich's appendix on modern poetry, all but four (Diego, Valéry, Krolow, and Kaschnitz) also appear in *Museum*.[23] Yet, while Enzensberger's anthology in major respects assimilates and then expands the modernist canon proclaimed in *Die Struktur der modernen Lyrik* (1958), it simultaneously combines this canon with an interrogation of modernism as it is defined by Benn in his address *Probleme der Lyrik* (1951)[24] Above all, the process of composition Benn advocates comes under considerable scrutiny because it isolates poetry from social responsibilities.[25]

With Friedrich, Benn locates the beginnings of modern poetry in France and cites Mallarmé as its central innovator (Benn 1951, 8–9). The pantheon of modern authors he invokes likewise incorporates many of the same French symbolists as Friedrich's, along with several German expressionists and dadaists, surrealists, and three Anglo-American authors (Auden, Pound, and Eliot). Those selections all find their parallels in Enzensberger's anthology. Benn in fact mentions only a few authors excluded by Enzensberger. These include Henry Miller (whose prose Enzensberger sharply critiques in a review [1957a]), Stefan George, and Hugo von Hofmannsthal, whose conspicuous absence from the anthology is subjectively justified in the afterword as a matter of personal choice, an editorial decision much criticized by reviewers (Holthusen 1967, 191).

Significant differences between Benn's and Enzensberger's positions, however, emerge in the account the two authors give of the process of composition and in their radically different views of how the work of art functions in its social and cultural context. Enzensberger boldly suggests that his *Museum* exists not as a static mausoleum for dead authors and the past but as a dynamic workplace for contemporary poets:[26]

> The museum is an establishment whose purpose has become obscure. It is generally considered an attraction, not a workplace. It would be more appropriate to think of the museum as an annex to the atelier; it should not mummify things of the past, but instead render them usable, not put itself out of reach of criticism's grasp, but expose itself to it. Thus the literary museum plays the same role in relation to the writing desk of contemporary productive work as the means does to the ends. (1980 [ed.], 766–67)

The trope of the dynamic museum, of ongoing importance in Enzensberger's work, and of its counterpart, the mausoleum with its dead exhibition of objects, seem to allude to Adorno's essay "Valéry Proust Museum," in *Prismen* (1955b; *Prisms* [1967b]), although Reinhold Grimm has proposed André Malraux as a likely source for the allusion.[27] Valéry, in Adorno, regarded museums as cemeteries for art that neutralized the effects of culture (1955b, 215). Proust, by contrast, reveled in the museum as a site for reflection and aesthetic contemplation (Adorno 1955b, 219). "Valéry feels himself at home in the studio," Adorno writes, "Proust strolls through an exhibition" (1967b, 180). Enzensberger, who does not mention Adorno in this connection, fuses the museum and the atelier to create a dynamic new literary institution by appropriating the terms of his argument.

While neither Benn nor Friedrich strictly opposed the use of tradition—Friedrich, in fact, saw appropriation as the mark of great poets (1958, 107–8) and Benn acknowledged that poems are in a sense the product of many hands (1951, 20)—Enzensberger's destabilization of a fixed canon and his argument in favor of rigorous manipulation of literary tradition are more radically conceived (1980 [ed.], 767). Benn speaks of the isolation of the writer (1951, 31), of a focus on words during the act of creating poetry (18–19), and thus implicitly of originality as an individual act. Enzensberger, by contrast, casts poetry as entangled in its surroundings, hence profoundly political in its drive to overturn existing aesthetic and social conventions. This conception emphatically contradicts Benn's formulation of the lyric genre as absolute and immutable (1980 [ed.], 777).[28]

Despite the fact that both authors trace the lineage of their thinking on this subject to a common source, Valéry, Enzensberger reaches far different conclusions about the nature of poetic creation.[29] With remarks dismissing inspiration as a romantic notion and proclaiming form central to the lyric, Benn suggests that since an author works and reworks poetic language, the poem becomes anonymous by the time it reaches its final state (1951, 20). The point leads Benn to propose "das absolute Gedicht" (the absolute poem), a text which achieves a level of abstraction and timelessness distanced from reality that renders it comparable to the rarefied subjects investigated by physics (1951, 42). Intent on redirecting the argument, Enzensberger adroitly blends scientific and technological metaphors to describe composition as a consequential, machinelike process of creation. His analogy should be read as an answer to Benn.[30]

Enzensberger is drawn to Benn's proposition that poets work scientifically, but to connect with this argument he explicitly cites Poe's "Philosophy of Composition." He writes about the "Poet als Technologe" (poet as technologist), a literary engineer who assembles verse—an account of poetry production that appears strikingly American (1980 [ed.], 775). This comparison is, in contrast to that of Benn's esoteric scientist, pragmatically conceived. While reminiscent of the language of futurist and other modernist manifestos, Enzensberger's description promotes an essentialist view of craft that emphasizes the way in which poetic language can operate according to cause and effect. This renders the lyric genre accessible to nonelite audiences. Nonetheless, Enzensberger makes clear that in his view, poetry, unlike common consumer products, does not conform to limiting cultural norms or bourgeois tastes. "The poem is the anti-commodity pure and simple: that was and is the societal significance of all theories of *poésie pure*" (1980 [ed.], 776–77), he writes, claiming that even the most aesthetic forms of the lyric are politically subversive and hence resistant to convention. That depiction of the lyric genre, reminiscent of Adorno, allows him to dismiss the false dichotomy of "ivory tower and agitation-propaganda" (1980 [ed.], 777) as unproductive.[31] By the late 1960s, of course, Enzensberger would be famously questioning the political efficacy of poetry entailed in the second part of this dichotomy.

The account of the working poet as assembler of language using pieces supplied by a literary canon denaturalizes the creation process by defining it as intentional (even mechanical), hence different from private poeticizing or patriotic effusions in verse. It also mirrors the construction of the essay itself, which juxtaposes the positions of Friedrich, Benn, and

Adorno through a montage of language. Older modernists cited—Poe, Mallarmé, and Valéry—function as proxies in his disputation with the unnamed opponents, who are played off and against each other through careful choice of wording. This strategy avoids the pitfall of defining contemporary poetry in terms of a split with the immediate past along the lines of older and younger writers.

Despite his obvious admiration for modernism's innovations, Enzensberger does not sanction gratuitous imitation of its poetic technique. Two sections in the afterword to *Museum*, "Schlechte Avantgarde" ("Bad Avant-Garde") and "Warnung vor Ismen" ("Warning about -Isms"), caution against this unreflecting imitation; and an additional essay from the period, "Die Aporien der Avantgarde" (1976b), critiques self-styled innovators. Ironically noting that few great artists, especially not in his estimation the most respected—Kafka, Proust, Faulkner, Brecht, or Beckett—would ever have called themselves "avant-garde," Enzensberger cites the tendency of artistic movements to define their positions antagonistically by creating a myth of generational conflict (1976b, 52).[32] His analysis, which anticipates typologies developed by Harold Bloom in *The Anxiety of Influence* (1973), dismisses the model of generational conflict as an explanation for new art, yet it does not quite align him with conservative aesthetic values. Critics, Enzensberger reminds his readers, often contribute to the creation of false aesthetic categories by admonishing artists to conform to cultural norms (1976b, 53), rendering older artists harmless through labels like "Classics of Modernism" (53) or misguidedly praising the mediocre over the truly innovative (55). The paradox for Enzensberger consists in the circumstance that almost as soon as avant-garde art comes into being, it becomes past history. "The only thing that can be stated with certainty is what *was* ahead, not what *is*," he observes (1976b, 62).

Given Enzensberger's avowed interest in revitalizing German culture, his categorical rejection here of tachism, *art informel,* monochrome painting, serial and electronic music, concrete poetry, and the beatniks as movements that show few signs of enduring or making a significant contribution (1976b, 68) would seem paradoxical were it not for the focus of this part of the critique on the manner in which movements become positioned within the public sphere rather than on artistic technique per se. Pondering the power of critics, Enzensberger voices concern about the influence of the art market, which by his account had become a veritable "Bewußtseins-Industrie" (consciousness industry; 1976b, 62).[33] His charge that potentially lockstep aesthetic programs promulgated by avant-garde movements constitute a dangerous tendency toward blind mysticism represents an extension of the author's repeated warning that artists will evade their social responsibilities if the role of the intellect in the production of creative works becomes diminished. Thus Enzensberger rhetorically refuses to apply the term "experimental" to any form of art out of concern that artists use this label to shield themselves from the true risks of producing art (1976b, 75). His perspective on this subject comes from the prominent public role played by European writers and intellectuals at this time, for Enzensberger excuses Jack Kerouac and American variants of the avant-garde, commenting, "The harmless naiveté with which they proclaim barbarism almost seems endearing in comparison to their European counterparts" (1976b, 69).

His reactions to techniques are more differentiated. Embedded within Enzensberger's critique of the avant-garde as an institution lies an endorsement of intentional innovation. Wary of dogmatic approaches, Enzensberger prizes artistic autonomy and hence remarks, for example, "Surrealism was granted an enormous impact, but it only became productive in those who freed themselves of its doctrine" (1964f, 79). His reviews and afterwords for various works bluntly voice skepticism about an increasingly Americanized society. Disdain for "low" aesthetic tendencies and ambivalence about class status also fuel his invectives against the cheap, mass-produced "jukebox of the culture industry" (1962a, 119). With intellectual confidence, Enzensberger critiques the hasty superficiality—which he terms "the dilettantism of the half-educated"—in the work of Henry Miller (1957a, 90), yet quite ironically designates *Tropic of Cancer* a "modern classic" (1964a), a problematic label, given his arguments against using this epithet in "Aporien" (1976b, 53). As a self-styled connoisseur, he scathingly dismantles Jack Kerouac's *On the Road* as poorly written gibberish.[34] A review of *Beat: Eine Anthologie* for *Der Spiegel* sets forth what he regards as seven tenets of the group—which he regards as shallow—with a plea for critics to judge literature on its merits rather than on affiliation with a movement (1962a, 118).[35] In sum, these accounts of modern literary tradition and the avant-garde, above all the American beat movement, look back past contemporary authors to the modernist generation of William Carlos Williams, to whom Enzensberger repeatedly turned when he sought workable models for his own writing.

This witty skepticism about the avant-garde signaled Enzensberger's wariness about the uncritical emulation of foreign literature. Emphasizing the productive aspects of an international perspective, particularly in his afterword for *Museum* and "In Search of the Lost Language," his arguments simultaneously acknowledged concern about the direction German literature was taking. The intense preoccupation with foreign works had, as we have seen, sometimes bordered on escapism from German concerns and at other times resembled mere aesthetic imitation. One of the foremost mediators of international poetry in the early 1960s by virtue of *Museum* and his own translations of foreign literature, Enzensberger responded to the influx of foreign literature in a characteristically twofold manner. On the one hand, he ardently encouraged writers to absorb these new impulses; on the other, he acknowledged the vitality captured by specific local character.

His is neither the response of categorical openness to the reeducation efforts of the 1940s nor the skepticism of authors in the 1950s about the potential of foreign literature to overwhelm the market. Instead his anthology makes the claim that German literature can stand on equal footing with an international canon.[36] In this context, Enzensberger's references to "world literature" and to the "provincial" serve the purpose of illustrating why the two concepts constitute a false dichotomy. Writing for *Museum* under the title "Weltsprache der modernen Poesie," Enzensberger swiftly dispensed with the customary division between rural isolation and the cultural center of the metropolis: "The particular, the dignity of the provincial, is saved from its reactionary inhibitions, from the insular, rooted-to-the-soil local museum and assumes its own rights. It does not disappear into the generality of the poetic world language, but instead actually creates that language's very vitality" (1964f, 20). The provincial in these terms denotes not the political isolation of the Nazi era disdained in "In Search of the Lost Language" nor writing ignorant of larger literary context but rather a form of authenticity.[37] As Enzensberger expresses this relationship, the universality of a work is not inversely proportional to its provincial character but rather intrinsically depends on it. Thus, contrary to what one might expect, Enzensberger elevates authors to an international context for the very reason that they do exhibit regional qualities.[38] This valorization of the provincial is consistently reiterated in reviews and afterwords for works by American authors, including Carson McCullers, Thomas Wolfe, Sherwood Anderson, William Faulkner, and William Carlos Williams. Ultimately it enables a self-presentation and self-understanding of Germany that values authenticity per se more than foreign or provincial traits.

The favorable assessment Enzensberger gives McCullers's *Clock without Hands* and several other American works hinges on local color, with explicit reference to what German writers might wish to attempt. "Whoever reads novels in Germany knows his way around there [America] better than at the marketplace in Schleiz or Geestacht or Passau. Compared with the distant USA, Germany is an unnarrated land. All great American novels are precisely located, down to the neighborhood block" (Enzensberger 1963a, 65). Enzensberger's afterword for the Norwegian translation of Anderson's *Winesburg, Ohio* similarly comments that although modern literature had become known as a phenomenon of the big city, provincial settings often proved more fruitful than the metropolis in producing compelling characters and microcosmic detail (Enzensberger 1964a, 213–14). His essay on William Carlos Williams mentions the regional quality of his verse while it underscores esteem for Williams as an international figure (1962a [trans.], 188–89). Ironically, as will be seen shortly, Enzensberger's translations of his verse muted aspects of local color in favor of generalized language that would be more accommodating to a European audience.[39]

The afterword to *William Carlos Williams* asks whether there is a specifically American mode of poetry. Enzensberger contends that Williams's work is both highly original and uniquely American, unlike that of Eliot and Pound, whom he portrays somewhat despairingly as turning away from their origins to reorient themselves toward Continental traditions. At the same time, however, he distinguishes Williams from those he considers mere regionalists (Vachel Lindsay, Edgar Lee Masters, and Carl Sandburg). These authors he describes as mediocre imitators of Whitman (Enzensberger 1962a [trans.], 172–74). His subsequent profile of Williams details continuities between the biography of the author and stylistic features of his texts.

Enzensberger portrays Williams as independent-minded, politically pragmatic, and free of poetic posturing, characteristics he believes elicit an indifference to Williams's work on the part of both the literati and the iconoclastic avant-garde. Stylistically, Enzensberger notes three Williams-esque qualities: the "opacity" of the descriptions (a notion attributed to Pound), his "antipoetic" subject matter (a term taken from Wallace Stevens), and the centrality of "glimpses" in framing the poems (a technique compared with James Joyce's "epiphanies"). Enzensberger makes much of Williams's opacity, noting it especially in a newspaper article published in advance of the translations in 1962, "Ein Gedicht ist eine Maschine" ("A Poem Is a Machine"). "This way of writing aims not at interpretation but rather at evidence. It consistently renounces 'depth' and instead offers the surface of appearances with the greatest precision: from this arises its impenetrability, that quality that Pound termed 'opacity.' In this manner the insignificant becomes delicious, the refuse becomes exquisite" (Enzensberger 1962c). This observation rehearses the language Enzensberger uses in his afterword to the translations; it also strikingly parallels the terminology he employed to describe himself and Williams in other essays. Enlarging on his conclusions about opacity, Enzensberger characterizes Williams's poems as similar to the German *Ding-Gedicht* (object poem). Their subject matter, however, according to his explanation, is appropriate to a mid-twentieth-century iteration of that genre because it involves themes of destruction, the quotidian, civilization's wreckage, and a mythologically conceived Paterson.

The affinities that draw Enzensberger to Williams become more evident when we compare the language of the afterword to the Williams translations with descriptions of his own poetry.[40] In the afterword, Enzensberger recapitulates that "[t]his way of writing aims not at interpretation but rather at evidence" (1962a [trans.], 183). Now Enzensberger elaborates on the "opacity" and quotidian content of Williams's verse by enumerating how the American, in his view, resisted conventions that prescribed "that the family, the daily routine of a normal house, the intimacy of a kitchen or a bathroom may not appear in a modern poem" (188). He comments about his experience with the translations, citing the idiomatic and colloquial range of the language as particularly difficult: "His [Williams's] succinctness is unattainable in German. Colloquial language is alien to our poetry, indeed to our literature as a whole" (187).

These observations intersect with Enzensberger's descriptions of his own poetry, for although they address the syntactic gap between American English and German literary language, they continue a discussion found in the essay "In Search of Lost Language." There Enzensberger sketched his own poetic accomplishments and those of Grass and Rühmkorf, representing himself and them as having a Williamsesque stance, content, and style: "[T]hey share a common aversion to all solemn attitudinising, to the traditional pose of the poet, to bragging of the so-called 'higher values.' Fragments of everyday life, scraps of slang, words from the world of consumer goods force their way into the poetic text" (1963d, 49).[41] While Patrick Bridgwater, William S. Sewell, and Dieter Lamping have elucidated the philosophical affinity between Enzensberger and Williams, what interests me is the process by which Enzensberger appropriated Williams's language. My concern with that development has to do with pursuing the relationship between Enzensberger's poetic language and the language invented for his translations of the American author's poetry. Williams was not the only poet whose work Enzensberger emulated—he also wrote at length about and translated works by Vallejo and Neruda—but the effects of this engagement proved uniquely enduring.

In Enzensberger's case, a new, or to put it perhaps more accurately, a rediscovered language resulted at least in part from the process of translating Williams's poetry; and it emerged between the appearance of his first verse collection in the late 1950s and publication of his third in the early 1960s. By the time *Blindenschrift* appeared, Enzensberger had adopted the particular fusion of domestic motifs with geopolitical concerns that he mentioned in connection with Williams. He dwelled on domestic vignettes in a poem dedicated to Günter Eich, "Abgelegenes Haus" ("Secluded House"), which still relates to German traditions in its synthetic structure. A complex of Enzensberger's poems written before and after the Williams translations were published, notably "Das Herz von Grönland" ("The Heart of Greenland") from *Landessprache* and "Doomsday" from *Blindenschrift,* treat the prospect of nuclear holocaust. Their subject matter links them to a comment Enzensberger makes in response to Williams's work and to language we have observed in "Die babylonische Bibliothek" and "In Search of the Lost Language," that "a particular taboo seems to urge itself on the poets of this century that the North Pole, the atom bomb and the minotaur are more worthy of their attention than the hand towel, the refrigerator and the night stand drawer" (1962b [trans.], 188). Indeed, Enzensberger breaks this taboo himself in *Blindenschrift,* a collection written at a time of heightened cold war tensions, whose dominant theme becomes the blindness of humankind to the deadly side of technology. At the same time, marked shifts in Enzensberger's handling of register, lineation, and audience accompanied this change in content.[42]

From Rhetorical Verse to Translation Practice

When "Lock Lied" ("Siren Song"), the initial text in *Verteidigung der Wölfe* (Enzensberger 1957b), and "Küchenzettel" ("Bill of Fare," or more literally "Kitchen List"), which opens the collection *Blindenschrift* (Enzensberger 1964d), are compared, the dramatic shift in poetic register and aesthetic position that occurs in the first three collections of poetry Enzensberger published becomes evident. These poems delineate two quite distinct formulations of the lyric genre, one following in a rhetorical tradition and the other clearly discursive. Each poem sets the tone for the collection it introduces, but while "Lock Lied" casts the poet as vigorously exercising the rhetorical potential of language, "Küchenzettel" depicts its first-person speaker as an almost invisible, neutral observer who detects commonalities among geographically and temporally disparate events. Both poems presume an essential connection between contemporary poetry and its predecessors, yet the two works construct this relationship in quite different terms. In "Küchenzettel," the productive relationship between Enzensberger's translations of poetry by Williams and his own verse becomes apparent; in "Lock Lied," the poetic mode employed represents a commentary on the German language.

"Lock Lied" declares a trio of poetic intentions in its three five-line stanzas, each of which ends playfully with the rather subversive call *Ki wit*. The call resembles the owl calls in Samuel Taylor Coleridge's "Cristabel" and copies the refrain of the telltale bird from the Grimms' fairy tale "Von dem Machandelboom" ("The Juniper Tree"). Readers may recall that this bird sings continuously until a boy's murder by his stepmother is avenged. The personified poet, speaking in the first person, initially instructs the reader to write out a text:

> Meine Weisheit ist eine Binse
> Schneide dich in den Finger damit
> um ein rotes Ideogramm zu pinseln
> auf meine Schulter
> Ki wit   Ki wit
>
>   (Enzensberger 1957b, 9)

> *My wisdom is a reed*
> *Cut your finger with it*
> *To paint a red ideogram*
> *On my shoulder*
> *Ki wit   Ki wit*

The phrasing relies on a literal interpretation of the term *Binsenwahrheit* (truism; R. Grimm 1984, 29) that incorporates the slight but crucial transposition of *Wahrheit* (truth) to *Weisheit* (wisdom) and a resequencing of *Binse* (rush) from this idiom. It also evokes a connection to concrete poetry through the term *Ideogramm* (Gumpel 1976, 194–95), which Pound had also previously employed in formulating his conception of imagist poetry.[43] The tone is presumptuous by design, with the cunningly androgynous speaker loftily asserting that some wisdom will be imparted and that the reader will ritualistically incarnate poetry by writing it out in the form of a character inscribed on the body (*Schulter*) of the poet. The second stanza then invites the reader to embark on a journey of the imagination on the shoulder of the poet. The island destination, however, has ambiguous qualities. The line describing that place restructures the word *Rauchglas* into glass (*Glas*) and smoke (*Rauch*), suggesting at once a site of occult magic (like smoke and mirrors) and the prophetic vision from Corinthians 13:12 that foresees clarity beyond the temporal world in which we can only apprehend things as though through a glass darkly. The third stanza adopts a menacing posture. The poet calls his voice "ein sanftes Verlies" (a soft dungeon), warns the reader not to be caught, and cautions, "Do not listen," because his *Binse* (clearly to be equated with a writing implement) is a silken dagger. This imagery oscillates between sirenlike, feminized allure (implied by the delicate *Binse,* lullingly rocked ship deck, tactile appeal of *sanft* [soft] and *seiden* [silky]), and the more masculine features of the poem that seem vaguely Homeric (the ship, *Verlies* [dungeon], and *Dolch* [dagger]), as if to allude to the crafty Odysseus.[44] This rendering of poetic elements is as destabilizing as the disjuncture posed by Enzensberger's handling of language. Whereas traditionally the male poet responds to the female muse, in "Lock Lied," reader and poet seem positioned in an ambiguous power dynamic on many interactional levels.

With deceptively simple language, manipulation of semantic convention, surrealistic juxtaposition of images, use of repetition rather than syntactic transitions to structure the text, and bold interjection of musical calls, the poem economically prepares the reader for the sections of "friendly," "sorrowful," and "angry" verses that follow in *Verteidigung der Wölfe.* "Lock Lied" simultaneously retraces inherited conceptions of the lyric genre as an intellectual, imaginative, or orphic enterprise, and distantly alludes to several iconoclastic contemporary trends (concrete poetry, surrealism, and sound poems). Combining "primitive faith in words and highly cultivated intellect"—antipodes identified by Reinhold Grimm in his definitive essay "Montierte Lyrik"—Enzensberger does, as Grimm asserts, demonstrate "a twofold relationship to language" (Grimm 1984, 40), evidenced in his reliance on and simultaneous dismantling of conventions.

Ultimately, however, this poem is about the tenacious coherence of language. In it, rhetoric possesses the power to persuade (even independent of actual content), and the lyric genre presupposes a triangulated relationship among linguistic text (written or spoken), author, and reader.[45] Consequentiality is implicit in this poem, for here language itself operates with relentless control. The reader *must* draw the ideogram because rhetoric commands this action, *must* also join the poet on the imaginative flight to an island and hence allow the poem to have an instrumental effect.[46] Poet, text, and reader each have prescribed roles. Only one choice is ostensibly left open, that broached in the final stanza: whether or not to listen to the poet's voice. Ironically, by this point the reader has through the act of reading the poem already "heard" the poet and text. The reader is enticed, then manipulated by language as if lured by a seductress, while the poet turns feminine powerlessness into manipulative power. Although lyric poetry fundamentally questions agency and malleability, "Lock Lied" does so with particular force by drawing the reader into a subtle entrapment. It unmasks how conventions of syntactic logic, relations of gendered activity or passivity, and the performative interaction between reader and text quite readily disintegrate. Logic, wit, gender, and syntax become caustic weapons in the invoked poetic arsenal.

By contrast, "Küchenzettel" relies on an evocation of images and sheer repetition, a strategy that invites imaginative play from the reader and a different kind of blurring of reader-poet roles. In each stanza, the poet gazes through an open kitchen door and observes household objects. These vary slightly but always include a cat dish, reading material, and two of three cookware items (milk can, cutting board for onions, and breadbasket). In each case, the first-person speaker in the poem declares that he has not read the telegram, letter, or newspaper that lies on the kitchen table. Experiential knowledge is thus given precedence over each mentioned form of writing. The poem applies this formula quite strictly to three different domestic settings (the poet's house, the image in a picture hung in an Amsterdam museum, and a summerhouse on the Moscow river).[47] Each verse mentions a different type of communication: writing, visual language, and political expression.

> an einem müßigen nachmittag, heute
> seh ich in meinem haus
> durch die offene küchentür
> eine milchkanne   ein zwiebelbrett
> einen katzenteller.
> auf dem tisch liegt ein telegramm.
> ich habe es nicht gelesen.

in einem museum zu amsterdam
sah ich auf einem alten bild
durch die offene küchentür
eine milchkanne   einen brotkorb
einen katzenteller.
auf dem tisch lag ein brief.
ich habe ihn nicht gelesen.

in einem sommerhaus an der moskwa
sah ich vor wenigen wochen
durch die offene küchentür
einen brotkorb   ein zwiebelbrett
einen katzenteller.
auf dem tisch lag die zeitung.
ich habe sie nicht gelesen.

durch die offene küchentür
seh ich vergossene milch
dreißigjährige kriege
tränen auf zwiebelbrettern
anti-raketen-raketen
brotkörbe
klassenkämpfe.

links unten ganz in der ecke
seh ich einen katzenteller.
                    (Enzensberger 1964d, 7–8)

One idle afternoon, today
in my house I see
through the open kitchen door
a milk jug   a chopping board
a plate for the cat.
A telegram lies on the table
I have not read it.

In a museum at Amsterdam
in an old picture I saw
through the open kitchen door
a milk jug   a bread basket
a plate for the cat.

A letter lay on the table.
I have not read it.

In a dacha on the Moskwa
a few weeks ago I saw
through the open kitchen door
a bread basket   a chopping board
a plate for the cat.
A newspaper lay on the table
I have not read it.

Through the open kitchen door
I see spilt milk
Thirty Years' wars
tears on chopping boards
anti-rocket rockets
bread baskets
class wars.

Low down in the left corner
I see a plate for the cat.

(Enzensberger 1994b, 33)

The poem constructs a tension between images (expressed by the verb *sehen*, "to see," the museum picture, and the framing effect of the door) and words (the telegram, letter, newspaper, and poem itself). The verb *sehen* occurs in the present tense in the first of these descriptions and in the past in the second two; each of these stanzas also provides a specific location (*in meinem haus, amsterdam,* and *moskwa*). The fourth stanza of the poem, which provides yet another similar description, does not locate its site geographically, instead connecting objects observed in the present with the span of modern European history. This penultimate stanza lacks the concluding phrase anaphorically applied in the verses that precede it ("ich habe . . . nicht gelesen"). When the poem ends, its two terse, free-standing lines note that the poet sees the cat dish in the far left corner. That gesture reinforces the primacy of image over text, generates the minimal formal closure afforded by repetition of a phrase, and yet suspends the completed text in an unresolved state since that bare statement draws no explicit logical conclusions for the reader.

Whereas a practice of overt citation underlies "Lock Lied" (involving construction of poetic language as if spoken by a narrator, as well as the disruption of linguistic convention through misquotation, as with the re-cast term *Binsenwahrheit*), "Küchenzettel" relies on the ability of language to evoke a sensory, visual impression and to suggest intervals of time sche-matically. It handles this mimetic task by calculatedly drawing attention to the limitations of the linguistic medium. The visual impression of space, which would be perceived rapidly by an eye gazing on the scene, is ren-dered schematically in a list form that emphasizes the linear construction and temporal interruptions of this written text. Meanwhile, apparently urgent texts that require a response are reported to be left unread in the poem. Without a reader, neither correspondence nor the briefs filed by correspondents in newspapers, nor poems for that matter, fulfill their so-cial function. Celan's famous suggestion that poems resemble *Flaschen-post* (messages in bottles) thrown out in the hope that someone might eventually find them is tested against the cold reality of armed conflict, where time, space, and responsive action cannot be taken for granted (1968, 128).

Yet "Küchenzettel" also draws the roles of author and reader more closely together than in "Lock Lied" by positing the first-person speaker (or poet) as a receptive observer whose apprehension of the scene has a function analogous to that of a reader experiencing the text. This con-structed immediacy contrasts with the carefully triangulated configura-tion of poet, text, and reader in "Lock Lied" and shows increasingly flex-ible absorption of literary traditions on Enzensberger's part. While "Lock Lied," as well as the accompanying poems in *Verteidigung der Wölfe,* posi-tion themselves antagonistically with respect to inherited rhetoric, German literary traditions, and even potential readers, "Küchenzettel" displays a selective absorption of influences that accepts intertextuality. Its approach minimizes differences in register and naturalizes citation practices. Not incidentally, this poem invites comparison with "The Red Wheelbarrow," a work translated by Enzensberger for his collection of verse by William Carlos Williams from 1962, in which the candid view outside into a wet garden sustains the entire poem. But the introspective direction of the pro-tagonist's gaze (into the house's interior rather than outside to the garden) and the musings on the threat of war distinguish Enzensberger's text from purely imagistic verse. The Williamsesque approach nevertheless allows for the creation of a poetic voice that seamlessly fuses the tone and particu-lar cadences of the international lyric it emulates with Enzensberger's pre-occupations with subject matter, textuality, register, and interpretation.

A more specific understanding of how this poetic voice evolved can be gained by examining Enzensberger's poetry and translations. Before Enzensberger becomes extensively engaged with translation and publishes *Blindenschrift,* parody, citation practice, and an eclectic interest in various American authors (chiefly Williams and Eliot) characterize his early verse. After his intense engagement with translation, a new poetic diction emerges. For this reason, Enzensberger's careful handling of register, lineation, syntax, visual images, and gesture in the Williams translations invites comparison with the innovations that surface in *Blindenschrift.* Some of the translator's solutions Enzensberger employs (notably terminology that evokes German contexts, slight transpositions of terms, and richly intertextual vocabulary) derive from his existing repertoire of poetic techniques. However, comparison of various translations Enzensberger made (especially his translations of poems by E. E. Cummings and T. S. Eliot) with his own poetry suggest specific instances in which the lessons learned while translating shaped poems by Enzensberger. Parallel readings of translated texts reveal a mirroring of lineation that is strongly related to the discursive mode Enzensberger comes to employ in his own lyric poetry. Moreover, when the construction of *Blindenschrift* as a poetic cycle is analyzed, it becomes apparent that it is those poems with a translation-like character that are used to establish a metapoetic framework for this book, which relies on the intertextual quality of the texts to authorize the new poetic voice Enzensberger explores.

Already in *Verteidigung der Wölfe* (1957b), Enzensberger's first collection, the poetry contained much evidence of encounters with American verse by Williams, Eliot, and Pound. "Letztwillige Verfügung" ("Last Request"), which parodically attacks the emptiness of military, church, and bourgeois funeral customs, echoes Williams's poem "Tract," for both share a critique of ritual, first-person address and a concluding blunt dismissal directed at a fictional listener (Melin 1992, 82–83). Another poem, "Tod eines Dichters" ("Death of a Poet") is dedicated to Rainer M. Gerhardt, who had published translations of work by Williams and Pound in the 1950s.[48] "Aschermittwoch" ("Ash Wednesday"), on the other hand, appears by virtue of its style, content, and title to stand in parodic relationship to the poetry of T. S. Eliot, whose work was widely circulated in Germany during the immediate postwar years, including an actual translation of "Ash Wednesday" published in 1948 (Eliot 1948). Later Enzensberger himself translated three other Eliot poems for *Museum.*[49] Enzensberger's detached mimicry of modernists was not, of course, limited to American authors. He also parodied Brecht in "Ins Lesebuch für die Oberstufe" ("Into the High-

School Reader") as well as Benn and many other German poets, such as Hölderlin.[50]

But while the poems in *Verteidigung der Wölfe* construct an opposi- tional relationship toward precursors (cf. Bloom 1973), those from the later collection *Blindenschrift* employ a more subtle, less antagonistically for- mulated mode of absorption that accompanied development of a poetic voice with strong affinities to Anglo-American antecedents. We can come to terms with these changes as something more than surface transforma- tion if we extend the argument that Anthony Easthope (1983) makes for reading poetry as a discourse that reverberates with and against the avail- able language conventions, ideology, and subjectivity of its time: briefly, we have to ask what connection this evolution of voice has to its back- ground, including the first large-scale protests in the Federal Republic of Germany (1957 demonstrations against nuclear weapons), the construction of the Berlin Wall in 1961, and the ensuing politicization of German litera- ture between 1961 and 1968.[51] If the stylistic changes in poetic voice that emerge in *Blindenschrift* do supply a reflective commentary on Germany's political status, readers are asked to try to decipher the discourse Enzens- berger is generating about the cultural function of poetic texts (Easthope 1983; Perloff 1998).

Close examination of Enzensberger's translations suggests, first, that he schooled himself in poetic techniques through a relatively long process of working with foreign texts. What he describes as the distinction between interpretation and evidence with respect to Williams's poetry corresponds closely to a gradual shift in his own work away from a poetry based on rhe- torical figures of speech, lexical manipulation, and a somewhat hierarchical relationship to readers as the recipients of texts. Naturalized voice, the use of line as the basic unit of meaning, and a more problematized construc- tion of text, author, and reader relationships become firmly established in *Blindenschrift* and remain throughout his later career. The role of the trans- lations in this development is clear from the quality of "closeness" they maintain to the originals and in the stylistic innovations used to mirror the originals' cadences. In Enzensberger's case, it is not feasible to speak about a coherent body of texts written before he began to translate at all, since he had already visited the United States in 1953 and his first three poetry volumes appeared parallel to his translations.[52] It is nonetheless possible to map strategies of interpretation, translation, and appropriation that he practiced by examining his renderings of T. S. Eliot, scattered translations of other Anglo-American authors (Auden, MacLeish, Cummings, Stevens, and Patchen), and his versions of poems by William Carlos Williams. Important considerations in this analysis are the textual matrix of form, line, register, succinctness, and aural quality.

These translations strive to preserve the original without pedantic insistence on each word, instead attending closely to how individual terms fit the context of sentences.[53] The German versions often achieve astonishingly close adherence to the originals with respect to poetic line length, the order of images, and even word-for-word correspondence of terms.[54] This adherence enables the translator to retain units of meaning systematically within the schema of line constructed in the original. Enzensberger, unlike many translators, consistently refrains from enlarging on content, although he does clarify syntax in instances in which English tolerates a greater degree of ambiguity than German allows. Often he employs cognates to do this, although he occasionally introduces a more regular line length than in the original text, evening out long or short lines to match the average space of others. Interpretive coherence combined with apt use of language enhances the readability of rhymed and unrhymed texts alike in translation. This deftness in reproducing cadence, devising syntactically economic solutions to translation problems, and preserving line is particularly evident with respect to rhymed texts. His rendering of T. S. Eliot's "Preludes," for example, masterfully establishes the poem's rhythms in the opening lines:

> The winter evening settles down
> With smell of steaks in passageways.
> Six o'clock.
> The burnt-out ends of smoky days.
> And now a gusty shower wraps . . .
>
> (Eliot 1972, 24)

> *Der Winterabend läßt sich fallen*
> *Mit Steakgeruch in die Passagen.*
> *Sechs Uhr.*
> *Verrauchter Tage tote Kippen.*
> *Bis sich in Regenschauern krallen . . .*
>
> (Eliot 1972, 25)

The language in German closely replicates the English iambic tetrameter and terminal stresses, despite the obvious difficulties involved in matching Germanic polysyllabic vocabulary with English monosyllables, espe-cially with respect to the use of prefixes, declensional endings, and the ac-centing of syllables. Rather than forcing a rhyme in the fourth line, then, Enzensberger sustains the acoustical coherence of the verse by means of the parallel endings (*fallen/Passagen/Kippen*) before reaching the suspense-ful conclusion to this climactic structure mediated by the insertion of the completing rhyme in the translation's fifth line (*krallen*). Similarly adroit renderings of Eliot's "The Hollow Men" (Enzensberger 1980 [ed.], 635), Auden's "In Memory of W. B. Yeats" (319), and MacLeish's "The End of the World" (458) display Enzensberger's ability to ply a formal poetic reper-toire that extends from nursery rhyme to ode and sonnet.

This formal competence depends on Enzensberger's inventive handling of syntax. English participial constructions, for example, which have no di-rect equivalent in German, are rendered as active verbs. Clause structure is simplified and genitive constructions unique to the German language employed.[55] Often Enzensberger splits a single image or description into two elements, using apposition to maintain their relationship to each other. Hence in "The Hollow Men," the lines "those who have crossed with di-rect eyes to death's other Kingdom" become "die hinüber sind, sehenden Auges, / ins andere, in des Todes Reich," where the terms for *other* and *Kingdom* become syntactically separated (Enzensberger 1980 [ed.], 634–35). A further technique, displacement of adjectives to position them after the nouns they modify, occurs, for example, when Enzensberger renders "unheard of manuscripts" in the poem "A Coronal" as "Handschriften unerhört" (1962b [trans.], 8–9).

The interpretive strategy common to these techniques is an insistence on the preservation of the particular elements of the original text in mini-mally altered form, and it relies on a practice that resembles the principle of *Entstellung* that Enzensberger elaborated in his analysis of Clemens Bren-tano's poetry. Here he explained Brentano's handling of genitive construc-tions as an intentionally polyvalent use of words (Enzensberger 1961, 58) and lauded the romantic poet's linguistic creativity in repositioning terms to make them poetically fresh (*neu verfügbar*) (1961, 28), terminology that seems to echo Pound's dictum, "Make it new" (Pound 1956, 147). What is striking, then, about Enzensberger's application of this technique to the translations is his use of it to make the translation language "new" while aiming to maintain fidelity to the original. In his own pre-*Blindenschrift* poetic practice, willful *Entstellung* and montage make ruptures between syntax and meaning visible; in the translations, such juxtapositions are minimized.

Beyond these practices for handling lineation and syntax, the translations Enzensberger made of poems by Eliot, Cummings, Williams, Stevens, and others share a succinctness arising from Enzensberger's use of an evocative, economic poetic language responsive to the German context in which he works. Enzensberger's translations of poems by Eliot—especially of "Preludes," "Rhapsody on a Windy Night," "The Hollow Men," and to a lesser extent "Triumphal March"—manifest a tendency toward a concentration of language, depersonalization, animation of the landscape, and intensely psychological descriptions. Combined with esoteric formulations, these are qualities reminiscent of expressionist and hermetic poetry. Indeed, his highly regarded rendering of "The Hollow Men" bears distinctly European features. Enzensberger translates the terms "kingdom" with *Reich,* and "meeting places" with the singular *Sammelplatz,* a term used to designate departure points for concentration camps. This practice extends across the spectrum of authors he translates. Such cultural accommodation can be found, for example, in his translation of Cummings's "My sweet old etcetera," where Enzensberger translates the lines "what everybody was fighting / for" as "welchen höheren / Sinn das Ganze hatte" and interjects key terminology such as *heldenhaft* (heroic) and *Feld der Ehre* (field of honor) to conjure images of both world wars (Enzensberger 1980 [ed.], 698–99). The effect of these inventive translations is to explicate content relevant to German deliberations about recent history by drawing on the language of public discourse. With respect to Eliot's "The Hollow Men," this accommodation results in a complex double intertextuality:

> Blind, es erscheinen denn
> Die Augen wieder
> Wie der ewige Stern
> Die vielblättrige Rose
> Des Todes-, des Zwielichtsreiches,
> niemandes Hoffnung,
> Hoffnung der leeren Männer.
>   (Enzensberger 1980 [ed.], 639)

> *Sightless, unless*
> *the eyes reappear*
> *as the perpetual star*

multifoliate rose
of death's twilight kingdom
the hope only of empty men.
(Enzensberger 1980 [ed.], 628)

Reaching back to German canon, Enzensberger echoes Rilke's verse "Rose, oh reiner Widerspruch, Lust / Niemandes Schlaf zu sein unter soviel / Lidern" (Rilke 1996, 394). In plying this multivalent language reminiscent of both Eliot's original and Rilke's even earlier text, Enzensberger displays a propensity for appropriating elements from many discourses, an attitude toward the poetic medium that, as will be seen shortly, also informs his own poetry.

Fundamental to this attitude is a respect for form and sheer line length, which pose challenges for translators because they directly affect the visual appearance of the poem on the page. Yet register and density, too, can alter length because they require flexible syntactic handling sensitive to the interplay of visual presentation of language, especially in the case of William Carlos Williams. Enzensberger cited his succinct, colloquial style as especially difficult to render in German: "The poems appear at first glance rather unprepossessing. The degree of condensation that they achieve only becomes apparent upon closer examination. Any attempt to translate Williams is a test by trial" (1962b [trans.], 187). Instances in which this difficult-to-render succinctness proved insurmountable can be detected in some translations in which Enzensberger does resort to poeticized language (for example using *gen* instead of *gegen* and *ward* instead of *wurde*), sanitized terms ("outhouse" translated as *Laube* rather than a more literal equivalent like *Außenabort*), or restructured statements that mesh less well with the colloquial register.[56] The fact that these instances are rare, however, speaks to the systematic approach to translating that Enzensberger took.

The succinctness Enzensberger cultivates for Williams's poetry carries over to other translations as well. His version of Stevens's "Thirteen Ways of Looking at a Blackbird" (Enzensberger 1980 [ed.], 534–39), shows reduction in the rephrased lines, "At the sight of blackbirds / flying in a green light," which is rendered as "Sähen sie Amsel fliegen im grünen Licht" ("If they were to see blackbirds flying in the green light"). Enzensberger's translation of Patchen's "The Grand Palace of Versailles" (Enzensberger 1980 [ed.], 473) addresses the issue of trilingual translation that surfaces at the end of the poem by curtly leaving the phrase "Good morning, Louis" in

English. Personal names, designations for plants and animals, profanity, and numbers, on the other hand, are only infrequently shifted to more European terms and usually to achieve a specific effect, as when "Lucy" in Cummings's "My sweet old etcetera" is glossed as "Minna."

Further examination of the Williams translations (Melin 1992, 86–87) reveals meticulous attention to acoustical patterning, vocabulary, and syntactic devices that allowed Enzensberger's work to surpass that of other Williams translators, including Erich Fried, Christine Koller, and B. K. Tragelehn. While these elements contribute to the impression of succinctness, they show Enzensberger's ability to match the conversational gestures that give the poems shape. Identification of these characteristic gestures allows for further comparison of the translations with poems by Enzensberger. Thus, the terse conclusions of many Williams poems, such as "A Fond Farewell," are echoed in several Enzensberger texts. In English and in the German version the verses read:

> Take what
> you might give
>
> and be damned
> to you. I'm
> going elsewhere.
>
> *Wie du mir*
> *so ich dir.*
>
> *Geh meinetwegen*
> *zum Teufel. Ich*
> *komm nicht wieder.*
> (Enzensberger 1962b [trans.], 112–13)

The use of disconnection (the unelaborated shift from a command that the "you" take something to the statement that the "I" goes elsewhere), of free indirect discourse,[57] of conversational exchange rather than an image or sententious statement as the closing moment of a poem, can be found already in the repertoire of Enzensberger's own early verse. This gestural technique for closing the poem, however, stands in close proximity to his interest in Williams, for it first appears in "Letztwillige Verfügung," which parodies Williams's "Tract" by musing in the final lines, "Um die Auferstehung des Fleisches inzwischen und das ewige Leben / werde ich mich, wenn es euch recht ist, selber bekümmern: / Es ist meine Sache, nicht wahr?

Lebt wohl. / Im Nachttisch sind noch ein paar Zigaretten" (Enzensberger 1957b, 34).

In *Blindenschrift*, where the influence of Williams on Enzensberger's work is most apparent, a closing gesture can be recognized in "middle class blues," which asks "What are we waiting for?" (Enzensberger 1964d, 33). This mimicry of gesture locates meaning in the speech act itself, rather than in the pronouncement's rhetoric. Enzensberger's techniques for minimizing the surface texture of citation, montage, and intertextual allusions in poem texts also become enlarged through the practices of lineation, imitation of register, and gestural handling of content in the translations, all of which he uses to approximate the discursive style and populist sensibility he admired in Williams.

Discursive Style, Democratic Forms

Blindenschrift is preoccupied with intertwined aesthetic and political reflections. The weaving together of these two matters occurs within individual poems, such as "Küchenzettel," and also through a juxtaposition and careful counterpointing of texts within the collection. Each of the three sections in *Blindenschrift* offers explicit commentary on the situation of Germany in the early 1960s through individual poems—"Abendnachrichten" ("Evening News," which broods about how distant wars in Asia may affect Europeans), "Auf das Grab eines friedlichen Mannes" ("For the Grave of a Peace-Loving Man," an ironic commentary on the ultimate complicity of a citizen who simply wanted peace during historically tumultuous years), or "Bildnis eines Spitzels" ("Portrait of a House Detective," an adroit identification of how cold war paranoia, euphoria over the *Wirtschaftswunder*, and suppressed memories of Hitler coexisted). Meanwhile, other poems map the aesthetic agenda: the first section, subtitled "Camera Obscura," begins with "Küchenzettel"; the second section ("Blindenschrift") incorporates "Weiterung" ("Expansion"); and the third, "Leuchtfeuer" ("Beacon"), the poem by that name. Both "Weiterung" and "Leuchtfeuer" bear comparison with Enzensberger's translations. The largest grouping of metapoetic texts (which includes "Mehrere Elstern" ["Several Magpies"] and "Windgriff" ["Gust"]) occurs in the fourth section, creating a disposition of materials that frames the collection as a work much preoccupied with the capacity of the lyric genre for meaningful expression. The specific intertextuality of these individual poems deepens Enzensberger's exploration across *Blindenschrift* of how language functions, for it establishes the need to read each text as a work informed by companion discourses emanating from cultural and political areas within and outside Germany.

To locate this intertextuality, we return again to Enzensberger's work as a translator. His approach to translation reflects an openness to the language of other poets. In *Blindenschrift,* the original poems "Weiterung," "Windgriff," and "Mehrere Elstern" in fact mirror three specific Enzensberger translations, for these poems stand as interlinear rewritings of texts by E. E. Cummings, Wallace Stevens, and Williams. All three reformulate and modify their antecedents. The mode for doing this, however, is not antagonistic or parodic—as in the case of "Letztwillige Verfügung"— but appropriative. Whereas "Letztwillige Verfügung" follows the general structure of Williams's poem "Tract" with heightened rhetoric, "Weiterung" and "Windgriff" by Enzensberger seamlessly interpolate phrases to such an extent that their relation to American texts is barely disclosed. The third poem in this group, "Mehrere Elstern," more obviously refers to Stevens's "Thirteen Ways of Looking at a Blackbird," while an additional companion poem from the same collection, "Flechtenkunde" ("Lichenology") stands in oblique relationship to the Stevens model.

"Weiterung" has been widely interpreted by Enzensberger scholars as a response to Brecht's "An die Nachgeborenen" that was the concluding selection in his *Museum* (Buck 1976, 14; Mayer 1969, 50). Brooding in "Weiterung" about the possible annihilation of the human race through nuclear catastrophe, Enzensberger contemplates the prospect that there may be no future generations. Brecht, as German readers would have known, had petitioned future generations to understand the acts of his contemporaries: "You who will emerge from the flood / In which we have gone under / Remember / When you speak of our failings / The dark time too / Which you have escaped" (1967a, 319). Enzensberger reformulates this plea, asking by contrast "[w]ho is to emerge from the flood if we go under in it?" (1964d, 50). Brecht's lines, which would have been very familiar to Enzensberger's German readers, provide an adequate vehicle to describe contemporary rearmament issues. Even where Enzensberger departs from Brecht to formulate questions rather than to commission his audience to action, to rhyme *untergehen* with *weitersehen,* and to conclude the verse with prosaic, laconic phrases that offer no comfort to the reader, the earlier "An die Nachgeborenen" stands as an instructive, essential point of contrast.

The middle section of the poem "Weiterung," meanwhile, contains a formulation strikingly similar to Enzensberger's translation of Cummings's "My sweet old etcetera," which, like "An die Nachgeborenen," was included in *Museum* (1980 [ed.]). Continuing on from the initial Brecht-inspired lines, Enzensberger spins out the poem through a series of playful word combinations:

> das wird sich finden,
> wenn es erst soweit ist.
>
> und so fortan
> bis auf weiteres
>
> und ohne weiteres
> so weiter und so
>
> weiter nichts
>
> keine nachgeborenen
> keine nachsicht
>
> nichts weiter.
>   (1964d, 50)
>
> *that will be found out,*
> *only when it gets that far.*
>
> *and so henceforth*
> *until further notice*
>
> *and without further ceremony*
> *so on and so*
>
> *furthermore nothing*
>
> *no descendants*
> *no forbearance*
>
> *nothing more*

The second half of Cummings's poem is similarly punctuated by free use of the word "etcetera," a feature carefully preserved by Enzensberger's use of the term *undsoweiter* in the translation in *Museum*. Enzensberger's translation of "My sweet old etcetera" and the poem "Weiterung" thus share the intrusion of decontextualized language (the *undsoweiter*). This word disrupts normal syntactic semantic context, and its repetition turns into an ironic elaboration heightened to the point of paradox. Techniques from the translation surface again in "Weiterung," notably the division of the phrase *undsoweiter* after *so,* which allows the final term *weiter* to accrue its own semantic value and function independently in the subsequent line. Further, the use of *soweiter* (in the translation of "My sweet old etcetera") or *so weiter* (in "Weiterung") as an autonomous unit and the conclusion of the verse with the very term that originally inspired the poetic variation are present in both the *Museum* translation (as *deiner Undsoweiter*) and Enzensberger's own text (*nichts weiter*).[58]

These intertextual connections established by Enzensberger's language (his allusions to Brecht and Cummings) underscore the political position of the author, for although all three poems address the impact of war on everyday life—Cummings the First World War, Brecht the Second World War, and Enzensberger the cold war—this text makes clear that in light of the prospect of total nuclear destruction, national identification becomes meaningless. The allusions to the American Cummings and the German Brecht compel the reader to notice that what is at stake is world peace. Cummings achieved his effect ironically by first observing the war in Europe and then moving to the distant vantage of the United States, where he retold its history as an event in the past. He finally contrasted the father's patriotic interjections about the glory of battle with the earthy, more authentic sensations of the poem's protagonist, who lay in the battlefield mud dreaming of "your smile / eyes knees and of your Etcetera" (Enzensberger 1980 [ed.], 698). By contrast, Brecht, brooding from afar on the dark days of Hitler's regime ("Wirklich, ich lebe in finsteren Zeiten" [Enzensberger 1980 (ed.), 757]), appeals as a German to a German audience. For Enzensberger, the situation is immeasurably more difficult. Should he admonish Germany from the perspective of the international community, react with personal anecdotes, or lay out the intellectual issues as one German speaking to others? Will any of these perspectives matter if the world ends? The role of Cummings's poem in this configuration must be construed as doubly ironic, given the fact that American modernist verse was disseminated as part of reeducation programs designed to foster democracy and world peace.[59] Enzensberger's unparodic absorption of the Cummings model introduces an element of co-optive subversion that sets it apart from the antagonistic forms of parody practiced in *Verteidigung der Wölfe,*[60] for this appropriation tacitly raises the issue of whose national identity can possibly inform the perspective of a pacifist. Once the textual model has been borrowed, the poetic language broadens and becomes autonomous, unfettering itself from the cadences modeled in a distant original, as if to underscore the way in which poetry, as Enzensberger argues elsewhere, always resists an explicit political agenda.

In the second half of *Blindenschrift* (1964d), Enzensberger consolidates his aesthetic position in a series of other texts related to translations he made. The first of these, "Windgriff," stands in close proximity to two poems by Williams, "Porous" and "The Term," the latter of which Enzensberger published in translation. While "Porous" describes cattail fluff blown in the air, "The Term" details a scene in which a sheet of brown paper (the medium of writing) rotates in the wind. Enzensberger's translation of "The Term" establishes a direct, colloquial tone by employing short word forms (*etwa, lang, drüber*) and substituting the present tense verb *treibt* in the fifth line for the expected past participle *getrieben* (to be driven). "The Term" describes how a paper rises, a feat accomplished with suspense in both the English and the German translation through the isolation of phrases within short lines and radical enjambment, especially in the conclusion (lines 13–18):

> Unlike
> a man it rose
> again rolling
>
> with the wind over
> and over to be as
> it was before.
>
> *Ein Mann*
> *wäre nicht wieder*
> *aufgestanden,*
>
> *vom Winde Hals*
> *über Kopf über Kopf*
> *weitergetrieben.*
> (Enzensberger 1962b [trans.], 106–7)

"Windgriff" fuses the content of "Porous" and "The Term," employing simple language and an image of wafting wind. Its visual image points out that representation is the essence of poetry:

> manche wörter
> leicht
> wie pappelsamen

steigen
vom wind gedreht
sinken

schwer zu fangen
tragen weit
wie pappelsamen

manche wörter
lockern die erde
später vielleicht

werfen sie einen schatten
einen schmalen schatten ab
vielleicht auch nicht
   (Enzensberger 1964d, 88)

many words
light
as poplar seeds

rise
turned by the wind
sink

hard to catch
carry far
like poplar seeds

many words
loosen the earth
later perhaps

they cast a shadow off
a small shadow
or perhaps not

The laconic style, sparse language, calculated enjambment, and careful handling of short line verse evident here are features that generally characterize *Blindenschrift*. In previous volumes, Enzensberger had shown a penchant for long lines and long poems: "Schaum" ("Foam") from *Landessprache* (1960d), is, for example, over two hundred lines in length and reminiscent of David Ignatow's "How Come." Within *Landessprache,* Enzensberger employed other cohesive elements to support this profusion of words. These included participles, often in postnominal position (a technique observed in his translation from the English), and enjambment. With *Blindenschrift,* these stylistic features became less prevalent, while the isolation of single terms on a line and the foregrounding of a plain style stripped of the obvious use of cadence, rhyme, and acoustical device dominates. The poems move away from idiosyncratic voice and toward an unembellished conversational language that projects a naturalized connection between poem and speech.[61] In "Windgriff," the function of this type of voice is closely related to the translative style of the poem, for the terse language, visual image, and tight handling of line underscore the text's deliberations about the meaning of words, their mimetic capacity, and language's efficacy beyond itself. As in the case of "Weiterung," intertextual references enhance the metapoetic position taken by the poem.

Turning from "Windgriff" to poems from *Blindenschrift* that respond to another translated text, "Thirteen Ways of Looking at a Blackbird" by Wallace Stevens, we can observe how Enzensberger uses Stevens to pragmatically recast philosophical reflections on the notion of *poésie pure.* The availability of the Stevens original in translation at the time when *Blindenschrift* appeared prompts a reading of "Mehrere Elstern" and "Flechtenkunde" from *Blindenschrift* as works that explicitly construct intertextual relations. Whereas Williams's "Tract" was not known in German translation when Enzensberger's parodic "Letztwillige Verfügung" appeared, Stevens's poem existed in the very version provided by Enzensberger in *Museum der modernen Poesie* (1980 [ed.], 534–39). Indeed, Alfred Andersch recognized Enzensberger's indebtedness to Stevens in his contemporaneous review of *Blindenschrift* (Andersch 1965, 83–84). To a greater extent than the other texts under discussion, "Mehrere Elstern" explicitly points back to a source by retracing and interrogating the aesthetic positions Stevens delineated in "Thirteen Ways of Looking at a Blackbird."

Despite formal and substantive similarities between "Mehrere Elstern" and "Thirteen Ways of Looking at a Blackbird," Enzensberger uses the text by Stevens to locate an antithetical aesthetic position. Stevens is concerned with distilling a pure correlation between poem and reality, Enzensberger with capturing the messy contest between art and life. Both poets define the relationship of poetry to sources of inspiration, but where Stevens isolates a visual impression of the silent blackbird, Enzensberger inserts cheeky magpies. In the English poem, a glass coach that signifies the artificial poetic perspective contrasts with genuine blackbirds in stanza eleven. "Mehrere Elstern" contains a parallel event—a counting of the birds (an act of categorization and organization antithetical to the disorder of reality). That act, however, provokes an anger not found in the Stevens text, for the magpies refuse to cooperate. Whereas Enzensberger's magpies are characterized as *unentbehrlich* (indispensable) in the sixth stanza, Stevens writes, "the blackbird is involved / in what I know," a line made even more personal in Enzensberger's translation "Dreizehn Arten eine Amsel zu betrachten" (*Museum,* Enzensberger 1980 [ed.], 535–39) through use of the possessive article ("meines Wissens / Mitwisserin ist die Amsel"). The final stanzas of both poems describe the bird in the snow, but quite differently. While Stevens sketches an image of a bird on a branch, Enzensberger's text taunts defiantly that perhaps he himself can be refuted, but that magpies in the snow are proof (*ein Beweis* [1964d, 85]). Thus Enzensberger transforms Stevens's pure poetic repertoire of the symbolic blackbird into abrasive magpies who defy categorization as aesthetic creatures. The problem of signification, which lies at the heart of these texts, is handled quite differently by the two authors. If for Stevens the blackbird is a resonant symbol taken from reality and not an artificial creation (the "golden birds of Haddam," a phrase that indexes a real town in Connecticut), Enzensberger's magpies never become symbolic, for they take on their own life. Stevens's poetic persona gazes contemplatively upon an object. Enzensberger's clever birds grow increasingly independent of him ("they don't let themselves be tamed by me"), defy common convention ("they don't care about the slogans"), and at last co-opt the poet as one of their own ("as if I were a magpie").

Several other poems included in *Blindenschrift*—"Leuchtfeuer," "Trigonometrischer Punkt" ("Trigonometric Point"), "Schattenreich" ("Shadow Realm"), and "Flechtenkunde" ("Lichenology")—share with "Mehrere Elstern" a division into multiple sections and a preoccupation with defining the capacities of poetry.[62] Each of the poems treats metapoetic issues having to do with the representational capacities of language and what the lyric genre can say about the threat of a third world war. Though different in content and structure from Stevens's poem, they use the division into discrete sections to examine their subjects from various perspectives. Their common principle is detailed analysis in combination with a circular logic that gives the formal appearance of closure. Although the beginnings and conclusions of these poems closely resemble each other, as the formula repeats it yields subtle deviations and changes in meaning.

Of these poems, "Leuchtfeuer," which describes the repetitive flashing of a lighthouse, most noticeably follows the constraints of self-enclosed logic and linguistic restriction.[63] The opening discounts any particular significance to the lighthouse's warning by blandly cataloging what the poet observes, that "this fire proves nothing." An accumulation of details in the first three stanzas continues to downplay indications of danger: the foghorn is electronically timed, the light calibrated to project at a designated candlepower, and the tower made of reliable iron. The effect is uncanny, however. By the time the final stanza returns to the opening words, restating these as "it means nothing more / promises nothing more," the suspicions of the reader are clearly raised that this bland declaration belies its own content. Enzensberger concludes by warning his readers that even where a fire seems to mean nothing, there is nonetheless a fire to be noticed 1964d, 66–67).

With similar terseness, "Trigonometrischer Punkt"—the title a reference to Günter Eich (1981)—employs formal repetition of terse phrases that sketch a configuration of angle iron, beams, and rubble. Reminiscent of Eich's famous poem "Inventur," the poem first reassures its readers that "this is no stake / this is no sacrificial altar / this is not bloody scaffolding," only to shock them later by declaring that under the leaves in this place one will find "a dead partisan / from the next war" (Enzensberger 1964d, 80–81). Both poems therefore contrast reports of normalcy with an underlying condition of danger, drawing attention to the rift between language and what it signifies.

Of the segmented texts in *Blindenschrift*, "Flechtenkunde"—composed in some twenty sections—constitutes Enzensberger's most extensive experiment with multiple-section poems. The descriptions of nature (lichens) are carefully allegorized in linguistic terms. The poem's second section toys with the meanings of various German verbs and an allusion to one particular lichen:

> die flechte beschreibt sich,
> schreibt sich ein, schreibt
> in verschlüsselter schrift
> ein weitschweifiges schweigen:
> *graphis scripta.*
>
> (1964d, 71)

> *the lichen describes itself*
> *writes itself in, writes*

> *in encoded script*
> *a verbose silence:*
> graphis scripta.

The subsequent sections describe lichens as the earth's slowest telegram, meditate on a line from Georg Büchner's *Woyzeck* (duly cited by Enzensberger), and consider items reported to be difficult to decipher (the beard, papyrus, silhouette, brain). The poem then turns to a series of associations that connect the lichen with social issues. The poet calls it "the honorable communist," a cure for all ills, a witness to history, and a hardy survivor—as if it could serve any purpose demanded by society. This use of language unmasks the imposition of partisan rhetoric on neutral objects and, as in "Mehrere Elstern," sets in motion an oscillation between self-contained descriptions of nature and the poet's social concerns. The looser treatment of the multiple-section form (the verses are sometimes based on a central motif, at other times on a pun or even a seemingly random comment) corresponds to a more flexible handling of topics compared and contrasted in the text. Nature as represented by the lichens, an enduring life-form, becomes associated with the indecipherable. Humankind, which seems oblivious to natural forces, figures in examples that show man exploiting nature, living in peril of war, blind to dire prophecies, and unrealistically giving in to escapist dreams of easily obtainable manna, which the poet ironically observes was produced by the inconspicuous and endangered lichen. To reach this conclusion, the text crosses over into a discursive and highly introspective mode of presentation. In notes to *Blindenschrift,* the poem is duly referenced to definitions of terms gleaned from the *Brockhaus Encyclopedia,* making its reading and interpretation contingent on the reader's private labor to trace its meaning (1964d, 96).

The afterwords to *Museum* and *Williams* trace a modernist poetics that connects language with an opaque image to create a debatably "universal" basis for poetry. Exploring the limits of mimesis and voice in *Blindenschrift,* Enzensberger moves from the sometimes sheer verbiage of *Verteidigung der Wölfe* and *Landessprache* to a Williamsesque colloquial language through his handling of lineation and syntax. As a consequence, many poems in *Blindenschrift* are characterized by more diegetic and somewhat less mimetic representations of speech.[64] This diction gives the appearance of immediacy between poet and reader, but that solution creates representational degrees of distance by differentiating poetic language from common discourse on the subtle level of line and person of address rather than on the basis of the surface distinctness of rhetoric, image, and lexis.[65] While the new, more moderate tone of *Blindenschrift* at first appears to drive toward the aesthetic of synthesis characteristic of German poetry in the 1950s, Enzensberger actually subverts this harmony.[66] His innovation consists of a skilled absorption of foreign models that locates the strangeness of language not via lexical manipulation but through juxtapositions that problematize interpretative readings. Enzensberger's choice of models for this poetic program—Williams and his generation—is remarkable because he turned to the American modernists, who earlier in the twentieth century had been so intent on forming a cultural identity for their own nation in the early 1960s, as a separate German identity began to take clear shape for the first time since the war.

The succinctness he cited as a salient feature of Williams's verse is absorbed into his own work along with the solutions to problems of translation that Enzensberger employed (cliché, shortened forms, unpretentious diction, and the occasional heightening of content or transposition of discourse into dialogue). In Enzensberger's earlier poetry, speech was often represented in quite idiosyncratic manner, as in "Geburtstagsbrief" ("Birthday Greeting") from *Verteidigung der Wölfe,* which, notwithstanding its labeling of a "letter," initiates a dialogue with a second-person addressee that resorts to a telegraphic delivery of messages, punctuated only by colons. "Alt bist du: alt: wie Laub verdorrt das Lid: / die Schläfen schimmeln: geiles Moos erpreßt / die Rippen wie ein Verdacht" ("Old you are: old: like foliage withers the eyelid: / the temples go moldy: wanton moss extorts / the ribs like a suspicion") (1957b, 55). Slogans, commands, quotations, exclamations, and pronouns that define conversational relationships ("I," "you," "we," "all of you") also abounded in *Verteidigung der Wölfe* and *Landessprache.* Typical of this approach, "Schaum" from *Landessprache* relies on dialogue exchange: "ehrlich gesagt: warum nicht? und warum / keine rampen? sollen es unsere kinder vielleicht / besser haben als wir? aber woher denn!" ("to be frank: why not? and why / no launch pads? should our children perhaps / have it better than we? I should say not!") (1960d, 39). Such rhetorical devices are not sufficient to render Williams's work in German, nor do they represent spoken language that involves both dialogue and descriptive modes (see Holden 1986, 35). They do succeed, however, in distinguishing poetic language from other discourses (conventional rhetoric or literary antecedents). The direction Enzensberger takes from the heuristic practices of translating American poetry leads toward a more colloquial German poetic language.[67]

Colloquial tone, however, is not an easy or unproblematical accomplishment, for as poet and literary historian Jonathan Holden points out in his discussion of conversational poems, this form—popular among American poets—is one of the most difficult modes of writing:

> In the conversation poem, the problem of establishing the authority of the speaking voice is even more acute than in confessional. The speaker cannot lay claim to the ethical or moral authority of the confessional voice by virtue of testimony alone. . . . The reader must be willing to pay attention to a speaker about whom there is nothing inherently exotic or historically compelling. (Holden 1986, 33)

The authority to which Enzensberger sought to lay claim in his poetry and essays from the 1950s and early 1960s was expressly ethical and moral, as well as intellectual and artistic, and in this principled stance his texts departed from existing German models. Gottfried Benn, who had incorporated fragments of speech into his poetry, had done so as the extension of an elite, internal monologue. Bertolt Brecht had likewise drawn on colloquial language in crafting his verse but had stylized this language for both rhymed and unrhymed verse, validating it through explicit emancipatory intentions. Enzensberger's project is more complicated: how to write poetry after the Holocaust, and how to fuse the intellect with creativity in the face of nuclear destruction.

During the late 1950s, the most prominent German poets seemed to be writing about silence—Celan (1975, 167) about the "two mouthfuls of silence" of ruptured interpersonal conversation in "Sprachgitter," first published in 1959, and Bachmann (1978, 124) with eschatological pessimism about the impingement of the public language on internal reflection, asking where one can go "when the stillness of death enters" in "Reklame," first published in 1956. The radio play genre, which had enjoyed much success in the postwar era and indeed provided financial support to many authors, had captured many aural capacities potentially available to poetry as a performative medium.[68] In this literary context, Enzensberger chose to connect his writings with multiple public and private discourses—those about poetry and history and others that urged the autonomy of writers and translators. His tool for doing so was a new kind of language, one modeled after a desired construction of democratic speech that in its substance drew on the phrasing of translation. This language, for all its sur-face simplicity, was richly intertextual. Enzensberger's reflections on poetry after Auschwitz, the modernist canon, and universality versus provincial-ism have to do with linguistic signification, the authenticity of poetry, and its aspiration to legitimacy as a part of public discourse. Poetry's dilemma was how to persuade its reader to take action, a dilemma made more urgent by concern over nuclear armaments and cold war tensions that made the future existence of Germany seem precarious.

The consolidation of poetic voice that occurs in *Blindenschrift* is fraught with technical difficulties, bedeviled with intellect, but still very much a reaction against a 1950s sense of constraint and forced symmetries. The 1960s, in the words of Korte, witnessed a paradigmatic change in German poetry, a "discovery of reality" (1989, 100). With Fried, Grass, and Rühm-korf, Enzensberger anticipated and prompted the change that emerged in the poetry of Jürgen Becker, Nicolas Born, and Brinkmann (all of whom display interest in the work of Williams that Enzensberger presented), as well as Wolf Biermann, Helga M. Novak, Yaak Karsunke, Sarah Kirsch, Reiner Kunze, and Peter Paul Zahl (see Melin 1992, 92). Six years before the end of the 1960s, Enzensberger in *Blindenschrift* begins to look back in the poem "Erinnerung an die Sechziger Jahre" ("Memories of the Six-ties"), predicting pessimistically that current problems would not be re-solved (1964d, 65). The poems in the collection substantiate the ability of poetry to capture reality with the accuracy of a photographic journalist (as in, for example, "Camera Obscura" or "Schattenbild" ["Shadow Image"]), yet they undermine themselves by repeatedly disrupting the tranquillity of visual images with verbal gestures of self-deprecation. "Who might that have been? / whoever it was, / cross him out" the poem "Notizbuch" ("Notebook") muses, positioning and repositioning the poet (1964d, 17). The choices Enzensberger makes about diction, content, and form in *Blin-denschrift* thus push the lyric genre in a new direction, one overtly con-nected to theoretical, political, and aesthetic discourses.

Yet as the author experiments with poetic strategies that alter the rela-tionship of poet to audience—an emancipatory and arguably democratic project—a connection to prose and the language of theory comes into play that must be taken into account when reading Enzensberger's subsequent documentary poetry. "Hans Magnus Enzensberger," Wolf Lepenies com-mented in his 1998 laudation speech upon the award of the Heinrich Heine Prize to Enzensberger, "*The* liberal. The poet laureate of the nation, who at his own pleasure covers the space or the opponent, who locks up behind while marching at the forefront. The liberal par excellence. Speaking philosophically: the free man" (1999, 25). In the early 1960s, Enzensberger hardly seemed a likely candidate for such an esteemed role, and by the end of the decade, this poet whose country has no poet laureate appeared to have ceased writing in the lyric genre altogether.

3. Toward Open Poems and the Lyrical Prose of *Mausoleum*

Poetry Meets News and Theory

The poet speaking from experience, plying honest language, anchoring imagery in palpable existence—these mimetic conventions shape the poems in *Blindenschrift,* and yet there is nothing incontrovertibly "natural" about this poetry. The discursive mode of lyric that Enzensberger adopts in this collection presents itself to the reader as casual, but this is a carefully crafted artistic illusion. Furthermore, the language of *Blindenschrift* reflects historically specific assumptions about the status of literature that are informed by interrelated practices of scholarship and translation and referenced to late modernist aesthetic sensibilities concerning verisimilitude, rhetoric, lyrical density, reader response, and visual culture. The final poem in the volume, "Schattenwerk" ("Shadow Work"), commits itself to a practice of ephemeral self-effacement: "Shadows are my work," it concludes sagaciously (1964d, 93). That gesture allows the poet to transcend mere experience at the cost of drawing our attention to self-authorizing procedures available for poetry after the 1950s.

Consider that as the stakes changed for poetry after the 1950s, Enzensberger, along with other German writers, grappled with the tension between sincerity and artifice. What surfaces in *Blindenschrift* (1964d) grows even more acute in the long poem "Sommergedicht" ("Summer Poem"), also composed in 1964, and in the poetic cycle *Mausoleum* (1975). Before turning to this set of works, however, I propose to look at Enzensberger's intellectual and aesthetic commitments in the late 1960s and early 1970s by attempting to step back from the controversies of those times, as Charles Altieri advocates readers of poetry do when ideology becomes an issue (1984, 33).

For Altieri, who focuses analysis on American verse of the late 1970s, isolating a dominant ideological mode in poetry means considering discourse as a reflection of how ideas are organized, vested with emotions, and given value in literature. Rather than submerging us in political debates, this critical approach requires that we survey our assumptions about poetic craft in order to locate the pressures on the lyric genre and understand literary tastes. Altieri reminds us that for this purpose examples "work better than abstract definitions when our concern is for the ways in which beliefs get codified and issue in judgments" (1984, 34), especially in situations where poetic ideology consists of "a muddy blend of literary and existential values" rather than a set of "crisp poetic doctrines" (33). While Enzensberger had definite political allegiances during this time, he kept his poetics opaque to the reading public, hence my path through his poetic output begins with specifics.[1]

For a time after *Blindenschrift,* it seemed to many critics and scholars that Enzensberger had ceased to publish poetry. Dietschreit and Heinze-Dietschreit's extensive survey of the author's works goes so far as to state that aside from five poems in a 1967 issue of *Kursbuch,* no lyric work by Enzensberger appeared for over seven years (1986, 89).[2] When the period 1964 through 1971 is closely examined, however, a different picture emerges of what occurred before the appearance of Enzensberger's next collection of verse, *Gedichte 1955–1970* (1971b). After *Blindenschrift,* Enzensberger published nearly two dozen new poems in widely scattered venues: *Luchterhand Loseblatt Lyrik,* American little magazines obscure to the author's European audiences, and retrospective collections in translation that intermingled old and new work.[3] This was a slim but artistically significant body of texts. The *Gedichte 1955–1970* (*Poems 1955–1970*) revealed to German audiences that Enzensberger had surprisingly continued to write poetry, for it gathered together approximately thirty new poems, including many of the scattered pieces that had appeared in the preceding seven years. Others remained uncollected until much later in *Die Gedichte* (1983). Although in some cases these poems did not have the polished features or connection within a single coherent project that had characterized Enzensberger's previous verse collections, they do give evidence that the author was producing varied poem texts. Meanwhile, Enzensberger also delivered numerous speeches and published article after article that referred to the contemporary state of poetry (1964g, 144–48; 1966b; 1967c; 1967f); thus, if anything, his theorizing about poetry increased. The beginnings of *Mausoleum* lie in this period, as do indications of a fascination with postmodernism.

One signal of the change under way in Enzensberger's poetry was his cultivation of long poem forms, including step-down line texts, catalog poems, improvisations, serialized verses, ballads, and documentary texts. As was the case for developments that occurred between *Verteidigung der Wölfe* and *Blindenschrift,* transformations that affected the literary climate at large prompted the shift. Political altercations, social change, and a growing awareness of ecological issues marked German and international public discourse in the late 1960s and early 1970s (Schnell 1993, 310–20). For the lyric genre in German-speaking countries, these years brought enormous diversity and change (Korte 1989, 82–143). Postwar German verse had come into its own, branching out in several directions at once, some international in character, others mining the rich specifics of national context. Important volumes of hermetic poetry by Paul Celan, Nelly Sachs, and Rose Ausländer appeared; and in the GDR, poets who had emerged in the first postwar decade, such as Peter Huchel, Georg Maurer, and Erich Arendt, were joined by others including Johannes Bobrowski, Helga Novak, Volker Braun, Günter Kunert, Heinz Czechowski, and Sarah Kirsch, who responded with intensity to the landscape and political setting in which they wrote. Throughout Austria, Switzerland, and the two Germanies, experimental poetry flourished through the appearance of collections by H. C. Artmann, Claus Bremer, Ernst Jandl, Eugen Gomringer, Friederike Mayröcker, and Franz Mon, whose texts laid out a spectrum of approaches ranging from the international avant-garde to dialect verse. Gruppe 47 met in Princeton, New Jersey, in 1966 but dissolved after 1967. Meanwhile, the Americanization of language and consumer goods accelerated in West Germany even as the discontent of European liberals with U.S. foreign policy grew.

The unsettled, politicized intellectual climate inevitably privileged writing grounded in critical analysis or "found" sources. Literary texts that drew on documentary materials began to take precedence over open-ended, evocative modes of writerly reflection, especially the type of contemplation associated with the lyric genre. Agitprop verse, which achieved a stature validated by the political insights it forwarded, emerged with force. Rolf Dieter Brinkmann, whose efforts would transform German poetry by stimulating a reengagement with the quotidian elements that had fascinated Enzensberger, published *Die Piloten* (*The Pilots*) in 1968 and *Gras* (*Grass*) in 1970. When Brinkmann published the anthology *Acid* in 1968, it set off a new phase in the reception of contemporary American verse by mediating the work of Frank O'Hara, the beatniks, and younger poets to German audiences. At its best, political verse offered intellectual critique combined with linguistic repartee, as in the work of Erich Fried, Wolf Biermann, and Yaak Karsunke. Much of the agitprop verse, however, was formally simplistic or rhetorically direct—mere expression and quantity rather than fine poetry. Enzensberger, by this time an established (though not establishment) poet, distanced himself from such easy, tendentious writing, devising instead sophisticated connections between poetry and contemporary issues that allowed for a dissection of conceptual problems through the concrete immediacy of poems.[4]

Scholars have analyzed this middle phase of Enzensberger's career largely in terms of the author's political views as expressed in his prose.[5] By focusing attention instead on his modest poetic output, we face the knotty problem of how poetry relates to theory, for the content of Enzensberger's poems and essays are dialectically bound to each other. The transformation of poetic style between the lyric verse of *Blindenschrift* (1964d) and the prosey, narrative ballads of *Mausoleum* (1975) pushes Enzensberger toward underlying questions about the representational capacities of poetic language that had not been answered by him or his contemporaries. These questions centered on how to resolve the tension between the personal and the public and, by extension, between the imagination and the intellect. All the while, debates over militarism, political repression, education, social reform, and environmental issues had a discernible impact on the literary field of the 1960s.

This public discourse impinged on the kind of language available to the lyric genre, especially as crises caused ideological rifts within the writers' community. Postwar political imperatives had created a climate in which the claims of the lyric genre to separateness from tainted public affairs gave it value (as long as the dichotomous cold war political categories of Communist versus democratic thinking prevailed). Now the defining question was not how to keep aesthetic and social matters apart. Rather, the problem centered on what forms of writing could address situations in which these two elements had become inseparable. The dynamic at work in German poetry after the early 1960s resembled that synthesis of imagination and intellect that Stephen Fredman describes in his selective study of twentieth-century American prose poems (1990, 10). Although his assignment of ideological cause and effect simplifies the complex process of writerly choice, it captures a force that changes literature. Enzensberger's poetic output through the 1970s is responsive to pressures to transform and draws on lessons he had learned from American verse, where "poet's prose" (as Fredman terms it) had growing currency. The innovations with which Enzensberger experimented—cyclical structure, subtexts, heteroglossia, documentary techniques, and dynamic interactions with readers—are directed toward developing a form of poetic thinking that idealistically claims that poetry fuses the imagination and intellect, albeit with a dose of pragmatic self-irony.

The poem that announces this new trajectory in Enzensberger's work, "Sommergedicht,"[6] displays affinities to both William Carlos Williams and Charles Olson. Though it rejects the self-contained isolation of art, "Sommergedicht" is a highly self-referential text that recycles phrases from Enzensberger's previously published verse. Registering the disappearance of conventional art and pleading for more relevant art forms, the poem laments, "No great art in that / one should work upon that / which does not yet exist" (Enzensberger, 1994b, 69) and situates poetry amid "late news / and radio talks / on neo-capitalism and the avant-garde" (69). The poem proclaims literature's practical inefficacy, announcing that "a poem is not bread" (83), and then plainly advertises its own nature as a constructed spectacle by terming art, "a performance . . . so unique" (85). Finally, "Sommergedicht" questions the tendency toward commodification of the beautiful, interpolating a quotation attributed to Marilyn Monroe ("I just hate to be a thing").[7] These topics intersect with arguments voiced in debates from the mid-1960s about the long poem. Contention in Germany over long poems centered on what was acceptable canon (for poets, critics, and academics) and the quality of literary discourse. The boundaries that "Sommergedicht" establishes for the lyric genre are then extended in the convoluted narrative and discourse structures of *Mausoleum*. Ultimately, the poetical prose Enzensberger develops supplies powerful evidence of how the lyric genre, even in a time of ostensible marginalization, offered a venue for relational thinking not afforded by other forms of writing.

Open Poems

When William Carlos Williams died in 1963—the year after Enzensberger published a substantial collection of the author's poems in German

—his translator wrote a poem commemorating the American, "Zum An-denken an William Carlos Williams" ("In Memory of William Carlos Wil-liams"). The text, which appeared in the influential German weekly news-paper *Die Zeit,* celebrated Williams's precision and insight. Conceding that Williams was "not a 'representative figure'" and noting ironically that he was "not blind enough for *Look* and too lively for *Life,*" Enzensberger poignantly memorialized him as a poet who

> Sah die Finsternis und das Licht,
> vergaß die Hühner nicht,
> war genau
> und sonderbar heiter.
>
> (1983, 283)

> *Saw the darkness and the light,*
> *did not forget the chickens,*
> *was precise*
> *and strangely cheerful.*

This symmetrical dichotomy of abstract dark and light, punctuated by the immediacy of chickens (a reference to the poem "The Red Wheelbar-row" by Williams), evokes the aesthetic of "Momentaufnahme" that En-zensberger had cited as fundamental to Williams's work. The text reminds readers of poetry's capacity to capture visual images. Its economical presen-tation, careful control of line, and spare language are all features Enzens-berger valued in poetry by Williams. Enzensberger duplicates his previous descriptions of Williams as an outsider—a revisionist canonization of his work.[8]

The final lines of "Zum Andenken" offer a summation that emerges from a stratified text. The eulogist peels away layers of literary reception—allusions to the media (television, reviews, illustrated magazines), biog-raphies, and literary prizes—until he reaches the essence of his subject, poetry by Williams ("The Red Wheelbarrow") as translated by Enzens-berger. The poem pendulates among geographic sites with the trigonomet-ric oscillation characteristic of Enzensberger texts, mentioning Rutherford (where the poet lived)—a rural location underscored by Enzensberger's choice of the term *Landarzt* (country doctor) to describe Williams, the *Stockholmer Akademie* (referring to the Nobel Prize, which the poet never won), and New York (the metropolitan center to rural New Jersey). Poten-tially constrained by its own visual elements, imagist poetry is here enlarged to encompass historical depth and geographic expanse. Williams, represented as the active observer, apprehends the world with (in)sight although he is half blind. Only he notices the quotidian details that elude others. Such a conception of the lyric genre promotes dynamic over static representation.

"Sommergedicht" similarly advocates a dynamic poetry. Inspired by Williams's techniques, it moves away from the succinct language that characterized *Blindenschrift* and makes use of phrase-based lines reminiscent of the stepped-down verse of Williams's later works. This form broke stanzas into segments that then can be read both separately and as a unit. Further, for the English-language collection *Poems for People Who Don't Read Poems* (1968c), in which the translation "Summer Poem" first appeared, Enzensberger crafted a two-page statement describing his intentions. This "Note to 'Summer Poem'" emphasized his intent to synthesize political with erotic themes, coalesce widely disparate geographical locations, and establish provocative temporal juxtapositions. American readers would have detected affinities to Susan Sontag's 1964 essay "Against Interpretation," which concluded with the terse provocation, "In place of a hermeneutics we need an erotics of art" (1976, 14).

Enzensberger's familiarity with Williams's poems in stepped-down line can be assumed since these were among the first to be translated into German after 1945 (Williams 1951; see also Melin 1992, 85). The broken-line form, however, was not unique to Williams. Poems by Vladimir Mayakovsky and Paul Van Ostaijen using similar lineation appeared in *Museum der modernen Poesie* (Enzensberger 1980 [ed.]). More definitive connections to Williams surface in the "Note to 'Summer Poem'" that Enzensberger appended to the text in *Poems for People Who Don't Read Poems*. The poetic theory expressed there mirrors statements in "Chapter 50, Projective Verse" from *The Autobiography of William Carlos Williams,* where Williams liberally appropriates Charles Olson's theory of composition by field. Williams prefaces his lengthy citation from Olson with the observation that "[a]n advance of estimable proportions is made by looking at the poem as a field rather than an assembly of more or less ankylosed lines" (1967a, 329).[9] Enzensberger likewise echoes this formulation by underscoring the evocative structure employed in "Summer Poem": "Its formal principle is that of openness. One can regard poems either as closed and sealed, as impermeable structures, or as net-line constructions with which new experiences can be caught again and again—even when the writing of the text is finished" (1968c, 162).[10]

Like Williams, Olson was concerned with poetic line but also with invention of a "poetic process consonant with the mechanisms of perception" (1992, 18). Olson, as well as Williams, anchored poetry in sensory experience, following a conception of artistic creation akin to the kinesthetic foundations of action painting, whose aesthetic was expressed by the physical act of flinging, pouring, or building paint across the surface of a canvas. Similarly, Enzensberger endorses a notion of poetry as performance, for the text created unfolds in relation to the sequence and time needed for the utterance of speech. Enzensberger's discussion of content, too, bears comparison with Olson's understanding of poetic subject matter.

Olson had elaborated a kinetic description of verse, which contended that every part of a poem must be charged with equal energy. Stating that form must be an extension of content, he emphasized that one perception must lead to another and express a sense of movement. As Altieri points out in his discussion of Olson, this project situates poetry in a "liminal place between aesthetic and ontological experience" (1979, 96). Enzensberger's response to this aesthetic cum ontological imperative is to advocate new content, especially details that map geographical centers, which, he claims, are "not presented as landscape pictures, but are stations in a comprehensive network of communications in which 'all distances are the same'" (1968c, 162).[11] Widely traveled, Enzensberger had used extended sojourns in Italy, the United States, and Norway between the late 1950s and early 1960s as opportunities to search for meaning in a cultural and political sense. "Note to 'Summer Poem'" described capturing a "nexus," as he termed it, by incorporating into poetry movement ("flight and acceleration") and heteroglossia ("the 'parlar rotto,' the broken speech of our media, in the flood of distorted information from Dante studies to the *Peking People's Journal*").[12] But whereas Olson depicted poems as abstractly dynamic and freighted with the poet's heroic ego (Altieri 1979, 18), Enzensberger charts movement through a space-time continuum plotted out in specific instances beyond the self. "Mobility is not confined to the dimensions of space, but extends to time," he comments (1968c, 163). This rationale explains why "Summer Poem" leaps forward into the future and back into the past to Petrarch, a feat accomplished through literary allusions in which the phrases used in the poem are indexed to sources noted in the book's margin.

In summing up his intentions, Enzensberger contrasts overdetermined literary expression with the openness he sought to achieve through the manipulation of poetic line:

Literary language has a tendency to tie down anything that can be said. This text opposes the tendency by breaking up sentences. That is why the poem is dominated by a kind of syntax which classical grammar calls *apo koinou:* four sentence parts are related in such a way that the sentence can be read in several different ways. (1968c, 163)

His statement promotes the poetic medium as linguistically pliable, but it by no means advocates relativism that denies meaning exists. It also opposes the notion of lyric poetry as hermetic, condensed, and esoteric to a degree that would prevent the reader from understanding what is said. Instead, the reference to grammatical syntax signals a tension between conventions used to achieve coherence and the text's capacity for openness. Limiting the number of interpretations to "several" versions mildly restricts the openness that can be attained. Enzensberger's statement celebrates indeterminacy as an antidote to univocal language, making clear that both readers and authors should expect to respond to open texts differently than to conventional ones.

When Enzensberger asserts in the "Note to Summer Poem" that poetry must interrogate its own premises, he proposes conditions for the creation of text and its eventual reading that depend on a deconstruction of poetic language. Writing with exceptional passion, he concludes, "A poem intended to be, and to remain, open must make the critique of itself as part of its movement. It participates in the twilight of which it speaks and must finally vanish in it if it is not to give itself the lie" (1968c, 163). This practice of erasure, a powerful literary solution localized as a concluding gesture, resonates with the open form of "Summer Poem." The poem's visual presentation prepares for this gesture of effacement with broken lines, contradictory utterances, and overt references to sources that violate poetic conventions of signification. Interrupted syntax and conflicting instructions about how to read characterize all eight sections of the text. Moreover, at the right-hand margin of the page, bracketed references to Lao Tse, Francesco Petrarch, Karl Marx, Vladimir Ilyich Lenin, and Norbert Wiener provide readers with the sources for its interpolated phrases. This citation practice, which resembles the academic convention of footnoting, produces a "translative" text that allows the poet to incorporate linguistic fragments from many different languages, historical periods, and genre sources into the poem.[13]

"Note to Summer Poem" concedes that collage and simultaneity are not new literary techniques. Its references to the use of polysemantic language and themes (geographical, political, erotic, and poetic motifs) display an indebtedness to Williams (cf. Weaver 1971). The terms of the discussion echo the assessment Enzensberger gives of the epic poem *Paterson* in his essay on Williams, where he had noted the physician-poet's use of montage techniques, mythological aspects of American civilization, the natural history of the Passaic River, and nondoctrinaire references to politics. Enzensberger concluded that for Williams, "A brittle humor works against the pathos of the large form, the celebratory invocation against the internal irony of the empirical" (1962b [trans.], 189). In "Sommergedicht," a similar manipulation of elements occurs. Here, Enzensberger's meditation on mobility traversing time in order to push the imagination into "that which does not yet exist" mirrors one specific theme, the power of the imagination, adumbrated in the "Descent" section of *Paterson:*

> The descent beckons
> as the ascent beckoned.
> Memory is a kind
> of accomplishment,
> a sort of renewal
> even
>
> an invitation, since the spaces it opens are new
> places
> (Williams 1967b, 73)

A dynamic, cyclical interaction of old and new—a momentum fed by reflective memory and organic progression—emerges in Williams's text. Likewise in "Sommergedicht," Enzensberger maps the act of a poem coming into being as an event that opens imaginative potential:

> Etwas Neues
> ein winziger Schrei
> bricht auf
> etwas Neues
> das *alle Springfedern*   [Wieland
> *der Einbildungskraft und des Herzens*
> *zugleich*
> in einer alten Gasse
> *spielen macht.*
> (1983, 106)

> *Something new opens*
>
> > > *a tiny cry*
>
> *something new*
>
> > > since it brings into play   [Wieland
>
> all the spring of imagination
>
> and of the heart
>
> > > *in an old street*
>
> > > > simultaneously
> > > > (1994b, 71)

The disappearance of bourgeois works of art predicted in "Note to 'Summer Poem'" anticipates the sentiments that would soon be expressed by Enzensberger in the essay "Gemeinplätze, die Neueste Literatur betreffend" ("Commonplaces on the Newest Literature" [1968a]). Yet this radical notion of disappearance reiterates the complex relation of the arts to society formulated in the *Selected Essays* by Williams, which is liberally cited in Enzensberger's afterword to the German translation of his work. "Sommergedicht" remains intensely connected to Williams's poetry through the remembered scent of strawberries and astringent birches mentioned in the text, a smell that resembles the trope used by Williams in "Asphodel, That Greeny Flower" of a blossom that "has no odor / save to the imagination. . . ."[14]

In "Sommergedicht," synesthetic impressions become proof of a continuum between art and physical experience:

> das ist keine Kunst
>
> > > sagt der Kritiker
>
> das geht nicht mehr
>
> > > wirf die Metaphern weg
>
> das ist vorbei
>
> Und ich warf die Metaphern weg
>
> > > > ging in die Sauna
>
> und fand
>
> > Birkenlaub
>
> > > und diesen Geschmack
>
> nach früher
>
> > in meinem Mund . . .
>
> > > > (1983, 110)

> *no great art in that*
>> *said the critic*
>>> *you can't get away with*
>>>> *that now*
>
> *throw away the metaphors*
>> *they're a thing of the past*
>
> *And I threw away the metaphors*
> *and went to the sauna*
>> *and found*
> *birch leaves*
>> *and this taste of earlier times*
> *in my mouth*

(1994b, 77)

With these lines Enzensberger levels the division between aesthetics and ontology and alters the poet's compact with the reading audience. The declaration "That's no art," as well as another repeated terse comment, "proves nothing" (1983, 108–13), foreground the process of poetic construction and militate against the potential aesthetic hermeticism of the lyric genre by creating a Brechtian disruption of the reading experience. The poem denies the reader the privilege of an effete, purely private encounter with the text. Like the introductory "Anleitung zum Gebrauch" ("Instructions for Use") that Bertolt Brecht supplied for his 1927 work *Hauspostille* (*House Breviary*), Enzensberger's essayistic elaborations on "Sommergedicht" fabricate a didactic apparatus for readers. Still, "Note to 'Summer Poem'" says little about other obvious precursors of this poem: the linguistic experiments of Gottfried Benn, who imported fragments from everyday speech into poetry, or Ezra Pound's literary and nonliterary language in the *Cantos*. Certainly, the formal innovations of "Sommergedicht" superficially resemble contemporary work by the concrete and Vienna Group poets (Helmut Heissenbüttel, Friederike Mayröcker, and H. C. Artmann, for example). But "Sommergedicht" has a syntactic cohesion that distinguishes it from their montages. Where they emphasize disjuncture, Enzensberger's "translative" handling of language melds the words of widely separated authors into a single poetic voice.[15]

Admittedly, that voice is precarious. The use of marginal supplemental references, explanatory text, and notes in "Sommergedicht"/"Summer Poem" outweighs the apparatus for readers in Enzensberger's other poem collections. In *Landessprache, Blindenschrift,* and subsequently in *Mauso-*

leum, Enzensberger positions references at the end of the volume. This practice draws attention to the artificially complete, book-bound existence of poetry. "Sommergedicht," by contrast, displays the raw edges of its own construction by placing attributions immediately next to verse lines. The lithographic-montage texture of the piece on the page speaks for a poet who conceives of himself not as the originator of poetic language but as another erudite reader. The actual reader must piece sense together through constructive interaction with the text, an act that becomes the price of admission to reading:

> *Das Große entsteht aus dem Geringen*   [Lao Tse
> und dazwischen
> > > öffnet sich vielleicht
> > > > ein Gedicht
> > > (Enzensberger 1983, 106)

> From little things grow what is great   *[Lao Tse*
> *and in between perhaps*
> > > *opens*
> > > > *a poem*
> > > (Enzensberger 1994b, 71)

This Lao Tse aphorism about the autogenesis of a poem alludes tangentially to Williams, who asserted that poetry should take its materials from things. Thus even the simplest statements prove to be multiply significant text fragments, overdetermined by rhetorical convention, literary tradition, and the poet's drive toward precise language. Detail—the stuff that motivated the lyric poems in *Blindenschrift*—becomes entangled with an abstract exploration of the intellectual and artistic potential of poetry.

While reiterating the values of evidence over interpretation—around which Enzensberger had crystallized his understanding of poetry by Williams—"Sommergedicht" raises paradoxes regarding signification and poetic authority. This poem explicitly challenges lyric conventions by resisting univocality, linear cohesion, and closure. By design the text proposes new roles for readers and writers: the writer of such a work does not labor to create an internally perfected art object but rather an experience that will challenge readers, who are in turn charged with reflecting, researching, and rereading the poem. Its aesthetic challenge presages the debate over lyric poetry and long poem forms that took place in Germany, especially exchanges between Walter Höllerer and Karl Krolow in the literary journal *Akzente* between 1965 and 1966. These discussions drew heavily on the models of Williams as mediated by Enzensberger and on comments by Olson. At issue were the audience for poetry (the elitism of hermetic lyric versus a democratic conception of literature advocated by Höllerer), the instrumental value of poetry (whether or not it could effect political change), and questions of aesthetic rigor (about which Krolow worried when cautioning against what he termed the "monstrous" aspects of *Paterson* [Krolow 1966, 277]).

Although it is generally accepted that German forays into long poem forms remained tentative into the 1970s (Hartung 1985), it is important to note that even prior to "Sommergedicht," Enzensberger had already experimented with comparable modes of writing. These included the extended forms in *Landessprache,* the segmented poems of *Blindenschrift,* and the cyclically organized groupings of texts within volumes. By the time "Sommergedicht" was composed, Enzensberger's verse was characterized by heteroglossic speech, which appears to have arisen out of his translation projects, and accommodated the infiltration of prose elements into the lyric genre. Inevitably, long-poem experiments by Enzensberger and fellow German authors brought the lyric genre up against language and print-production forms affected by what Enzensberger termed the "consciousness industry" of the mass media. These mass-media modes of discourse, combined with a general sense of social crisis in the late 1960s, deeply affected German poetry. The resulting challenge to the lyric genre involved questions about authentic expression, ethical integrity, and artistic autonomy. *Mausoleum* represents this clash through a lyrical prose that fuses poetic and theoretical source texts using a sophisticated combination of formal devices, trenchant metonymy, and cyclical structures.

Poetry and Industry

When the critic in "Summer Poem" objects "no great art in that," and the poet responds, "and I threw away the metaphors" (Enzensberger 1994b, 77), the artist gains substance for poetry through sensory experience. Rarely do we encounter such an explicit statement about craft in a poem. The gradual disappearance of the text does not therefore signal the end of the writing but rather its alliance with reality. The poem breaks open (*bricht auf*), rises (*steigt*), and then exits (*verschwindet*), leaving the words on the page as a mere trace of themselves. "Gemeinplätze, die Neueste Literatur betreffend" (1968a), by contrast, sounds a funeral knell for bourgeois art. Enzensberger ironically tells his readers that the supposed death of literature is merely old news about something that had not occurred and perhaps never would. The difference between this hypothetical end of literature and the vanishing proposed in "Sommergedicht" has to do with the efficacy of literature and the entanglements of the publishing industry and literary scene. Examined in relation to Enzensberger's poetic program, the comments "Gemeinplätze" makes about critics, intellectuals, and the mass media demand an interpretation that diverges from the reading the essay has received as a critique of the intelligentsia or a proclamation of revolutionary vision (see Dietschreit and Heinze-Dietschreit 1986, 68–73). Its metaphorical language, which draws in part on Enzensberger's poetical writings, speaks with urgency about how power structures, public discourse, and modes of production constrain literature, especially the lyric genre.

By reading across "Gemeinplätze," "Bildung als Konsumgut" ("Education as Consumer Good") and other companion essays from *Einzelheiten* (*Details*), it becomes possible for us to establish a significant relationship between the innovations in form and content that were part of Enzensberger's poetic program and aspects of the culture industry that he critiqued in his prose writings over the course of several decades. This comparison locates the kind of internal contradictions and external pressures that Altieri connects in another context to the formation of literary taste and ideology. With this understanding of the aesthetic-ideological fault lines behind *Mausoleum,* the latter half of this chapter turns to an extended reading of that poetic cycle in order to discover what leads its poems so unswervingly toward prose and pastiche.

"Gemeinplätze" begins with a lengthy quotation from Franz Kafka's story "Josefine, die Sängerin oder Das Volk der Mäuse" ("Josephine the Singer, or the Mouse Folk") that describes intolerance for the true artist and predicts the disappearance of the singer Josefine. Enzensberger's essay itself depicts funeral preparations for literature, "Careful little tin wreathes are shaped for it. . . . The funeral procession leaves behind a dust-cloud of theories, about which there is little new" (1968a, 187). This artful conflation of Kafka and the death of literature is played out in terms that correspond to discussions of the *Stunde Null* (zero hour) represented by the end of World War II, as we can see by making a chronological digression.

Enzensberger's accounts of the rediscovery of German literature after 1945 in "In Search of the Lost Language" consistently mention his discovery of Kafka via English translations. "Letztwillige Verfügung" from

Verteidigung der Wölfe instructs listeners on how to mourn in terms that anticipate "Gemeinplätze": "Take the tin wreath from my breast, it tugs so," the speaker there commands (1957b, 33). "Gemeinplätze" thus reminds us that German society had cast literature in "a peculiar role" after 1945—the very public job of advertising that reform had occurred in Germany (1968a, 189). Central to Enzensberger's analysis is the conclusion that writers were co-opted by this agenda, which rendered literature ineffective, extended the bourgeoisie's control over culture, and consolidated the military-industrial complex's power to influence all forms of production, even that of literature. Poetry was to take the place of a social revolution that had failed to take place (1968a, 190). The essay voices disdain for abstract theory, empty platitudes about revolution, and literary criticism, as well as frustration with the ineffectiveness of poetry. Its remarks about the publishing industry, however, connect with Enzensberger's earlier publications about the *Bewußtseinsindustrie* (consciousness industry) as shaping all cultural media, a context that necessarily directs attention to the precarious status of the lyric genre in the late twentieth century.

Enzensberger's essay on the postwar rise of the paperback industry, "Bildung als Konsumgut," initially published in 1958 and subsequently revised in 1962 for *Einzelheiten,* had already registered the decline in literacy that created the precondition for the analphabetic attitudes disparaged in "Gemeinplätze." Examining contemporary book publications in terms of merchants, the publishing industry, publishers' programs, and readerships, Enzensberger concluded that an erosion of bookstore exclusivity had occurred. He linked this development to shifts in class dynamics, sardonically bemoaning the transformation of literary editors into mere programmers who fill industry production quotas rather than exercising aesthetic taste. "Bildung" argues that restrictive canons and tendentious pieces prove that contemporary readership has deteriorated into unreflective consumerism. The essay diagnoses in the postwar emergence of paperback publishing an abandonment of the emancipatory function formerly accorded literature. Once literature enlightened. Now, the author laments, publications are targeted to specialized readerships (urbanites, predominantly male readers, or younger readers). Few workers (the general audience) or the less numerous but traditionally important academic readers truly care about literature. None of these groups as described seeks education through the printed word. Rather, social status is the primary goal for German readers who, like the American white-collar workers the author regards as crass book consumers, are not analytic readers (1964e, 163). "Bildung" satirically concludes that publishers view literature as something that should be published only when it is risk free, a circumstance that inevitably detaches writing from politics (1964e, 160).[16]

This quite rhetorical argument simplifies the issues of readership to make the point that with the fragmentation of audience into specialized interest groups, the individual reader proves increasingly manipulable, a chance recipient of merchandise (1964e, 160). That faceless reader contrasts with the intense intellectuals who resemble the discerning audience of autonomous working poets to whom *Museum der modernen Poesie* is addressed. Accordingly, Enzensberger concludes that there is a sharp distinction between who buys books and who actually reads to learn (1964e, 164–66). His reified picture of marginalized literary production, as drawn in both "Bildung" and "Gemeinplätze," is eventually represented in *Mausoleum* through a plethora of metonymic details concerning book production, printed artifacts, and readers. By then, interest in poetry had declined. Enzensberger's poem "Gedichte für die Gedichte nicht lesen," which lent its title to an important edition of the author's work in English translation, *Poems for People Who Don't Read Poems* (1968c), wryly comments on that shrinking audience.[17] Given Enzensberger's pessimism in the late 1960s, the title of a contemporary anthology edited by Volker Hage, *Lyrik für Leser* (1980), might have seemed naive in its suggestion that the lyric genre could be salvaged through democratization. Yet that is the rescue Enzensberger himself eventually seeks.

The changes in the German literary market that "Bildung" inventories —plentiful paperbacks, mass-media technology, and commodified relationships among readers, publishers, and authors—have relevance to "Gemeinplätze" for their impact on literacy. The main purpose of "Bildung" is assessment of the damage that the narrowing of the sociopolitical niche available to literature has caused. This concern spills over into other feuilletons in *Einzelheiten*, where he even predicts that the consciousness industry will become "the key industry of the twentieth century" (1964e, 10).[18]

It seems that even as Enzensberger worked out matters of authenticity and voice in his poetry, translations, and poetical writings, a counterpoint of related, more intractable questions about literary production, readership, and the public status of literature surfaced. Similar circumstances in the nineteenth century have been analyzed by Pierre Bourdieu, who has suggested that the destabilization of cultural life has bearing on genre integrity. Arguing that shifts in the hierarchy of genres are "determined by modification of the chances of access to the literary field, and external changes which supply the new producers," Bourdieu contends that new literary products are developed for "socially homologous consumers" (1993, 55). The situation of German literary culture after 1945 was more than ripe for such radical, protracted transformation. Against this background we can see Enzensberger's cultivation of long-poem forms—which were audience and media sensitive (given the references to electronic media, news items, and reader response in the "Note to 'Summer Poem'")—as enmeshed with a fundamental restructuring of the lyric genre.

The infiltration of "unpoetic" elements—documents, proselike lineation, and neutral voicelessness—into *Mausoleum* expresses this transformation. Nonetheless, the external pressures on literature, which are reflected in both "Sommergedicht" and *Mausoleum* as intrusive discourses, arose long before the postwar era. In fact, Bourdieu dates these forces to the advent of the Industrial Revolution:

> The development of a veritable culture industry and, in particular, the relationship between the daily press and literature, encouraging the mass production of works produced by quasi-industrial methods—such as the serialized story (or, in other fields, melodrama and vaudeville)—coincides with the extension of the public, resulting from the expansion of primary education, which turned new classes (including women) into consumers of culture. (1993, 113)

Anticipating Bourdieu, Enzensberger argues for the open poem by recognizing the interconnectedness of cultural products, modes of production, and changing audiences. After "Gemeinplätze" Enzensberger demonstrates in *Mausoleum* that poetry and industry are emphatically conjoined by producing the collection as a kind of documentary work.

His project requires the assistance of theory. *Mausoleum* subtly insinuates to its readers that even in the lyric genre, intellectual categories of analysis can be used to identify the social crisis that poetry describes. Enlightening readers and providing guidance for analysis, *Mausoleum* continues in the direction Enzensberger charts for literature in "Gemeinplätze." Enzensberger is concerned with three issues in *Mausoleum:* textuality, theory, and readership. The first contested point, textuality, is called to our attention through his choice and nuanced handling of lyrical prose for the ballads. Thematically, the quasi-industrial apparatus of literary production is the conundrum Enzensberger examines as the machinery of literature interposes itself where genuine language, authors, and audiences should interact. Human expression becomes a mere cog in the impersonal, self-sustaining social machinery that even controls words; poetry is reduced to prose. This intellectual problem is not unique to Enzensberger, whose conceptual framework for describing systems of power is indebted to writings by Adorno, Benjamin, Foucault, and Habermas about cultural production. The ballads of *Mausoleum,* however, suppress the theories on which they are based even as they explicitly foreground obscure historical sources.

Like "Sommergedicht," *Mausoleum* calls for resistance to the stultifying nonaesthetic of mass consumption. Covertly the ballads create conditions for reading that demand that the audience experience the multilayered text through an intensely interactive process involving intellectual processing instead of passive acceptance. To view *Mausoleum,* then, not as a series of disconnected poems but as an extended composition, the reader must construct coherent social, historical, and cultural analyses to account for what is read. Fundamentally, the collection enjoins us to ask how it represents the interaction of writing and reading.

The complexly woven textual fabric of poetic musings, monologic quotations, and spliced documents in *Mausoleum* presumes an educated readership or at least an educable one interested in learning the truth about the "History of Progress." Such textuality, moreover, points to a poet who seeks language to express, however abstrusely, a consonance between individual perception and larger truths. Looking for a connection between the work of art and experience, Fredman hypothesizes that poetical prose appears in the work of Williams, Robert Creeley, John Ashbery, and contemporary language poets when these authors become fascinated with the interface between fact and imagination. Despite the limitations imposed by the generalizations he makes, Fredman proposes a germane distinction between French and American prose poems to explain the point. The former he characterizes as "a highly aestheticized, subjective, idiolectal artifact, a paean to the isolated genius" (1990, 10). "The latter," he claims, proceed on the conviction "that experience is shared rather than private, that the self is the center and circumference of democracy," with the result that "American poets ask their prose to articulate a shared world in which experience vouches for truth rather than for individual genius" (10). This assertion returns us to the question of how Enzensberger conceives of poetry and the culture industry, now in relation to theory.

Mausoleum—its title an ironic allusion to the distinction made between active exhibitions and dead museums in *Museum der modernen Poesie*—labored to unmask the pernicious consequences of isolated genius at a time when the basis for shared values was in extreme flux.[19] *Mausoleum* embraces poetry as a means to think through this problem of individualism and community in the medium of language. As a collection, it asks if the "progress" generated by technology and science impinges on the autonomy of expression itself.

The conceptual underpinnings of *Mausoleum* can be elicited through a comparison of the text with contemporaneous discourses from the field of social theory, for the ballads incorporate from them terms that pertain to technology, science, and social power. *Mausoleum*'s meta- and subtextual elements palpably echo the kind of discourse in Jürgen Habermas's discussion of technology in *Technik und Wissenschaft* (*Technology and Science* [1968a]) and of social evolution in *Legitimation Crisis* (1975). His familiarity with the intellectual currents represented by Habermas can be assumed for several reasons: Enzensberger had been introduced at his 1964 poetry lecture at the University of Frankfurt by Adorno, appeared in debates with Herbert Marcuse, and had his work critiqued by Habermas.[20] His study of the mass media had drawn on the critical theory of the Frankfurt school— Benjamin's deliberations on reproduction, Adorno's cultural analysis, and Marcuse's discussion of mass communication. Moreover, about the time when the first poems related to the composition of *Mausoleum* appeared in 1968, Habermas published an essay dedicated to Marcuse in the influential journal *Merkur,* "Technik und Wissenschaft als 'Ideologie'" ("Technology and Science as 'Ideology'"), which diagnosed a rationalization of society abetted by the social control exerted through the mass media (1968b, 100).

In *Technik und Wissenschaft,* Habermas postulates the organization of social structure around the concepts "Man-Machine-System" (1968a, 82). Although machines are ostensibly neutral objects that should not intrinsically embody political ideology (59), Habermas, following Marcuse, contends that the technology and science that have produced machines have taken on the function of a legitimation of power (74). Habermas further reasons that the elimination of a distinction between *Praxis* (praxis) and *Technik* (technology) in society will ultimately have an impact on language itself (91). This conclusion resonates with *Mausoleum,* where (pseudo-) scientific experiment, technological invention, linguistic expression, and politics form a web of control so thick that it degenerates. These thematic strands, part of the microstructure of the ballads, are laid down through graphic examples, especially montaged materials and "neutral" anthropological observations.

Meanwhile, on a macrostructural level, *Mausoleum* plots a Marxian account of history that corresponds to the stages articulated in Habermas's

Legitimation Crisis. Habermas (1975) suggests that societies are organized according to one of three formations—primitive social, traditional social, or liberal capitalist—categories represented in sequence in *Mausoleum* as antievolutionary. "Without a theory of social evolution to rely on," Habermas contends, "principles of organization cannot be grasped abstractly, but only picked out inductively and elaborated with reference to the institutional sphere (kinship system, political system, economic system) that possesses functional primacy for a given stage of development" (1975, 18). Only the discerning reader who spends time analyzing the surfeit of details in *Mausoleum* will comprehend the conceptual framework of social theory it imports. Enzensberger thus generates a literature that paradoxically welcomes the common ability of readers to grasp texts and yet delimits an exclusive readership among those who, through political solidarity with the author, already understand the analytical categories that shaped the text.

In analyzing the situation of German literature in "Gemeinplätze, die Neueste Literatur betreffend" (1968a), Enzensberger rhetorically despaired of both the "death of literature" and the dearth of literature capable of transforming society. His conclusion proposed a collaborative interaction between authors and readers:

> Teaching political literacy skills to Germany is a gigantic project. It would, of course, have to begin—as does any such undertaking—with the education of the educators. Even this is a protracted and arduous process. Furthermore, each enterprise of this kind depends on the principle of reciprocity. It is suited for him that constantly learns from those who learn from him. (1968a, 197)

An expression of this project, *Mausoleum* uses the flexible capacities of poetry to move readers to engage in inductive reflection as part of an emancipatory project.[21] This process, which brings together fact and imagination, is ultimately supported by Enzensberger's variable handling of the poetic medium, in particular his cultivation of lyrical prose.

Counterreadings and Counterfeiting

Mausoleum by its subtitle (*Thirty-seven Ballads from the History of Progress*) presents itself as a conventional collection of poems. However, like the stories fabricated about its subjects—around one of whom the text reports "legends of missing corpses, ballads mixed of magic and industry murmur" (1975, 37)—it handles this form in a free and highly evocative manner. The collection invokes the tradition of the German ballad detailed by Günther Witting (in relation to the genre theory of Wolfgang Kayser) and noted by Helga M. Novak (in her review of *Mausoleum*). It also echoes various international, twentieth-century models.[22] The texts resemble the "Graves" section of *Museum* and verse by Bertolt Brecht and Gottfried Benn (notably the latter's "Chopin"), whose work Enzensberger emulated.[23] Likewise, *Mausoleum* fits with portrait poems, including those by William Carlos Williams, the German expressionist poet Georg Heym, Edgar Lee Masters (*Spoon River Anthology*), and Robert Lowell (*Life Studies*). Ballads by Johannes Bobrowski (*Sarmantische Zeit/Schattenland Ströme*) and Helga Novak (*Ballade von der reisenden Anna*) as well as the prose poems of Walter Helmut Fritz (*Bemerkungen zu einer Gegend*) invite further comparison with Enzensberger's project. Such generalizations about formal heritage, however, need to be supplemented with discussion of *Mausoleum*'s textuality, theoretical grounds, and readership, which the collection itself, rather than external craft statements by the author, articulates.

Within *Mausoleum*, the branching, sublimation, and reemergence of themes lend a coherence that allows the collection as a whole to be read as an extended narrative. Devices that bridge sections, rhetorical gambits, and shifts between hypotactic and paratactic construction are conspicuously used.[24] Enzensberger handles multiple thematic strands at once in order to explore the nature of progress and stasis. The most obvious structural feature in *Mausoleum* is the diachronic progression through history — from Giovanni de' Dondi (1318–89) to Ernesto Guevara de la Serna (1928–67). At the same time, the individual ballads thickly interweave leitmotivs into a kind of postmodern pastiche about synchronic connections. This rich texture produces a paradox for the reader. In the early ballads, a sense of symmetry, proportion, and conventional poetic language exists, while the logic motivating the collection as a whole has not yet become completely clear. Later, the detail crowding the poems turns disproportionately dense, giving in to the influence of prose. The point becomes clear: what has been called progress in the past is actually devolution. Textuality mirrors the destabilized system of knowledge promulgated by postmodern theory; Enzensberger thus expounds a system of representation that rescinds conventions of readership.

The effect achieved is kinesthetic and at times bewildering. The dynamic force of historical chronology, human evolution, and technological advance generates a simulated forward motion in *Mausoleum* constantly contradicted by indicators of stasis: the death dates of the famous persons, the self-absorption of idiosyncratic inventors, and the formal closure of each ballad narrative. Linked from poem to poem, the themes that branch and proliferate across *Mausoleum* tangle into a crisis of the kind Andreas Huyssen has found corresponds to the exhaustion of utopian paradigms when "political demands have overloaded art's circuits" (1995, 99).[25] A surfeit of detail overwhelms the intellect of the reader overtaxed by sorting through the facts in these dystopian ballads. Enzensberger thereby claims the legitimacy of imagination, which alone remains viable when the authority of discourse is undermined.

It is not difficult to connect this dissolution of one form of authorization (factual data) and the rise of another (imagination) with contemporary political events and to move from that point to areas of theory relevant to *Mausoleum*. The year 1968 marked not only the height of protest against the war in Vietnam but also the apogee of agitation for educational reform in Europe, a situation adumbrated by Schnell as posing a particular challenge to *Germanistik* (52–56).[26] The sensitivity displayed in *Mausoleum* toward how discourses of many kinds exert power is moreover specifically grounded in the collection though an explicit reference to theorist Michel Foucault in the ballad "Carl von Linné (1707–1778)." The allusion is brief and not linked to a particular text by Foucault, and the index that is appended to *Mausoleum*, while citing Foucault, does nothing to distinguish him from minor figures in the volume. But Foucault's work supplies one heuristic underpinning for the book as a whole,[27] and the "Linné" poem accomplishes a critical, if understated, narrative summation.

The poem portrays Carl Linnaeus as consumed by "the madness of a classicist" (Enzensberger 1975, 31). The text relates how a collector's insatiability drove the laconic scientist to seek control over nature through inventories and nomenclatures. Foucault analyzes Linnaeus in *The Archaeology of Knowledge* to show that his systems are not based on logical systematicity (1972, 56). For Foucault, Linnaeus's work exemplifies procedures of intervention (1972, 57–59). Observing that phenomena at a given point in history are regarded differently even by interrelated disciplines, Foucault terms the rule for this response the principle of divergent perspectives. Enzensberger achieves his own divergences with layered narratives and heteroglossia; practices devised by Linnaeus—approximation, transfer, and systematization that form and filter content (Foucault 1972, 59)—resemble the rewriting *Mausoleum* endeavors.

Consonant with a sense of contemporary political crisis, *Mausoleum* asserts that the creation of art is not mere imitation of nature but a process that shapes the reader's response to its message. This reading of the collection as a constructive aesthetic project becomes all the more necessary when we recognize that Enzensberger consulted Hugh Kenner's *The Counterfeiters* (1968) while researching materials for *Mausoleum*.[28] When Enzensberger appropriates the counterfeiting technique described by Kenner, he alters poetic conventions of representation.

Attentive to the connection between technical craft and larger purpose, Kenner saw that even the most exacting reproduction of detail departs radically from the original and that this deviation marks counterfeiting as a form of creativity:

> But the craftsman is never really under control even when his hand is moving as we expect. For to ask him to do what has been done before is to ask him to counterfeit something, and the counterfeiter is never doing what we think. . . . We suppose that his work is an exercise in craftsmanship. It is not. It is an exercise in creative metaphysics. (Kenner 1968, 83)

Seizing this notion, *Mausoleum* re-creates the past through montaged authentic materials; its simulation unmasks contradictions inherent in the historical documents that would have been suppressed at the time of their actual creation.[29] The collection is replete with counterfeit markings. Passages manifest archaic spellings or parts of speech (for example, *"Apparate, mit welchen das Gut theils horizontal, theils vertikal von einer Vorrichtung zur andern die Maschine zugeführt wird"* [Enzensberger 1975, 59] [*"Apparatuses with which the Substance, in part horizontally, in part vertically, passes from one device to the next through the Machine so that any Manual Labour or Impurification are forestalled"*] [1976c, 58]) and rhetorical or classical devices (such as exclamatio: "O hilfloser Helfer der Menschheit! O mystischer Technokrat!" [1975, 122] ["Oh helpless helper of humanity! Oh mystical technocrat!"] [1976c, 137]). Blatant anachronisms, foreign phrases, and mathematical equations pepper the text. More than an "original," the resulting text calls on the perceptive reader to doubt the conceptual scaffolding around which it is built.[30] Although *Mausoleum* announces itself as a ballad cycle that traces social evolution, it adduces not the expected progress but a stifling of progression which only the poetic imagination can resist. The reader is enjoined to participate in this adventure.

Within Enzensberger's oeuvre, *Mausoleum* is a transitional text that shows the unraveling of modernist unity; it is a work fraught with linguistic play, illusionistic frames, and conceptual traps. Whereas in "Sommergedicht" a final gesture of disappearance vests the author with sufficient writerly self-consciousness to validate poetic expression, in *Mausoleum* the poet is conspicuously withdrawn and voiceless. Its counterfeited language interpolates, and interpellates, discourses that are revealingly heterogeneous, divergent, and contradictory. Cataloging and concealing its sources by turns, *Mausoleum* plays with the contours of the texts it collages. Whole blocks of text are inserted, in some cases reproducing the typography, layout, and punctuation conventions of the documents from which these pieces are taken. Portions of the text are conspicuously labeled as "Ansichtskarte" ("Picture Postcard"), "Aus dem Werkverzeichnis" ("From the Catalogue Raisonné"), or "Inventar einer Expedition" ("Inventory of an Expedition"). Other sections quote from anthropological records, legal paragraphs, or illustration keys ("Legende"), listing by number the various parts of grotesque inventions such as the guillotine. Typography draws visual attention to the quotations, as when italics distinguish imported commentaries.[31]

The semantically polyvalent language makes it extremely difficult to determine the mimetic value of any single word on the page. Everything seems to have equal importance in this dense matrix. The sharp photographic *Momentaufnahme* and succinct diction that had been equated with authentic expression in *Blindenschrift* are gone. *Mausoleum* houses a surplus of language: monotone reportage, interior monologue, and bland lists. Long lengths make it difficult for the reader to take in a ballad at a glance. In contrast to the expansive openness theorized for "Sommergedicht," here the manipulated prose syntax forces semantic closure without reaching conclusions. This artificial denouement generates suspicious silences that compel the reader to develop alternate readings—and to rely on the deciphering capacities of poetic imagination rather than on reason.

To get at the energies set loose by these operations of textuality, theory, and readership in the collection, I want to look at three poems from *Mausoleum* that place particular emphasis on the distinction between poetic thought and technological-scientific rationalization. I concentrate on the ballads that open and close the collection, "Giovanni de' Dondi (1318–1389)" and "Ernesto Guevara de la Serna (1928–1967)," and on "Bernardino Sahagún (1499–1590)," positioned at a crucial turning point in the history that the collection chronicles.[32] The framing ballads introduce and bring to formal conclusion the themes of technology, science, writing, memory, and history (or, in the alternate translation of the word *Geschichte,* the "story"). The middle one, about Sahagún, inserts the problem of genocide and Holocaust into the historical conversation. The three poems contrast nature and culture, the individual and the collective, and private writing and public language, supplying a commentary on contemporary Germany.[33] By considering first what these ballads represent as the purpose of the lyric genre, we will be prepared to understand how details in other poems further contribute to Enzensberger's radical interrogation of culture.

The opening poem in *Mausoleum,* "Giovanni de' Dondi (1318–1389)," is about an early inventor of clocks. It is preceded in Enzensberger's publications by several poems with related content, "Himmelsmaschine" from *Gedichte 1955–1970* (1971b, 122–23) and "Celestial Machine," Enzensberger's own translation of that text (1970a, 4). Comparison of "Himmelsmaschine" and "Giovanni de' Dondi (1318–1389)," with passing reference to the intermediary "Celestial Machine," helps foreground practices of poetic construction used in *Mausoleum.* Composed in free, yet rhythmical verse, with lines of two to four stresses, "Himmelsmaschine" interpolates a mere two dozen italicized quoted words, barely hinting at the prose pastiche that will later develop in *Mausoleum.* The *Mausoleum* version of the poem, "Giovanni de' Dondi (1318–1389)" begins tersely, mentioning in three lines the life's work of the obscure figure:

> Giovanni de' Dondi aus Padua
> verbrachte sein Leben
> mit dem Bau einer Uhr.
>
> Eine Uhr ohne Vorbild, unübertroffen
> vierhundert Jahre lang.
> Das Gangwerk mehrfach,
> elliptische Zahnräder,
> verbunden durch Gelenkgetriebe,
> und die erste Spindelhemmung:
> eine unerhörte Konstruktion.
>
> Sieben Zifferblätter
> zeigen den Zustand des Himmels an
> und die stummen Revolutionen
> aller Planeten.
> Ein achtes Blatt,
> das unscheinbarste,

wies die Stunde, den Tag und das Jahr:
A.D. 1346.

Geschmiedet mit eigener Hand:
eine Himmelsmaschine,
zwecklos und sinnreich wie die *Trionfi,*
eine Uhr aus Wörtern,
erbaut von Francesco Petrarca.
Aber wozu vergeudet ihr eure Zeit
mit meinem Manuskript,
wenn ihr nicht fähig seid,
es mir nachzutun?

Dauer des Tageslichts,
Knoten der Mondbahn,
bewegliche Feste.
Ein Rechenwerk, und zugleich
der Himmel noch einmal.
Aus Messing, aus Messing.
Unter diesem Himmel
leben wir noch.

Die Leute von Padua
sahen nicht auf die Uhr.
Ein Putsch folgte dem andern.
Pestkarren rollten über das Pflaster.
Die Bankiers
stellten ihr Positionen glatt.
Es gab wenig zu essen.

Der Ursprung jener Maschine
ist problematisch.
Ein Analog-Computer.
Ein Menhir. Ein Astrarium.
Trionfi del tempo. Überbleibsel.
Zwecklos und sinnreich
wie ein Gedicht aus Messing.

Nicht Guggenheim sandte
Francesco Petrarca Schecks
zum Ersten des Monats.

De' Dondi hatte keinen Kontrakt
mit dem Pentagon.

Andere Raubtiere. Andere
Wörter und Räder. Aber
derselbe Himmel.
In diesem Mittelalter
leben wir immer noch.

(1975, 7–9)

Giovanni de' Dondi of Padua
spent his life
building a timepiece.

A unique timepiece, unsurpassed
through four hundred years.
The gearwork manifold,
elliptical wheels,
connected by driving linkage,
and the first crown-escapement:
an incredible construction.

Seven dials
showed the position of the sky
and the mute revolutions
of all planets.
An eighth face,
the plainest,
gave the hour, the day, and the year:
A.D. 1346.

Forged with his own hand:
a celestial machine.
Purposeless, ingenious, like the Trionfi,
a clock of words,
built by Francesco Petrarca.

But why squander your time
with my manuscript
if you are unable
to emulate me?

Duration of daylight,
nodes of lunar orbit,
movable feasts.
A mathematical engine, and also
heaven once more.
Of brass, of brass.
That's the sky we still
live under today.

The people of Padua
didn't give the clock
the time of day.
Putsch upon putsch.
Plague-carts rolled through the streets.
The bankers
settled accounts.
Food was scarce.

The origin of that machine
is problematic.
An analog computer.
A menhir. An astrarium.
Trionfi del tempo. *Leftovers.*
Purposeless and ingenious
like a poem of brass.

No Guggenheim sent
Francesco Petrarca checks
the first of the month.
De' Dondi had no contract
with the Pentagon.

Different predators. Different
words and wheels. But
the same sky.
That's the Dark Age we still
Live in today.

(1976c, 1–3)

Initial stanzas replete with technical terminology detail the mechanical features of de' Dondi's timepiece; the fourth stanza notes its status as an artifact analogous to a work of poetry: a labor of love and beautiful creation with no practical purpose. A pendulating, almost ticking rhythm sounds midway through the text. The poem first presents de' Dondi as laboring without constraint on the construction of the clock, but Enzensberger rapidly, and with marked irony, alludes to the emergence of a hierarchical economic system based on class distinctions ("The bankers settled accounts. / Food was scarce."), patronage affiliations ("No Guggenheim sent / Francesco Petrarcha checks / the first of the month."), and an incipient military-industrial complex ("De' Dondi had no contract with the Pentagon" [1976c, 7–9]). With the fifth stanza, the text introduces comparisons with the contemporary context, underscored by use of the phrase "That's the sky we still / live under today," which the final lines then repeat in slightly varied form.

The description of the clockwork, right down to the sequence of mechanical parts (weight-drive, verge-and-foliot escapement, elliptical gearwheels, and linkwork) nimbly imports terminology used in an account of the same invention by Derek de Solla Price, "Celestial Clockwork in Greece and China" (1975). A source Enzensberger cites in *Gedichte 1955–1970* (1971b), where the poem "Himmelsmaschine" appears, Price mentions the clock's "inconspicuous dial" and the fact that no similar machine was built until centuries later (1975, 31).

Enzensberger's self-translation "Celestial Machine" mirrors "Himmelsmaschine" by using an epigrammatic quotation from de' Dondi, eleven stanzas, and a line-by-line correspondence of content, but its language remains somewhat dry and unembellished. "Giovanni de' Dondi (1318–1389)," a refinement of "Himmelsmaschine," adumbrates principles of originality, efficacy, and craft that become important in subsequent ballads of *Mausoleum*. Enzensberger enlarges on the observation Price makes that de' Dondi's clock seems to have been utterly unprecedented merely because no antecedents survived. The gesture frames the alternative history of progress articulated in *Mausoleum:* a series of anomalies rather than rational evolution. This first ballad establishes one of several historical arcs, a chronology that culminates in the Enlightenment midway through the collection. While Price dates de' Dondi's invention to Padua in 1364 and compares the clock's spectacular ingenuity with seventeenth-century products, Enzensberger emphasizes the continuity between the early Renaissance and the German Enlightenment of the 1700s, terming the clock a machine unsurpassed for over *four hundred* years.

Even in counterfeiting, Enzensberger substantially reworks Price's presentation of de' Dondi in order to link poetry metaphorically with mechanical inventions. For example, Price tells readers about an early manuscript describing the planetary equatorium, a tool used to calculate the location of the planets, and he cites the device as one that strongly influenced later theologians, scientists, and the Renaissance poets Dante and Chaucer.[34] Discussing the relationship of artifacts to developing technology, Price observes that often tools had no practical application but that "in the sixteenth and earlier centuries the world was already full of ingenious artisans who made scientific devices that were more wondrous and beautiful than directly useful" (1975, 29). Similarly, Enzensberger comments that both de' Dondi's clock and Petrarch's poetry were "zwecklos und sinnreich" (1975, 7–9), or "[p]urposeless, ingenious" (1976c, 1–3).

Enzensberger thereby sets up an interface between poets and scientists, as Price had done, but specifically connects de' Dondi's clock with Petrarch's *Trionfi del tempo* (*The Triumph of Time*). The rest of this stanza collapses de' Dondi's and Petrarch's work into a single concept. Here Enzensberger establishs the parallel positions of poetry and technology, thereby announcing his project in *Mausoleum:* Petrarch, the artist, becomes just as emblematic of the principles of originality, efficacy and craft explicated in "Giovanni de' Dondi (1318–1389)" as is the scientist de' Dondi.

The fourth stanza of "Giovanni de' Dondi (1318–1389)" incorporates an epigraph by de' Dondi—"Why, my Reader, should you waste your time studying this manuscript of mine if you are not capable of building clocks yourself?"—which had opened both "Himmelsmaschine," where this epigraph stood in externalized, dialectical relationship to the text, and "Celestial Machine," in which the question was directed toward eliding the distinction between writing and reading. At the same time, variations in computational terminology (*Rechenwerk, Rechenmaschine,* and *analog computer*) among the three poem texts reveal semantic drift toward the thematic cluster of machinery-writing-social relations of *Mausoleum.* Ultimately "Giovanni de' Dondi (1318–1389)" shifts the technological jargon of the earlier two poems to generalized formulations. Enzensberger's *Einladung zu einem Poesie-Automaten,* published some twenty-five years later, comments that the literary stagnation circa 1975 drew him to speculate about creating a computer-type device to produce poetry. These poems provide contemporary evidence of that fascination.

Once the ballad "Giovanni de' Dondi (1318–1389)" has established the metaphor of poetry as technology, *Mausoleum* makes machines the literal coproducers of texts. In the cycle, writing falls victim to a limiting metonymy, and systematic, scientific notation supplants free poetic expression. The first ballad thus marks the beginnings of modern poetry and also its end, for the equation of writing with mechanical production undermines artistic autonomy. That trope can be traced back to Enzensberger's afterword to *Museum* of 1960, which refers to Poe's account of poetry as handiwork "aus Triebrädern und Riemen" (1980, 776) and to his 1961 essay "Scherenschleifer und Poeten." Enzensberger had also called poetry creation mechanical (re-)production in the essay "Die Entstehung eines Gedichts" (1962b), which cites this phrase from Poe's "The Philosophy of Composition" again (39) and lists other authors who expounded similar views (including Baudelaire, Mallarmé, Benn, Pound, and Valéry). He in fact comments that Mayakovsky drew on Poe's descriptions of poetic gears and belts in creating a Marxist aesthetic that encompassed all productive forces, including poetry creation (1962b, 41).

But *Mausoleum* deliberates on the consequences of this logic. A gradual metamorphosis narrows writing to a mere technical means of media production, yet this evolution leads to an apostasy of progress that does not leave Marxism unscathed. We can see the pernicious consequences of aligning poetry with mechanical production by systematically tracing the language that describes writing through the cycle of poems. The second poem in *Mausoleum,* which is about Gutenberg, marvels at the potential of the print medium while pondering the limitations of reproduction ("The same book, not the same" [1975, 10]). It concludes by drawing attention to the physical poem, the blackness on the paper and the art of artificial writing (11). That statement prompts the reader to ponder the constructed nature of literature, its mimetic conventions, and actual production. Subsequent poems mention texts, acts of writing, and fragmentary traces of verbal expression. Third in the cycle, "Niccolò Machiavelli (1469–1527)," terms Machiavelli a "model for all history writers" (1975, 12) and "Ghostwriter" (13) for the Borgias, a poet whose lies often tell the truth.

"Bernardino Sahagún (1499–1590)," however, briefly recovers claims to credibility and truth-telling. This ballad has the special purpose in the collection of preserving the last traces of an indigenous population that will be decimated by genocide, and it anticipates subsequent barbarisms. The poem refers to "the old hieroglyphs" of the Native Americans (1975, 15), the "illegal copies" written by Sahagún's pupils, grammars, and glosses (16). Its precise anthropological recording procedures (interview techniques, crosschecking, transcription rules) contrast with the obliteration of knowledge about the native population. Italics distinguish first-person observations gleaned from the early anthropological source from the ballad's third-person commentary on Sahagún. This pristine documentation—which mimics Enzensberger's own habit of producing literature as a traveler abroad—makes writing an ethical act that protests genocide but makes it public (see esp. Enzensberger 1964h). The fate of the Native Americans is a historically transposed record of the Holocaust. European social "evolution" is shown to be inhumane, "primitive," in contrast to the coherent society that existed in the Americas before Christian conquerors arrived.

Three of the ballad's passages voice the perceptions of the Native Americans. "The Omen" employs eloquent hypotactic construction to describe prefigurations of the Spaniards' arrival. "The Mountain" and "The Cave" are linguistically reduced to constricted, paratactic construction. Their language is fragmented and repetitive, an accumulation of terse phrases that mirrors the progressive silencing of the massacred.[35] These sections anticipate other ballads that reverse the categories of "primitivism" and "sophistication" by revealing the primitiveness of crude, self-absorbed experimenters in later history. *Mausoleum* reassigns the labels that identify what is primitive, simple, old, and forgotten and what is advanced, complex, new, and historically remembered. In "Bernardino Sahagún (1499–1590)" the "new" lands are "discovered"; elsewhere astronomy "redefines" the universe. The intelligent reader knows that such attributions of origination and agency are bald manipulations of language by the dominant class.

From here, Enzensberger continues to make the case for poetry that culminates in "Che." "Tyge Brahe (1546–1601)," on Tycho Brahe, further erodes our confidence in scientific perception and reprises the terms *Astrolabien, Uhrwerke,* and *Druckerpressen* (1975, 20) used in "Giovanni de' Dondi (1318–1389)." Other figures who follow in *Mausoleum* rely on machines and facts as sources of information, dismissing intuitive insight and physical perceptions, and thereby allow Enzensberger to introduce the topic of control over political and erotic thought. The subsequent ballad, "Tommaso Campanella (1568–1639)," relates how manuscripts were stolen, then handed over to the Inquisition (23). Incorporating a legal document, the ballad lists regulations of sexual behavior to suggest that even the most individual, private acts are reducible to public statutes (25).[36]

Vastly overwhelmed in *Mausoleum* by science and technology, its status as a viable genre undermined, poetry—that expression of an "erotics of art" vaunted in "Note to 'Summer Poem'"—loses value as an instrument of bourgeois aesthetics. Only a few individuals in *Mausoleum*, those who immerse themselves in eccentric research, seem more independent, notably

Carl Linnaeus ("Carl von Linné (1707–1778)" [1975, 31]) and Alexander von Humboldt ("Alexander von Humboldt (1769–1859)" [62]). Their credibility stands in inverse proportion to the extent of sociotechnological control over their research. Other intellectually sophisticated figures, for instance Leibniz, exhibit rudimentary social and moral development. Their emotional primitivism equates with the mechanical primitivism and the automaticity of machines.

This evolutionary arc in which progress and normative bourgeois aesthetics suppress the imagination leads to a devolution of art objects, writerly verse, and creative magic and to a longing for poetry. "Gottfried Wilhelm Leibniz (1646–1716)," which follows "Campanella," defines how the imagination is restricted through discourse and connects a lack of sexuality with moral corruption. Portraying Leibniz as cut off from emotions and sexual urges, the text calls him an artifact (Enzensberger 1975, 27). Enzensberger expresses his disfunctionality with use of passive constructions and repetitive syntax. The ballad notes in a monotone that Leibniz has produced a jumble of abstractions of abstractions (27). Leibniz corresponds widely in letters (28) but does not interact directly with people. He is the subject of voyeuristic CIA spying. Enzensberger carefully interweaves succinct commentary with italicized quotations by Leibniz to pass judgment on the philosopher. This pliable, lyrical prose challenges the reader to reflect on the authorial position of the person who generates it, for it wavers among types of speech with variable mimetic capacities—free indirect discourse (the exclamation "Ach ja!" ["Ah yes!"]), grammatically marked indirect speech ("er habe . . . sich damit befaßt" ["someone, anonymous, claims"]), and figurative language ("Gold aus dem Kot . . . das Licht aus der Finsternis" ["gold from excrement, diamonds from cesspools"]) (1975, 30; 1976c 27–28).[37]

The next poem in the cycle, "Carl von Linné (1707–1778)," though more positive about its subject, turns the potentially creative work of "collecting, cataloguing, and naming" into an obsession. "Meaningful. Meaningless. Meaningful," the text prattles, as if counting off the petals of a flower as they are plucked to the familiar incantation of "loves me, loves me not." The chant echoes the terms "zwecklos und sinnreich" (1975, 7–8), or "[p]urposeless, ingenious" (1976c, 1–3), used to describe de' Dondi's fabulous clock.

From this ballad on, all art becomes ever more imperiled as machines increasingly threaten to replace human creativity. "Jacques de Vaucanson (1709–1782)," called a *Künstler* (artist), proposes the possibility of an endless machine—a machine capable of building machines in endless succession. His achievement is consummately normative creation. As fantasy wanes and sensuality shrivels into perversion, writing and art undergo a commensurate reduction. "Raimondo di Sangro (1710–1771)" speaks of "ballads mixed of magic and industry" (1975, 37), while the next poem "Giovanni Battista Piranesi (1720–1778)" muses about artists who merely catalog (41). "Lazzaro Spallanzani (1729–1799)" announces the development of a class of intelligentsia "like scorpions" (46) and denounces the insufficiency of their writings (47). "Charles Messier (1730–1817)," who relies on minimal technology (sharp eyes, a pendulum clock, a quadrant, and a shabby telescope [48]), leaves a correspondingly minimal legacy ("Only a letter recalls him" [49]).

In emphasizing the writerly preoccupations of *Mausoleum*, I do not want to imply that we should overlook Enzensberger's social concerns. My point is that in the absence of a coherent teleology, the tension between rationality and irrationality becomes an increasingly central issue in *Mausoleum,* as it had in German society. Enzensberger draws on social theory to bring this project to maturity, as can be seen from a comparison with the account of social evolution formulated by Habermas in *Legitimation Crisis* (1975). As a group, the latter ballads in the collection show a proliferation of systems that for all their sophistication only lead to greater confusion. Habermas is concerned with the loss of legitimacy that occurs when flexible liberal-capitalist social formations supplant feudal-aristocratic social hierarchies. Demonstrating that new forms of control are imbricated with the old, *Mausoleum* overlaps with their histories by covering the Enlightenment (1975, 27, 34), French Revolution (52, 54), and the ever-accelerating Industrial Revolution (57). It intimates the advent of a postcapitalist society in the poems about Bakunin (94) and Che Guevara (126) and debates plausible explanations for the evolution of humanity. The ballad about Darwin perversely lavishes attention on his working habits, while slighting his theory (86). Neither system suffices, for *Mausoleum* instigates its own "legitimation crisis."

The collection offers damning evidence of how the rationalization of society quashes creative impulses. "Joseph Ignac Guillotin (1738–1814)" and other ballads about Enlightenment figures contrast human slaughter with reason. Metaphors of light and dark (Enzensberger 1975, 51) underscore this failure. Guillotin himself is depicted as a plump speaker given to *Wortschwall* (verbosity). "Antoine Caritat de Condorcet (1743–1794)," which describes terror, revolution, and machinery, reduces language to "the usual epithets." "Oliver Evans (1755–1819)" remarks on the outmodedness of words (58) and the autogenesis of machines (59). "Thomas Robert Malthus (1766–1834)" turns to solipsism, referring to "Herren Godwin und Condorcet" (60) and directing the reader back to the figure of Condorcet in a previous ballad, a gesture of dangerously inbred hermeticism. "Alexander von Humboldt (1769–1859)" then emphasizes the work of Humboldt not as writer but as painter (65), thereby marking the rise of visual culture.

Inevitably the pendulation between rationality and irrationality falls out of sync. A ballad about "Charles Fourier (1772–1837)" remarks on the mixture of madness and insight in the French writer's work (1975, 67). "Charles Babbage (1792–1871)," concerning the English mathematician, cites an exchange with Tennyson mentioned in Kenner's *The Counterfeiters* that illustrates the loss of nature as a source of poetry:

> Als aber der arme Tennyson ihm seine Verse zusandte
> (*Every minute dies a man/Every minute one is born*),
> schlug er ihm vor, *in der nächsten Auflage*
> *Ihr treffliches Werk dergestalt zu verbessern,*
> *daß es lautet: "Täusche dich nicht, in jeder Minute*
> *erblicken eins Komma ein sechs sieben Menschen das Licht."*
> (1975, 71)

> *But when poor Tennyson sent him his verses*
> (Every minute dies a man/Every minute one is born*)*,
> *he suggested that in the next edition of your excellent poem*
> *the erroneous calculation should be corrected as follows:*
> *Every minute dies a man/and one a sixteenth is born.*
> (1976c, 74)

In this same ballad Byron's daughter, Lady Lovelace, appears at Babbage's laboratory door (Enzensberger 1975, 72). Now even the muse figure seems to participate in the reduction of poetry to machinery, which has substituted mere fact for metaphor. Further destabilizing our world, the next ballad, "Louis Auguste Blanqui (1805–1881)" ends with the image of the scientist recording his observations on "cell development" and "an astronomical hypothesis" (78), data extremes at both ends of the measurement scale that nonetheless thwart analytic discrimination. *Mausoleum* does not seek to dispense with the sense of crisis that it propounds. Instead, an iron framework of disciplinarity is imposed on every new event that occurs. The system becomes more and more hermetic.

But then Enzensberger interrupts the "evolution" by introducing Robert-Houdin. His ballad questions the status of art by turning reader attention to the "art of deception" that Robert-Houdin practices. He thrills to deceive his audiences, blinding reason with reason (Enzensberger 1975, 81). This interlude cautions readers not to take the rational elements too seriously as they proceed through the rest of the collection. The succeeding ballad, which is about the English engineer Brunel (82), abruptly returns readers to history and a fulminating imperialism ("Metastasen des Empire"). This provocative pairing of Robert-Houdin and Brunel—illusion/fact, poetry/politics, or decadent art/virulent nationalism—is ironically diffused by the conclusion of the Brunel ballad, which comments that historians dismiss it all as legend. Similarly, two ballads later in "Charles Darwin (1809–1882)," the protagonist reacts with disgust to himself, commenting that he is only a machine condemned to consume books and then reproduce them in altered form to throw upon the dung heap of history (88).

Notwithstanding this protest, rationalization proceeds on its own momentum. Each ballad extends control over nature and by alienating humanity from the physical world with an estrangement that builds the subsequent sequence of texts about the city planner ("Baron Georg Eugène Haussmann (1809–1891)") and the musician ("Frédéric Chopin (1810–1849)"), the revolutionary Bakunin, a physician (Semmelweis), a camera inventor (Marey), an efficiency expert (Taylor), and a film director (Méliès). Technology grows more brutal while language becomes progressively more prosaic, as if poetry were quashed by the rigidity of socioscientific discourse. A final quartet of texts concerns dubious figures: Ugo Cerletti (the inventor of electroshock therapy), Molotov (the Russian politician), Wilhelm Reich (psychotherapist), and Alan Turing (a quirky mathematician preoccupied by the potential of computers).[38] Increasing cross-referencing with the earlier poems in the collection meanwhile forces the serious reader into a laborious recursive process of rereading.[39]

The progression of *Mausoleum* through time follows neither uniform intervals, expected highlights, nor a conventionally telescoped acceleration across the modern period. It is erratic. Some personages alluded to in some ballads are contemporaries of the reader; other figures exist in anachronistically conceived spaces. A few inhabit mutually exclusive parallel universes, as is the case for the last two in the collection, Turing and Che Guevara. Although neither figure is cognizant of the other, both suffer from asthma, sharing a kind of artistic sickliness that is intensely personal.

The final ballad, about Che Guevara—"Ernesto Guevara de la Serna (1928–1967)"—opens with a riddle that conceals his identity and returns *Mausoleum* to questions of how culture is constructed. This puzzle entices the reader to meditate on time. "For a time thousands wore his cap on their heads," it teases (Enzensberger 1975, 126), evoking scenes of mass protest demonstrations. Guevara, unlike those persons in the volume who disdain the world of literature, is an avid reader, both of fantastic novels by Jules Verne and of French symbolist poetry, especially Baudelaire, whose work he knew by heart (127). His cult-figure status is established through references to legendary attributions, such as the Christlike appearance of his corpse and allusions to a dubious afterlife among downcast hippies and in boutiques. Here poetry is recovered not only in the allusion to verses by Baudelaire but also through a reference back to Sahagún: "The silence of the Indians was absolute, as if we came from another world" (127). This remark reverses the earlier configuration of insiders and outsiders by isolating Europe on the margins of the world.

That reference to the *Indios* recalls the question of genocide under which German postwar poetry had toiled mindful of Adorno's caution about the barbarousness of writing poetry after Auschwitz. The references to bloodshed in "Bernardino Sahagún (1499–1590)" and now the palpable suppression of the pasts by dominant histories undo these silences. The evocative power of poetry draws out these unspoken stories because it continues to move the reader. Guevara recognizes the estrangement between himself and the Indians, as did Sahagún. The concept "eine andere Welt"/ "another world" (1975, 15, 127) stands in diametric opposition to that of "die neue Welt"/ "the new world" wrenchingly created by conquest, invention, and technological progress.[40]

Mausoleum does not in the end seek a glib poetic restitution for crimes against humanity, nor does it offer closure. Instead, it creates conditions for a model of reading consonant with the project of "teaching political literary skills" announced in "Gemeinplätze." The solution Enzensberger devises is quite different from those applied by other contemporary poets. Rather than agitating, the poet relies on the sheer complexity of language—the writerly medium. In cultivating lyric prose, Enzensberger seeks compatibilities between theory and the lyric genre, yet without rejecting the concrete texture of words in favor of abstractions. The shift toward prose in *Mausoleum* (a genre presumably more accessible to contemporary audiences than poetry) in fact complicates the text. It compels the reader to discover nuances, follow disparate narrative strands, and adjust interpretations as the poems are experienced. This participatory reading process itself takes time and, hence, reflection. As a work, then, *Mausoleum* challenges the contradictory roles conventionally assigned to poetry: the voicing of exclusively private concerns and the yoking of content to overtly political messages.

Embracing an emergent postmodern aesthetic of pastiche, *Mausoleum* sets up conditions for its own reception. As a text, it draws attention to its own constructed nature through visual signals, linguistic discontinuities, and a stubborn resistance to closure of meaning. The ostensibly neutral language of historical reportage suppresses private elements; public language is unmasked as inherently controlling. Enzensberger's use of prose discourse drawn from atypical sources opens up interstices where sensitivity to the rhetorical, affective, and historical qualities of words becomes critical. Otherwise the reader would perceive the literary language of *Mausoleum* as mere ordinary prose. To play with reliability, *Mausoleum* manipulates the signifying conventions of factual texts, rendering their contents strange in a manner that exceeds the polyvocal language of "Sommergedicht" (which relied on variable semantics) and the practice of "Entstellung," which foregrounded dissonances through juxtaposition. *Mausoleum* presents its readers with occasions for analysis. Equating writing with machinery, it revives clichés about the dark of ignorance and the light of truth. The analytical instruments of academic-theoretical discourses (analysis, argument, data, experiment, history, and catalog) shape the language of the ballads. The tools of poetry—evocation, imaginative connection, narrative sequencing—guide the reader in understanding the collection as a whole. *Mausoleum* is legitimated not by its content or authentic voice but rather by the capacities of the lyric genre. For its audience, which shared a sense of history deeply marked by postwar concerns about memory and the past, *Mausoleum* reflected the 1960s and 1970s aesthetic ruptures, burgeoning consumerism, and political turmoil by holding up the clouded mirror of history.

In his commentary on *Museum der modernen Poesie*, Enzensberger had postulated a readership consisting of working poets who would actively make use of the poems he collected. *Mausoleum* assumes a broader but no less vigorous audience, one eager for information and prepared to unravel complicated cyclical patterns, myriad details, and a bricolage of allusions. Far from staging a pessimistic retreat into post-1968 lethargy, the collection advocates reflective learning and presupposes, however tentatively, a common, progressive community. While the figures portrayed naively take for granted the validity of their own positions, their temporally fixed perspectives are undermined by the external insights of history.[41] Dichotomies of right/wrong, public/private, inner/outer, and intellect/experience become effaced. The lyrical prose of *Mausoleum* uses the conceptual means of theory (logic, analysis, systematicity) in concert with the elements of poetry—its spontaneity, recourse to the sublime as a source of inspiration, and joy in language itself. This "dance of the intellect among words," Pound's *logopoeia,* ends with rupture. "The text breaks off and the answers rot on," the final ballad concludes, as if announcing a sequel (Enzensberger 1975, 128). In Enzensberger's next major work of poetry, *Der Untergang der Titanic* (*The Sinking of the Titanic*), the strands of intellect and imagination meet in an exploration of chaos theory, ecological crisis, and the recovery of poetic voice that recasts the relationship between poetry and theory in concrete terms.

4. Poetic Survival

Chaos Theory and the Recovery of the Lyric

Der Untergang der Titanic (*The Sinking of the Titanic*) opens with an emphatic assertion of the poet's identity that honors the lyric genre as a mode of expression: "There is someone who listens, who waits, / holds his breath, very close by, / here. He says: This is *my* voice. // Never again, he says, / is it going to be as quiet, / as dry and warm as it is now" (Enzensberger 1980b, 1). The delivery of these lines is deliberate—their cadences grow from the speaker's voice, the at-first isolated sensory perceptions, and the temporal-linear character of poetic texts. Pauses, breaths, and shifts in breathing signaled by laconic itemization and punctuation mark the palpable rhythm. This physiologically grounded pattern recalls Charles Olson's assertion in his 1950 work "Projective Verse" that in the writing of poetry, "the line comes (I swear it) from the breath, from the breathing of the man who writes" (quoted in Williams 1967a, 331). The breathing also evokes Paul Celan's statement in his 1960 Büchner prize speech, "Der Meridian" (1972), or "The Meridian" (1999a), which called poetry a turn of breath (1972, 141).[1] Written in free verse, the first canto in *Der Untergang der Titanic* develops into a monologue as the third-person discourse gives way to a poetic "I" through phrases that show the poet finding voice: "This must be *my* voice. / I wait," "I have been waiting for a long time," and "I tell myself" (1980b, 1). Each verse consists of a three-line stanza, an unusual strophe form that resembles the triadic, stepped-down lines of "Sommergedicht." The language is condensed, eerie, and lyrically evocative.

In contrast to *Mausoleum,* where prose and rationalizing thought impinge on poetry, *Der Untergang der Titanic* labors to free elements fundamental to the lyric genre. The epic relies on spontaneity, coincidence, and imaginative synthesis. Openly raising questions about what obtains aesthetic value, the text recovers traditional sources of poetic inspiration—nature, the muse, and perceptions of the senses. While like *Mausoleum* it reflects on historical events and sustains tension between private and public expression, *Der Untergang der Titanic* turns to chaos theory, drawing on a companion discourse from the physical rather than social sciences for focus. Enzensberger has termed *Der Untergang der Titanic* his best work (1995a, 13). It is a complex, self-consciously constructed text that recounts the tale of its own composition, thinks about the art of Old Masters, and meditates on aspects of translation. This work evidently preoccupied its author for over a decade, for the text reports on its own initial writing in Cuba (where Enzensberger resided in 1968). Published in German in 1978 and produced in radio play version in 1979, *Der Untergang der Titanic* was then issued in 1980 in an English translation authored by Enzensberger himself, *The Sinking of the Titanic.*

When it first appeared, the epic received interpretation as a work that expressed the mood of resignation among German intellectuals after the collapse of 1960s activism. Analysis of *Der Untergang der Titanic* in connection with Enzensberger's subsequent publications, however, uncovers not pessimism but a reengagement with the possibilities of poetry that takes the author in a strikingly different direction. As my previous chapters have shown, Enzensberger had already sought to enlarge the means available to the lyric genre by contesting, absorbing, and rewriting nonpoetic language. Grappling with chaos theory in *Der Untergang der Titanic* and other works, he appropriated a daring structural paradigm and uncovered a fresh source of linguistic material. Put simply, chaos theory explains that within unpredictable systems, an underlying order exists. Many of Enzensberger's publications starting with *Der Untergang der Titanic* (1978a)—especially the poetry collections *Zukunftsmusik* (*Music of the Future* [1991c]), *Kiosk* (1995b), and *Leichter als Luft: Moralische Gedichte* (*Lighter than Air: Moral Poems* [1999e]), explore that critical tension between order and disorder by indexing chaos theory. Others, his poetry guide *Das Wasserzeichen der Poesie* (*The Watermark of Poetry* [1985]) and the textbook for German-language beginners, *Die Suche* (*The Search* [Enzensberger et al. 1993]), playfully use physical presentations of text that mirror the kinds of patterns science associates with chaotic events for didactic purposes. Several essays by Enzensberger also mention the science of chaos, and it even surfaces in one of his books for children, *Der Zahlenteufel* (1997a), also published in English as *The Number Devil* (1997b), which includes a chapter on fractals (1997b, 189–210).

While the terminology of chaos theory that figures in *Der Untergang der Titanic* is best illustrated with examples from the text itself, two science findings broadly inform the work as a whole and can provide us with a conceptual framework for its interpretation. First, chaos theory treats small- and large-scale phenomena as equally important, and it looks for patterns that clarify their underlying regularity. Second, chaos science recognizes that "neutral" observation cannot exist because in the physical world the scientist (or scientist-poet) and the subject observed are both subject to the laws of cause and effect. These principles operate on several levels at once in the epic. Linguistically reproducing small chaotic effects, *Der Untergang der Titanic* mimics the phenomena that gave rise to chaos theory and resists deploying large conceptual categories and theoretical language, as *Mausoleum* had. Moreover, in *Der Untergang der Titanic,* Enzensberger tests a composition process that involves the long-term redaction of texts. The technique, which follows the principle of constellations Enzensberger identified in Brentano's poetry, is consonant with the notion of emergent patterns articulated in chaos theory. Each involves a process of seemingly spontaneous centering around foci. In the constellations of rewriting, as Enzensberger defines them, the author returns again and again to a set of linguistic material (themes and phrases) and reworks these elements in different texts. Within Enzensberger's oeuvre such constellations entail exercises in self-translation that link his practices as translator and his endeavors as poet over long periods of time—and with brilliant result. Throughout *Der Untergang der Titanic* and related texts, the association of chaos theory with an effort to recover poetic values connects Enzensberger's ironic deliberations about poetry as an anachronistic "old medium" with his anarchic speculation that even the smallest line of verse has the ability to overthrow all expectations with which the lyric genre has been freighted.

Chaos Theory

One of the problems disclosed by *Mausoleum* was that coherence could be lost amid a surfeit of data and rationalized explanations because, Enzensberger argued, in the end poetry and not just intellect is needed to produce clarity.[2] In appropriating chaos theory in *Der Untergang der Titanic,* Enzensberger seeks to address modern and postmodern fragmentation by insisting that we notice that contemporary science has procedural means for finding order in stochastic phenomena. His allusions to science in *Der Untergang der Titanic* and subsequent publications draw the lyric genre back to two areas that had been largely abandoned by German literature in the latter half of the twentieth century—didactic verse and nature poetry—albeit with a radical modification of those traditions. *Der Untergang der Titanic* gives poetry license to address intellectual dilemmas through playful, lyrical, and sensorially evocative means; and within the continuum of expressive registers Enzensberger wields, it comes to stand opposite *Mausoleum* in much the way that *Blindenschrift* had an inverse relationship to *Verteidigung der Wölfe.* Initially Enzensberger explores chaos theory as a means to resolve a logical (and arguably postmodern) impasse that literature shares with science, namely, that all-encompassing, hierarchical theories inadequately account for particulars. He returns to the topic several times in widely dispersed texts and finally directs deliberations on chaos toward a reconsideration of the status accorded literature in the contemporary sociocultural context.

In a 1976 essay, "Bescheidener Vorschlag zum Schutze der Jugend vor den Erzeugnissen der Poesie" ("Modest Proposal for the Protection of Youth from the Products of Poetry"), which he delivered as an address at the annual meeting of the American Association of Teachers of German, Enzensberger indulged in an intricate digression about scientists who observe "millions of inconspicuous elemental events . . . always hoping to find significant rules in the chaos of minimal reactions that occur there" (1976a, 427).[3] A fundamental skepticism about man-made, cerebral systems emerges in Enzensberger's characterization of these invented macrostructures as "a gigantic intellectual toy that our aestheticians never even let themselves dream of" (1976a, 427). His interrogation of these constructs leads to his "modest" proposal that interpretation—such as German teachers prescribe for their students—be abolished. The rhetorical art of Enzensberger's speech shapes the substance of the argument, which reasons that interpretation unjustly shackles a text to a single reading and that no single reading should be presumed valid. While Enzensberger's earlier writings about literature, in particular the "Note to 'Summer Poem,'" presage the conclusion's dismissal of interpretation, the terms of the debate are here more ironic and extreme. Poetry, the poet declares, is as unquantifiable as the phenomena studied by those few enlightened physicists who, eschewing the prospect of absolute, universal laws, "came upon the nearby thought that there are micro-occurrences which do not allow for an exact prognosis and about which only probabilistic statements can be made, and even then only if they occur often enough" (1976a, 427).

Although "Bescheidener Vorschlag" is laced with ironic characterizations of poetry as infinitesimal, politically ineffective, and anachronistic, for Enzensberger—and for the scientific community in the late 1970s—the articulation of chaos theory coincided with a paradigm shift that legitimated the study of small, aleatory pieces of evidence. Paradoxically, this theory proposed a new notion of coherence at the very moment when it seemed that the last coherent systems had been lost. Enzensberger's evocation of chaos science in connection with the lyric genre thus serves to reassert the value of poetry by attaching the lyric to a robust new paradigm, one grounded in the very particulars of the natural world. This engagement with chaotic effects returned the author to principles once enunciated by Adorno concerning the stubborn resistance of artworks to societal norms.

What chaos theory seems to offer Enzensberger is a way to resolve a vexing aesthetic problem also found in science. James Gleick summarizes the scientific matter as follows in *Chaos: Making a New Science:* "Simple systems give rise to complex behavior. Complex systems give rise to simple behavior. And most important, the laws of complexity hold universally, caring not at all for the details of a system's constituent atoms" (1987, 304). Dripping water, weather changes, electronic oscillation, turbulence, and heartbeats all exhibit quite similar, loose patterns with chaotic variation comprehensible only under this kind of scrutiny. When a faucet leaks, for example, the seemingly monotonous fall of droplets is impossible to predict using sophisticated equations because the drip frequency is in fact irregular. Only chaos science supplies the means to describe the apparent uniformity in such variable patterns. N. Katharine Hayles explains in her introduction to *Chaos and Order: Complex Dynamics in Literature and Science,* "The science of chaos seeks to understand behavior so complex that it defeats the usual methods of formalizing a system through mathematics. Hence the science of chaos has also been called the science of complexity—or more precisely the sciences of complexity, for fields as diverse as meteorology, irreversible thermodynamics, epidemiology, and nonlinear dynamics are included within the rubric" (1991, 1).

Contending that chaos theory displays affinities to postmodern thinking outside the field of science, Hayles locates the origins of chaos science as much in literature and literary theory as in previous scientific history. The writings of Jacques Derrida, Fredric Jameson, Jean-François Lyotard, and Luce Irigary serve as her illustrations of this point.[4] Other scholars who have explored the connection between chaos theory and literature, notably David Porush (1991) and Peter Stoicheff (1991), detail additional parallels between complex narrative forms (for which metafiction is a prime example) and such scientifically observable phenomena as nonclassical relationships between macro- and microstructures, the "butterfly effect," fractals, attractors (a form of self-organization within chaotic systems), and bifurcation points (Porush 1991, 70–73). Enzensberger's texts, especially those dating from the late seventies, seem compatible with this kind of analysis.

To elicit the particular connection between *Der Untergang der Titanic* and the science of chaos, however, it is necessary to consider how Enzensberger absorbs the basic findings of chaos theory, a general interest in science, and specific terminology. In his texts, problems illuminated by chaos science (proportionality, observer involvement, and self-organization) as well as pattern elements figure as structures and vocabulary. Among the salient terms Enzensberger gleans from this discipline are the "butterfly effect" (the notion that a small change in initial conditions could burgeon to cataclysmic proportions), bifurcation (a sudden splitting off from regular events, which can be diagrammatically represented as a branching), and fractals (a term used to describe a family of shapes that exist in the natural world and are characterized by jagged irregularity).[5]

The merging of *Naturwissenschaft* (natural sciences) and *Literaturwissenschaft* (literary science), which has antecedents in Enzensberger's project of redefining German poetry around 1960, matures considerably in *Der Untergang der Titanic*. The dynamics of loosely defined chaotic perturbations that seem to have fascinated Enzensberger in the early 1960s involved asymmetrical or shifting relationships between parts and the whole (or between the micro- and macrostructures), discipline-transgressing patterns (of discourse or content), and subjective effects (under which the observer or experimenter comes to influence the experiment). His initial definitions of modernism had evoked the subject of chaos in generic terms, sometimes with reference to the writings of Adorno. At stake was the vital tension between prescriptive and emancipatory aesthetics that we saw in Enzensberger's account of unsystematized literary abundance in "Die babylonische Bibliothek" (1960b) and his definition of poetry vis-à-vis experimentation for *Museum der modernen Poesie* (1980 [ed.]) in connection with both Edgar Allen Poe's "Philosophy of Composition" (1965) and Gottfried Benn's *Probleme der Lyrik* (1951).[6] Enzensberger's first three volumes of verse and essays from *Einzelheiten II* (1964f) hint as well at the metaphorical affinity artistic creation has to scientific work. But a more urgent sense of contingency surfaces in the essay "Gemeinplätze, die Neueste Literatur betreffend" (1968a) and the poem "Hommage à Gödel" ("Homage to Gödel") from *Gedichte 1955–1970* (1971b). Their quandary carries over into *Der Untergang der Titanic* (1978a), which makes explicit recourse to chaotic principles to illustrate Enzensberger's skepticism about systems.

For the earliest allusions to scientific theory in Enzensberger's work, we need to look at his discussion of modernist literary values. His poems regularly refer to science, technology, progress (or the lack thereof), and impending apocalypse. Titles such as "Die großen Erfindungen" ("The Great Inventions"), "Isotop" ("Isotope"), and "Gespräch der Substanzen" ("Conversation of the Substances") from *Landessprache* (1960d) and "Bibliographie" ("Bibliography"), "Carceri d'invenzione" ("Prisons of Invention"), "Doomsday," "Countdown," "Historischer Prozeß" ("Historical Process"), and "Flechtenkunde" ("Lichenology") from *Blindenschrift* (1964d) evidence a preoccupation with the history of science and contemporary scientific issues. Likewise, his description of work by Günter Grass and Peter Rühmkorf in the essay "In Search of the Lost Language" (1963d), which promotes international modernism by claiming that quotidian language equates with political activism, proposes a type of linguistically transgressive poetry that foregrounds aleatory and stochastic elements—objects of study in chaos science (49). Enzensberger's challenge to a traditional, fixed aesthetic of proportional relationships emerges in his praise for unexpected combinations of items, especially in his comments about the safety pin, Rapacki Plan, jukebox, and cough drop having "the same right and the same naturalness as the moon, the sea, and the rose" in lyric poetry (1963d, 49).

Over time Enzensberger enunciates related observations in quite varied forms and contexts. His essay "Bewußtseins-Industrie" ("The Consciousness Industry") from *Einzelheiten I* (1964e), which critiques the illusion of intellectual autonomy, concludes that objectivity has become impossible. In his own translation of the text for the *Partisan Review,* "The Industrialization of the Mind," Enzensberger remarks, "It is a measure of their limitations that many media critics never seem to reflect on their own position, just as if their work were not itself a part of what it criticizes. The truth is that no one can nowadays express any opinion at all without making use of the industry, or rather, without being used by it" (1969b, 110). In this instance, the reflexive element marks the difference between general criticism and the thorough analysis the author advocates. Enzensberger determines that any formulation of a position must acknowledge the contingency of the observer, anticipating a similar conclusion by Jürgen Habermas, whose *Legitimation Crisis* commented, "The crisis cannot be separated from the viewpoint of the one who is undergoing it" (1975, 1). That entanglement mirrors a phenomenon foregrounded by chaos theory: that the scientist always impinges on what is investigated.

The ideological considerations that gave fresh impetus to Enzensberger's interest in disorderly phenomena, meanwhile, became more acute in the late 1960s under the pressure of social turmoil. When his important essay "Gemeinplätze, die Neueste Literatur betreffend" (1968a) concludes with a call for literature based on principles of reciprocity (*Gegenseitigkeit*) in the production and reading of texts, he conceives something more radical than the interpretive hermeneutic circle—a system that acknowledges that author and reader are inextricably intertwined (like author and subject matter). That self-analyzing authorial gesture, which foregrounds the inconsistency of aesthetic, political, and social systems, incorporates a recognition of the observer's intervention that meshes well with chaos science principles. "Hommage à Gödel," *Mausoleum,* and *Der Untergang der Titanic,* which appear after *Kursbuch 15,* evidence Enzensberger's turn to scientific theory in search of a discourse that accounts for such impingement.

A meditation on the entanglement of the observer in studied phenomena underlies Enzensberger's poem "Hommage à Gödel" from *Gedichte 1955–1970.* Its sentiments participate in the debate about the literary movement New Subjectivity, which critics faulted for shrinking poetry to merely personal expression (a problem the style shared with contemporary American verse). The mathematician Kurt Gödel had formulated a proof that recognized that systems could internally contain contradictory propositions that could be proven only through reference to other, external systems. Enzensberger reformulates this in layperson's terms as a matter of language:

Du kannst deine eigene Sprache
in deiner eigenen Sprache beschreiben:
aber nicht ganz.
Du kannst dein eignes Gehirn
mit deinem eignen Gehirn erforschen:
aber nicht ganz.

(1971b, 168)

You can describe your own language
in your own language:
but not quite.
You can investigate your own brain
by means of your own brain:
but not quite.

(1994b, 105)

This poem, which significantly concludes *Gedichte 1955–1970* (1971b), contrasts Gödel's seemingly modest theory (*unscheinbar*) with tall tales about Baron Karl von Münchhausen. In emphasizing the recursive, contradictory nature of proofs, "Hommage à Gödel" foreshadows the treatment of science as a discipline in *Mausoleum* (1975), where Kurt Gödel also figures. Given the mathematician's obscurity at the time, the annotation concerning his theories in *Gedichte 1955–1970* provides scant orientation to the importance of his work, for it cites only the 1931 publication in which the theorem appeared.

"Hommage à Gödel" shares with "Giovanni de' Dondi (1318–1389)," the first poem in *Mausoleum* (1975), a sense of contingency, focus on the adjective *unscheinbar* (insignificant), and a presentation of instructions to the reader. Read together, these texts show an oscillation between optimistic and pessimistic formulations of the same problem, a maneuver that is both characteristic of Enzensberger and itself Gödelian. Whereas the *Mausoleum* poem chides the reader for not acting on the text (But why squander your time / with my manuscript / if you are unable / to emulate me?) (1975, 8), "Hommage à Gödel" orders the reader with a Brechtian imperative to take its sentences in hand and pull (1971b, 313). This admonishment commanding the recipient to unravel the text defines the relationship of book to audience instrumentally. The poem assumes it will prompt the reader to action. The mathematician in "Hommage à Gödel" stands in inverse relationship to the gloomy figure of Alan Mathison Turing in *Mausoleum*. Gödel explored principles of indeterminacy; Turing, by contrast, tried to produce theorems and computing devices capable of absolute predictability.[7]

Despite its pessimism, *Mausoleum* pushed for a radical rethinking of assumptions about the lyric genre by placing language on the precarious edge between the reflective contemplation of poetry and a rigidly rational system of prose. Enzensberger's subsequent rendering of *Edward Lears kompletter Nonsens* (*Edward Lear's Complete Nonsense* [1977 (trans.)]), which appeared just two years later, embraced playful experimentation as an artistic principle as fully as *Mausoleum* suppressed it; and as readers recently learned through the much-delayed publication of *Einladung zu einem Poesie Automaten* (*Invitation to a Poetry Automat* [2000]), he continued to work on connecting mathematics and poetry.

Acknowledging the failure of the automaticity and absolute certainty sought by Turing, the *Mausoleum* cycle begs for adventurous reading that will recognize how contingent any order is. The pedestrian macrochronicle of progress from which science emerges triumphant is thwarted by the unconventional critique proffered by contradictory microdetails. The manipulation of texts and discourses confronts the reader with a destabilized account of history full of micro- and macrophenomena.[8] Such disproportionality foils the powers of deductive thinking. The interplay of text and subtext weaves the kind of discursive formation articulated by Michel Foucault: not "an ideal, continuous, smooth text that runs beneath the multiplicity of contradictions, and resolves them in the calm unity of coherent thought . . . [but] rather a space of multiple dissensions; a set of different oppositions whose levels and roles must be described" (1972, 155). *Mausoleum*'s juxtapositions and dissensions call into question the persona of the writer (authorial reliability), the status of the text, and the responsibilities of the reader (as the reflective or nonreflective recipient of texts).

Partially concealing its sources (like *Mausoleum*), published two years after Enzensberger's "Modest Proposal," and complemented by companion essays, *Der Untergang der Titanic* incorporates essential pieces of chaos science into its very structure and terminology. The conclusions it draws suggest that art should again be recognized as a medium that synthesizes complex aesthetic and social impulses, much in terms previously envisioned by Adorno, Barthes, and Benjamin. Diagnosing an antagonistic relationship between art and politics, Adorno had written in *Ästhetische Theorie* that "the more art is forced to resist the controlled, standardized life mandated by the ruling apparatus, the more it is reminiscent of chaos" (1970, 404–5).

As it approaches the subject of chaos, *Der Untergang der Titanic*—as Adorno had noted of revolutionary art—takes on the orderly chaos of chaos theory. For rather than abandoning a coherent narrative entirely, the epic deploys the thematic constellation of "sentence/thread/narrative," terms that had concluded "Hommage à Gödel." The narrator muses continuously about losing the thread of the narrative. These musings fuss about variability (versus reliability) and the nonconclusive end points of historical events, human experiences, and literary forms. The epic juxtaposes the 1912 nautical disaster against two other time frames: Cuba in the late 1960s and Berlin in the 1970s. Working simultaneously from three temporal perspectives, the poem considers how an author composes a text, the meaning of historical events, and the role of the intellectual in contemporary society.

Rich in literary allusions,[9] aspects of which are detailed in Lehmann's interpretation of *Der Untergang der Titanic* (1984), the text has affinities to the writings of Joyce, Pound, Neruda, Poe, and Dante.[10] Enzensberger's interpellation of social conditions further connects the epic with the tradition of the ship of fools, a literary topos dating back to the fifteenth century whose history is detailed by Michel Foucault in *Madness and Civilization* (1965, 14). Quite apart from these literary antecedents, the *Titanic* itself occupies a unique position in cultural history both in the United States and abroad. Memorialized in numerous popular songs and films, the disaster became the subject of Thomas Hardy's poem "The Convergence of the Twain" (which is mentioned by Reinhold Grimm [1984] in connection with Enzensberger's epic). Elizabeth Bishop's "The Imaginary Iceberg" (from the 1955 volume *North and South*) also obliquely recalls the tragedy. Bishop celebrates the power of sublime spectacles of nature, observing "We'd rather have the iceberg than the ship, / although it meant the end of travel."[11] Enzensberger reports about other choices and losses, modern doubts about technology, and a poem manuscript that disappeared, only to be painstakingly reconstructed. Class inequities (expressed through references to *Titanic* passengers, foreigners, and mock political speeches), comparisons between the work of painters and poets (creation, restoration, and counterfeiting), and a thorough intermingling of high- and low-culture artifacts complicate the tableau.

As the epic's narrative unfolds, elements acquire an organic relationship to each other. The text introduces isolated details (sounds, occurrences, topoi) as chaotic phenomena, then shows through recursion that they too

belong to a pattern. Gradually the reader perceives that phases of randomness are punctuated by interludes of organized consolidation in *Der Untergang der Titanic.* Those cycles organize the seemingly random events, details, and literary allusions, finally producing an inductive framework for
the epic. These operations generate the illusion that the content (rather
than the poet) drives the writerly medium, hence that the agency needed
to construct a work of art has its origins in nature, not in the hands of the
idiosyncratic author. At the same time, the nonclassical proportionality of
micro- and macrophenomena marks the epic as something that seems to
be naturally given rather than artistically (or artificially) made.

In chaos theory, the "butterfly effect" accounts for, in Gleick's words,
"sensitive dependence on initial conditions" (1987, 23). Applied to the field
of meteorology, this principle suggests "the notion that a butterfly stirring
the air today in Peking can transform storm systems next month in New
York" (8).[12] In other words, phenomena of infinitesimal size may have enormous impact *and* still elude science's predictive abilities. If we extrapolate
to *Der Untergang der Titanic,* we notice that the ship's collision with the
iceberg promised on the book's cover is curiously displaced from a central
role in the epic, which forces us to turn our attention instead to faint, ominous sounds: breathing, white noise, and a pulse. These poetic elements
so seemingly insignificant that they might otherwise escape notice are, in
light of the "butterfly effect," no longer noise signifying nothing but rather
symptoms of distant causality.

The iceberg's whiteness is a product of weather, crystalline fractal formation, and oceanic currents—three of chaos theory's important phe-
nomenological sources—and it is huge. Yet, in the first poem in the epic
cycle, it is noticed only by the attentive poet, and only as an odd scraping: "A scraping sound. A creaking. A crack. / This is it. An icy fingernail /
scratching at the door and stopping short" (1980b, 2). And for a moment
even the poet questions the significance of this portent:

> Do you mean to say
> that was all?
> Yes. We've had it.
>
> This was the beginning.
> The beginning of the end
> is always discreet.
>   (1980b, 2)

After this introduction, the poem hastily catalogs the physical damage to the ship and, somewhat more slowly, the silent disappearance of the iceberg into darkness. Line length, syntactic structure, and a deft manipulation of consonance against assonance control the subtle shifts in the poem's tempo by slowing it to a largo.[13]

The actual sinking of the *Titanic* lasts nearly a hundred pages while water drips incessantly in the background. The slow process of the ship's demise continues as the narrative pendulates across large expanses of time and space. The second canto dwells on specifics about the ocean liner (the coordinates marking its position, the names of various passengers, and the music the band played). An account of a fifteenth-century artist painting a picture of the apocalypse follows, then a canto about Enzensberger's 1968–69 sojourn in Havana, and next a poem on aging ("Verlustanzeige"/"Notice of Loss").[14] To put this in terms of chaos theory, self-organization around certain attractors develops as an appearance of regularity forms from these pendulations. The reader follows the epic poem into a metafictional narrative pattern that circles asymmetrically around the geographic-temporal locations of *Titanic*, Cuba, and Berlin. Indeed, as if to reinforce the progression from obscure event to pattern, one-third of the way into the text the epic inserts a second "butterfly effect": a small indication of Enzensberger's own literary beginnings.

The context for this occurrence is a poetic interlude entitled "Abendmahl. Venezianisch. 16. Jahrhundert" ("Last Supper. Venetian. Sixteenth Century"). In this poem, the poet assumes the persona of a painter named Solomon Pollock,[15] who muses about various works he has executed, especially a favorite composition, *Saint Anne, the Virgin and Child.* Under the saint's throne in this canvas, he has, quite oddly, painted a soup turtle but then obscured it. He calls the painting "not my most famous work, but perhaps my best," and adds, "[n]o one except me knows why" (Enzensberger 1976c, 25).

Brecht, in an allegorical poem from the 1940s, "Im Zeichen der Schildkröte" ("Under the Sign of the Turtle"), had written about a tortoise carrying an olive branch who triumphed over a malevolent eagle (a symbol for Nazi Germany) by consuming its eggs (1967a, 855–56). The incongruous turtle in *Der Untergang der Titanic* appears, however, to be a cryptic reference to Enzensberger's own early career, for Reinhard Lettau in his copious documentation of Gruppe 47 reports on a certain young writer, Enzensberger, who read a work entitled "Die Schildkröte" ("The Turtle") at one of the group's meetings. The author, according to Lettau, was excoriated by his fellow writers and never published the piece. Some twenty years[16] after the fact, the allusion implies that this incident led to *Der Untergang der Titanic*.[17]

To this self-reference *Der Untergang der Titanic* adds others about its elusive author. Presented as if they had only to do with an invented protagonist, the generic references establish a tension between the seemingly impersonal detachment of the narrator and the autobiographical elements of the epic, which include scenes Enzensberger witnessed in Cuba, asides about the loss of his original manuscript for the poem, and remarks concerning its later reconstruction (1978a, 14, 18, 80). We know that Enzensberger admired the recycling of Brentano's constellations—his technique of reworking language, themes, and rhetorical gestures. Repeated statement, correction, and redaction in *Der Untergang der Titanic* in connection with chaos phenomena introduces an added twist.

Reading *Der Untergang der Titanic* as "a form of epistemology" (Lehmann 1984, 315) in which the loss of narrative coherence is mirrored by Enzensberger's "art of active forgetting" (325), as Hans-Thies Lehmann does, leads the audience to the conclusion that poetry has become an untenable act because human perception fails to locate ultimate coherence. But as Lehmann quite accurately observes, Enzensberger's subversive strategy in the epic is to undermine modernist assumptions about culture, ideology, and coherence exactly by celebrating art's demise (333). The loss of textual cohesion and the ensuing "death of the author" (ritualistically staged and performed in the concluding cantos) is ironically constructed in this epic. Chaos theory tells us that there are always limits to human perception but that this fact does not confound analysis. Hence, *Der Untergang der Titanic* argues, we can resolve the (post)modern impasse literature faces, for through long-term process (science instructs us), disparate, chaotic phenomena ultimately form a kind of continuous narrative.

Transcending the poet's self-deprecating feelings of powerlessness is not easy (cf. West 1981). Yet the gaps the epic registers, which are caused by a loss of memory (or the missing manuscript), begin by their sheer existence to constitute what is absent. Concretely, in "Verlustanzeige" ("Notice of Loss") the poet records the loss of hair, nerve, weight, of world wars, and other sundry objects, thus validating their existence (1978a, 11). Meanwhile, intangible experience is represented as a pattern arduously learned as real things or abstract ideals are lost—teeth, coins, or paradise, the elements named in "Verlustanzeige." Insofar as it accounts for this more complex unity, the paradigm of chaos theory thereby supplies the epistemological lens needed for discerning the epic's underlying consistency. Challenging old conventions, artificial continuities, and habits of consistency, *Der Untergang der Titanic* points to a new order grounded in physical reality, with all its discontinuities. The reworking Enzensberger supplies of his own writings in *Der Untergang der Titanic* advances this perspective by signaling moments of recursion and reflection.

"Weitere Gründe dafür, daß die Dichter lügen" ("Further Reasons Why Poets Do Not Tell the Truth"), a poem that rephrases the translation the author made of T. S. Eliot's "The Hollow Men" for *Museum der modernen Poesie*[18] (while also alluding to Nietzsche's Zarathustra), plays a pivotal role in this regard. By acknowledging uncertainty, the poem allows for a brief consolidation of chaotic impulses in the epic. Temporal markers, tokens of class status, and apocalyptic elements previously introduced in *Der Untergang der Titanic* reappear and are used to prompt the reader to question the status and reliability of authors. Meanwhile, on another level, "Weitere Gründe" outlines a writerly program of intentional redaction. The poem demonstrates that exact signification is impossible. It also shows, however, that when inexact expressions accumulate, these "chaotic" poetic tracings ironically reestablish the author's presence. The poem starts with the pendulation from one antagonistically defined opposite to another (characteristic of modernist aesthetic formulations), yet that movement opens up a new space for poetry, advancing the lyric genre toward a postmodernism in which such distinctions are irrelevant. The poem's multiple intertextual allusions serve to interrogate language's expressive capacities (with respect to semantic, symbolic, and temporal issues) and to foil critical-intellectual analysis.

> Weil der Augenblick,
> in dem das Wort *glücklich*
> ausgesprochen wird,
> niemals der glückliche Augenblick ist.
> Weil der Verdurstende seinen Durst
> nicht über die Lippen bringt.
> Weil im Munde der Arbeiterklasse
> das Wort *Arbeiterklasse* nicht vorkommt.
> Weil, wer verzweifelt,
> nicht Lust hat, zu sagen:
> "Ich bin ein Verzweifeldner."

Weil Orgasmus und *Orgasmus*
nicht miteinander vereinbar sind.
Weil der Sterbende, statt zu behaupten:
"Ich sterbe jetzt,"
nur ein mattes Geräusch vernehmen läßt,
das wir nicht verstehen.
Weil es die Lebenden sind,
die den Toten in den Ohren liegen
mit ihren Schreckensnachrichten.
Weil die Wörter zu spät kommen,
oder zu früh.
Weil es also ein anderer ist,
der da redet,
und weil der,
von dem da die Rede ist,
schweigt.

(1978a, 61)

Because the moment
when the word happy
is pronounced
never is the moment of happiness.
Because the thirsty man
does not give mouth to his thirst.
Because proletariat *is a word*
which will not pass the lips of the proletariat.
Because he who despairs
does not feel like saying:
"I am desperate."
Because orgasm and orgasm
are worlds apart.
Because the dying man,
far from proclaiming:
"I die," only utters
a faint rattle,
which we fail to comprehend.
Because it is the living
who batter the ears of the dead

with their atrocities.
Because words come always
too late or too soon.
Because it is someone else,
always someone else,
who does the talking,
and because he
who is being talked about,
keeps his silence.

(1980, 50)

"Weitere Gründe" gains form as it unfolds and retraces itself and canonical texts. Reperforming Eliot's conclusion to "The Hollow Men," Enzensberger subtly counterfeits in the manner we know from *Mausoleum* (1975) and Kenner (1968). The poem appropriates Eliot's major contrasts (the dichotomies of idea/reality, motion/act, emotion/response), the dialectical structure of "The Hollow Men," and to a certain extent its linguistic register. In paraphrasing Eliot's trio of unbridgeable gaps, which begins with the lines "Between the idea / And the reality / Between the motion / And the act / Falls the Shadow" (Enzensberger 1980 [ed.], 638), "Weitere Gründe" includes his categories of conception/creation and existence/essence, but these contrasts are here absorbed in a translative poetry that performs in a radically different context.

For the German reader, the term *Augenblick* (moment or, literally, blink of the eye) evokes the question of temporality and mortality focused on in Goethe's *Faust* (as well as the aesthetics of postwar poetry), while the title of the poem recalls Nietzsche's section "About Poets" from *Thus Spake Zarathustra* where Zarathustra responds (with several nods to Goethe) to the question "Why do you say that poets lie too much?" (1982, 130). The overdetermining of intertextuality goes even further since Enzensberger also reformulates Bertolt Brecht's observations on the difficulty of discerning the truth. Describing the trivial surface fact that satisfies hack writers, Brecht commented that many are content merely to be painters covering the walls of sinking ships with still lifes (1967b, 15). More immediately, the poem seems to reference the proposal Jürgen Habermas makes in his discussion of social crisis, where he evokes the contradiction between abstractions and facts to observe, "All the more sensitively, however, must bourgeois society react to the evident contradiction between idea and reality.

For this reason the critique of bourgeois society could take the form of an unmasking of bourgeois ideologies themselves by confronting idea and reality" (1975, 23).

Unlike in *Mausoleum,* where embedded theory linguistically constrained the ballads, in *Der Untergang der Titanic* Enzensberger redirects the poem away from mere theorizing. The coldly neutral and rather formal abstractions of the beginning of "Weitere Gründe" (the thirsty one, working class, despairing one, assert, hear) give way to simple language, even monosyllables, in the last several lines after the logical caesura interjected by the compound *Schreckensnachrichten* (horrifying reports). Rather than establishing a distance between poetry and the present through abstract language, cerebral rationalization, and the relegation of the lyric genre to the past, the poet illustrates how these boundaries break down under pressure from real, terrible events. He thereby connects language with problems of the real world and advocates a naturalized relationship to words.[19]

This renaturalization of poetic discourse resonates with an aspect of chaos theory that for N. Katherine Hayles explains linguistic events. Language, Hayles writes, is, like natural phenomena, a "vital medium that has its own currents, resistances, subversions, enablings, pathways, blockages. As soon as discovery is communicated through language, it is also constituted by language" (1991, 5). *Der Untergang der Titanic* stumbles around, insinuates chance linkages, challenges poetic univocality with its restatements. But like matters studied in chaos science, the language of "Weitere Gründe" and other cantos in the epic starts to self-organize, anchoring its subjects with the strange attractors that turn out to be the dichotomies of current intellectual debates. Language is no longer a strictly sequential medium. The text sets aside the modernist aesthetics exemplified by Eliot, opting instead for the sheer linguistic revelry represented by Pound.[20] The process of writing itself—and the texture of words—become central to the epic.

Beyond these aesthetic ramifications, the paradigm of chaos theory has social implications for *Der Untergang der Titanic* as well. Enzensberger represents the postapocalyptic moment after the *Titanic* has sunk (and the narrative has ended) with a description of the flotsam left behind after the huge vessel breaks apart.[21] The minute debris of this conclusion matches in size the small sounds at the poem's beginning. In thus framing the epic with the obscure, that quotidian detail valorized by "In Search of the Lost Language," Enzensberger connects us with the potential for social commitment. Detail—what we experience—establishes a naturalized relation between people and events. In thinking through the question of why the chaos paradigm operates on the human scale, Hayles observes that when order and disorder become merged in literary texts, "[t]his reconstitution makes clear that the world as humans experience it is a collaboration between reality and social construction" (1991, 14). Enzensberger's insistence on including both the large and the small recovers a viable position for the lyric genre by revisiting some of the most basic assumptions shaping post-1945 German poetry. At a time when, as poet Erich Fried put it, New Subjectivity seemed to direct writers to perceive always more of less until one could "finally see everything of nothing" (1978, 115–16). Enzensberger offers a literal refutation. The epic's recourse to traditional poetic content (the ship, poet cum artist persona, and vast nature) juxtaposes these grand elements against the insignificant scale—junk, human fallibility, and meteorological inconveniences. An aesthetics of chaos accommodates these factors nonhierarchically. *Der Untergang der Titanic* manages to rescue poetry's capacity to respond affectively to the human condition (to express nostalgia, passion, or hopelessness, for example) without giving in to the temptation to make the lyric genre into mere personal expression.

Manipulating apparently stochastic and aleatory elements, Enzensberger creates a provisional restitution of the author. Order and authorial presence gradually emerge through repeated but never quite identical elements. These fragments neither subordinate themselves to rigid orderliness nor free the author to locate himself outside the text he creates. The diminished role Enzensberger rhetorically ascribes to contemporary poetry in "Bescheidener Vorschlag," as well as the limitations of the lyric genre acknowledged in *Der Untergang der Titanic,* paradoxically ensure a robustness greater than that of the "macroscopic order," which the "modest proposal" disparaged in standard interpretations (1976a, 428). Imagination and attentiveness are instead nurtured by a poetic sensibility. This conception of poetry's function is consonant with Enzensberger's previous reflections on the genre, yet heightened, for now the reader must attend to small details, read skeptically, and decode messages that are part of an ever evolving poetic language. Rather than use theoretical prose to assert that poetry remains vital—the tack taken in the original appendix to *Museum der modernen Poesie*—Enzensberger relies in *Der Untergang der Titanic* on the subtleties of the poetic medium itself to convey this message.

Although this approach means that poem and aesthetic theory are merged, becoming poetry as theory, the poem does not harbor an unreflected sense of what words can accomplish. The "Nineteenth Canto," which follows "Weitere Gründe," recounts the discovery of a Japanese survivor whom no one could understand, floating on a table (1980b, 51). These lines register a disjuncture between articulated speech and comprehensible utterance. The latter half of the epic multiplies the instances in which language and reality diverge. "News Wires of April 15, 1912," which presents a series of telegraph reports (texts that represent factually accurate, objectively mediated information), concludes with blatant falseness: according to Reuters, all passengers have boarded lifeboats (1980b, 53). Statistics about those who perished (in the "Twenty-second Canto") are vehemently challenged in the "Twenty-third Canto." An intervening lyrical text, "Model toward a Theory of Cognition," provocatively describes the opening of a series of Chinese boxes in an infinite series in which the final, imaginary box is completely empty, a construction favored in metafictional narratives. "Identity Check," which follows these three sections, interrogates the nature of identity. It begins with the phrase "This is not Dante" and concludes with its reversal, "This is Dante" (1980b, 65). Temporal sequence breaks down toward the end of the poem as past and present merge and coherent syntax unravels. The "Twenty-ninth Canto" registers this dissolution through a description of the loose wreckage over the disaster site: "Something always remains—/ bottles, planks, deck chairs, crutches, / splintered mastheads—/ debris left behind, / a vortex of words, cantos, lies relics—" (1980b, 83).

The collapse brought by the formal dissolution of narrative, temporal, and conceptual order unmasks the denaturalized, constructed nature of advanced societies. A renaturalized coherence emerges, then, late in the epic through tiny details. The "Thirty-first Canto" recounts the assembly of survivors in a fictitious location, "The Berlin Room." The breathless, shrouded survivors force their way into the room and then discuss one of the dead—obviously an or the author—whose works they now wish to amend: "Gut, daß er tot ist. / Jetzt können wir . . . streichen, was uns nicht paßt" (1978a, 108), or "It's just as well that he's dead. / Now we . . . / can finally cut out / . . . / whatever we do not like" (1980b, 91), they shout. This group debates the author's shortcomings with vehemence, yet shows confusion about what to do next. The poet quells this argument by interjecting a summary that labels the collective experience of survival. At the end of the "Thirty-first Canto" the poem returns to the trope of breath adumbrated at the opening of the text—now an acknowledgment of ultimate, if coincidental, social connectedness: "Wir waren übrig, wir atmeten. / Ein

Zufall, irgendein Zufall / hatte uns hierher verschlagen. / Wir saßen alle in einem Boot" (1978a, 112), or "We were left over, / we went on breathing. / We had ended up here by chance. / We were all in the same boat" (1980b, 95). Everyone is in the same predicament. Everyone shares one experience, seemingly by chance. And chance, which is viewed as purposeless coincidence under conventional paradigms, lies at the heart of chaos theory, which regards it as an occasion for self-organizing patterns—or the reconstitution of communities.

Chaos theory acknowledges that there can never be endings and beginnings, and in *Der Untergang der Titanic* there are multiple endings. The first is happy, with saved passengers—and every reader knows this to be a false report. Other equally plausible and implausible finales punctuate the epic. Some are part of *Titanic* mythology, particularly ditties and musical renditions. The "Twentieth Canto," based on African-American songs about a folk hero, Shine, cleverly references another end point in its opening lines, the Nazi capitulation ("Am achten Mai, war das ein Ding, / als die Titanic unterging" [1978a, 65]; "The eighth of May was one hell of a day, / when the *Titanic* was sinking away" [1980b, 54]). The "Thirteenth Canto" interweaves popular songs and the sentimental hymns reportedly played by the band on the sinking luxury liner.[22] The concluding "Thirty-second Canto" and "Thirty-third Canto" provide divergent models of closure. In the first, a muselike figure approaches the poet. She is reminiscent of a figure in "Sommergedicht" and modeled after Marilyn Monroe, who is subsequently named with a large cast of characters from the epic in the "Thirty-third Canto." The penultimate "Thirty-second Canto" offers the more traditional and aesthetic of the two endings:

> Die Unbekannte vernahm seine ruhigen Atemzüge,
> beugte sich über ihn in der Dunkelheit,
> verschloß ihm den Mund, küßte ihn
> und nahm ihn mit, mit ihrem einzigen Mund.
>
> (1978a, 113)

> *The unknown woman heard his even breath,*
> *stooped down to him in the dark,*
> *closed his mouth, kissed him,*
> *and with her one and only mouth*
> *took him along.*
>
> (1980b, 96)

The gesture symmetrically takes back the breath, heard and felt as physically palpable sensation—the starting point of the epic—and repositions the muse within the epic, albeit as a departing figure. But even in this most poetic gesture, the reader must notice Enzensberger's irony in playing with literal and figurative meanings, for, after all, the iceberg itself has itself already been termed "ein Schauspiel von atemberaubender Schönheit" (1978a, 55), or "a breathtaking spectacle" (1980b, 44).[23]

The final canto, by contrast, delivers a postmodern pastiche in which the falsetto warnings of the poet/anarchist go unheeded by the motley survivors. Its witty, iconoclastic tone is reminiscent of Archibald MacLeish's "The End of the World," which appeared in *Museum der modernen Poesie* (Enzensberger 1980 [ed.]). Ever wary of the aporias of the avant-garde, Enzensberger carefully skirts a fresh declaration of literature's end by insisting on an open ending. *Der Untergang der Titanic* concludes with much self-irony: "schwer zu sagen, warum, heule und schwimme ich weiter" (1978a, 115), or "Dimly, hard to say why, I continue to wail, and to swim" (1980b, 98). With this gesture, Enzensberger returns to the ambitious project of "[d]ie politische Alphabetisierung Deutschlands" ("the political education of Germany"), outlined in "Gemeinplätze, die Neueste Literatur betreffend" (1968a), by announcing a resolve to continue.

Mausoleum had harshly critiqued the artificial inventions of modern science. *Der Untergang der Titanic* poses a more sympathetic yet still scientifically grounded model that allows the poet to convince us of his aversion to deterministic, closed systems—be they scientific, social, or aesthetic. In describing the paradigm shifts precipitated by Newton, Einstein, and chaos theory, Gleick comments, "Of the three, the revolution in chaos applies to the universe we see and touch, to objects at human scale" (1987, 6). It is this relationship to the human world and celebration of open-ended phenomena that drives Enzensberger's exploration of the chaos theory paradigm. The radical rethinking of poetry begun in *Der Untergang der Titanic* continues to be worked out in Enzensberger's subsequent publications.

Indeed, arguably *Der Untergang der Titanic, Das Wasserzeichen der Poesie,* and *Die Suche,* whose story is by Enzensberger, share a preoccupation with finding an epistemological framework adequate to address the contemporary human condition. While caution is warranted in correlating aspects of a collaboratively produced work such as *Die Suche* and the anthology *Das Wasserzeichen der Poesie* with a text written by a single author (*Der Untergang der Titanic*), these works employ similar writerly strategies.

Each makes use of layered, open-ended, self-organizing systems. *Die Suche* guides students in developing skills for decoding details, locating the author, and connecting "literature" with life. Learners are asked to read patterns mediated by clues, instructions, and conceptual frameworks. The last page delivers to the student a final mystery. Deciphered, the jigsaw puzzle reads, "For the search goes on. The best is yet to come" (Enzensberger et al. 1993, 192). This cryptic riddle seems emblematic of Enzensberger's latest projects.

Cryptograms, Didactics, and Poetry

Das Wasserzeichen der Poesie (Enzensberger 1985), a book about the art of poetry, anticipates the dramatic illustrations of *Die Suche* (Enzensberger et al. 1993). A lavishly produced tome, it is subtitled *The Art and Pleasure of Reading Poems,* and it announces itself as "One Hundred and Sixty Styles of Play Presented by Andreas Thalmayr." The name is a pseudonym for Enzensberger, who has openly acknowledged his hand in authoring this work, which appeared as part a series he edited for *Die Andere Bibliothek.* The anthology offers texts that involve radical experimentation and formal tradition, and it promotes a diverse canon by disguising itself as a pseudo-traditional poetry manual. The specialized poetic vocabulary and esoteric games used in *Wasserzeichen* seem to imply that poets are the first audience of poetry, but its subtitle declares a larger educational mission that reaches out to other groups. The appealing physical design of *Das Wasserzeichen* is clearly meant to enhance the reading experience of any book-loving audience and warrants consideration as an important aspect of the work itself.

The white cover of the book displays a circular labyrinth in its midsection. A Minotaur occupies the maze's center; a female figure is positioned below the labyrinth between a bear (on the left) and two boars (on the right). In the upper third of the visual space, two man-beast figures occupy the corners, one a male body with a wolf's head, the other a bird's body and head with human legs. Convoluted vinelike tendrils twist across the lightly textured background, connecting the labyrinth, female muse, animals, and man-beast figures. The white binding is complemented by a red-and-gold book label on the spine of the volume. Its clear dust jacket displays the full title of the work in blue and two stars with an emerging ray; one aligns with the center front (positioned precisely over the Minotaur), and the other is placed in the center of the back cover. This careful attention to the visual presentation of the volume has the performative function of raising the expectation that this handbook is an item for connoisseurs of poetry, a particularly exclusive item.

Das Wasserzeichen der Poesie is divided into nine sections—each titled a *Hauptstück* (main piece)—which collect examples of poems and responses to poetic texts that exhibit rhetorical devices, linguistic playfulness, or formal techniques. Readers must coordinate the explanations provided in the table of contents with individual texts. After doing so, a list of sources at the back of the book must be consulted. That division prescribes a threefold referencing process. The introduction to the work bemoans the overproduction of tedious poetry, lamenting, "Wenn es nach der Zahl der Produzenten ginge, wäre die Poesie ein Massenmedium" ("If things went according to the number of producers, poetry would be a mass media" [1985, V]). As an alternative, it suggests that the volume could be regarded as a compendium or "Lehrbuch der Poetik" ("Handbook of Poetics") (VII). The authorship of the volume is rather loosely disguised, for the name of one of the "contributors" is Serenus M. Brezengang (an anagram for Magnus Enzensberger). The collection further encompasses poems and translations by Enzensberger (including that of work by William Carlos Williams), texts by international modernists alluded to in his own work, and elaborate commentaries written with the incisiveness for which Enzensberger is famous. It is replete with flourishes, such as a section entitled "Puzzle," which contains poems laid out as a visual puzzle (346–47), and a "Round Poem" (353) written in concentric circles that resemble layouts later used in *Die Suche.*

By design, *Das Wasserzeichen* structures interactions with the printed text that insist on the kinds of readerly practices demanded by *Mausoleum* and *Der Untergang der Titanic* (index checking, attention to heteroglossia, and reading as an act of constituting the text). Readers need to muster a synesthetic response to the medium as well, for they must synthesize perceptions of visual elements, linguistic symbols, and acoustic events. The evocation of this sensory input and the relatively equal weight given sensual elements in the experience of reading the text emphasize the significance of palpable and apparently spontaneous phenomena.

The interactive, pedagogic reading scheme promoted by *Das Wasserzeichen der Poesie* informs Enzensberger's subsequently published *Die Suche* (Enzensberger et al. 1993). This textbook, an ingeniously designed curriculum built around a detective story that Enzensberger wrote, is noteworthy for the extensive instruction in decoding strategies that it provides. Such strategies are now recognized as important to language learning, but in the early 1990s they were not often explicitly taught through textbooks. The plot of *Die Suche* renders such decoding essential, for the text becomes an allegory about reading. Two bumbling detectives pursue a mysterious woman, who in the last pages of the text turns out to be their employer. This female protagonist enlists the help of her identical twin to test the two protagonists before deciding to assign them to a more serious case. The language learner reading this story works alongside the detectives to find clues. In an initial exercise, for example, students match nouns with pictures presented on assorted puzzle pieces represented on the first page. They then sequence the shapes and use the words to fill out a crossword puzzle. Their next task resembles the long sequence of white noise at the opening of *Der Untergang der Titanic*. Students look at two pages of photographs, listen to recorded sounds that match images, and mark the route they hear by identifying relevant photographs.

Elsewhere *Die Suche* contains references to Enzensberger that the beginning German student would likely miss. Small reproductions show details from Peter Brueghel the Elder's "The Hunters in the Snow" and Caspar David Friedrich's large canvas "The Sea of Ice."[24] These two paintings, alluded to in *Der Untergang der Titanic* and cited in scholarly essays (Lehmann 1984; Künzel 1980; Nägele 1984), appear midway through the textbook. Eventually, one character declares with a confidence that only slightly intensifies sentiments expressed in the *Der Untergang der Titanic*, "Do you know an author who doesn't lie? That's the beautiful part about writing. You must think of our readers. They should also have their fun. Fantasy is expensive and novels cost money" (Enzensberger et al., 105). Later *Die Suche* encourages students to develop predictive reading strategies by asking them to consider what several writers have to say about why they write. One unnamed author offers the wisdom, "Writers are spies who have no boss and no employees—and they invent their secrets themselves" (109). The corresponding photograph shows Enzensberger.

In asking students to decipher a wide range of visual, auditory, textual, and grammatical clues, *Die Suche* emphasizes the importance of microstructure, yet reassures them about the existence of macrostructures. When the topic of narrative perspectives and time frames is introduced, *Die Suche* visually displays how four narrative strands operate in concert by inviting the reader to connect sentences that identify narratives with corresponding pictures of characters, authors, and readers (Enzensberger et al. 1993, 69). Students need to match one of these statements—about authors—with a tiny portrait of Enzensberger.[25]

Such self-references, which are abundant throughout Enzensberger's later work, cajole the reader and allow the author to maintain a secretive presence in the finished text. *Die Suche* diagrams its story's frameworks for the student as three concentric circles. These circles represent the time frame of the main character ("Schlock-Time"), that of the action ("Plot-Time"), and finally that of the narrator ("Narrator-Time") (Enzensberger et al. 1993, 69). By supplying the details to fill out these schematic presentations, the learner constructs the kind of temporal-geographical patterns that we encountered in *Der Untergang der Titanic*. Without distinction as to differences between general readership practices and the specialized skills needed for reading poetry and other genres (including film narratives), Enzensberger in *Wasserzeichen* and *Die Suche* thus asks the reader to become a participant in the "experiment" of coconstructing a text.

This turn to potentially cryptic writing practices can be accounted for by Enzensberger's concern about the compromised status of poetry. The chaos paradigm of *Der Untergang der Titanic,* gaming strategies of *Wasserzeichen,* and explicit didactics of *Die Suche* compensate for obstacles to deciphering texts by making the author's own travail to address disorder and order a spectacle to watch. Enzensberger's effort to save coherence depends on prompting readers to appreciate texts in fundamental ways via modes of engagement that seemed to have eluded the lyric genre. I want to look at more of his self-references and how they involve a cryptography of writerly coding and readerly decoding because they play an important role in his works from the 1990s. My analysis focuses on "Valse triste," a poem eventually published in *Zukunftsmusik* (1991c), whose redactions display subtle repairs that Enzensberger's recent poetry has made to the discursive mode of expression we first encountered in *Blindenschrift* (1964d).

Enzensberger's writerly practices of drafting and revising poems remain relatively less well understood than some other facets of his work. Tweaking motifs, appropriating preexisting literary materials, and making autobiographical asides, he closely follows the generative poetic process his dissertation detected in Brentano's texts and termed constellations: the invention and reworking of a single poetic element (the term *Linde* [linden] and its associations for Brentano, for example) in multiple texts.[26]

In Enzensberger's constellations, translation and self-translation play a prominent role (see Melin 1987). As we have seen, in publications through *Blindenschrift* (1964d), translation served Enzensberger as a heuristic procedure for studying new types of poetic language, importing fresh content, and, most important, establishing poetic voice. Text manipulation in *Mausoleum* (1975) involved a reworking of found prose language, especially public discourse, that unmasked false claims to authority. Enzensberger's self-translations, on the other hand, function quite differently, for they initiate questions about the interplay of public and private elements in contemporary poems. The self-translations make public the intimate process of creating literature by showing the author at work. Paradoxically, however, some of the most extensively reworked texts by Enzensberger display both great distance from their origins and an uncanny ability to mimic spontaneity. Thematizing the problem of self-translation, *Der Untergang der Titanic* allegorized the work of the poet as that of the restorer and presented his labor as a craft that is intrinsic to the artist's being. The act of making art—priming the canvas, penciling outlines, brushing on the paint—ties the producing of art (or poetry) to visible, natural origins in physical labor and deeply personal experience.

"Valse triste et sentimentale" from *Zukunftsmusik* (1991c) offers one of the more intriguing examples of the paradox of the reworked poem. While in a few instances—such as *Der Untergang der Titanic* (1978a) and the poem "Automat" (originally from *Kayak*)—the translations Enzensberger made of his own texts stand as intermediate versions between earlier and later German versions of a particular work, an even more complex revisioning practice stands behind "Valse triste et sentimentale" (1991c, 64–65). Its title already evokes multiple literary and musical antecedents—a symphonic piece by Jean Sibelius ("Valse triste"), Wallace Stevens's poem "Sad Strains of a Gay Waltz" (1972, 116–17), a poem by Gottfried Benn entitled "Valse triste" (1960b), and an experimental text written by Rainer M. Gerhardt (1965/66, 24–26).[27] Enzensberger's "Valse triste et sentimentale" itself appeared in an earlier version under the same title in *Lyrische Hefte* (1972b, 4–5). This first publication occurred at a point when the climate for German poetry was changing, as agitprop verse had lost its hold and New Subjectivity was beginning to emerge. The first version's reproduction of panic-filled questions in quotations ("What should I do? / What do I want do?") economically sketches a mood of vague aesthetic and political disorientation. The closing lines ("Don't let me see you around here again!") are reminiscent of concluding gestures employed by William Carlos Williams.

The 1991 version of the poem intensifies this sense by amending the command to, "Close the door / and don't let me see you around here again!" (1991c, 65).[28]

As was the case for the discursive poems from *Blindenschrift,* "Valse triste et sentimentale" *seems* to give voice in an immediate way to the experience of the poet because it structures perceptions of reality around an apparently unmediated connection between the "I" and "you" of the poem. The nostalgic longing of the poem derives from a subtle manipulation of symmetries—*ich/du,* contrastive phrasing ("Mit oder ohne" [with or without]), the implied temporal contrast (*früher* [earlier] versus the present)—the use of paratactic construction, abstract content, and the evocation of a Williamsesque conclusion. These writerly devices heighten the retrospective quality of the poem and suggest a longing for modernist aesthetics. But as a text with a history of some twenty years, this poem invites—indeed, demands—a reading that foregrounds Enzensberger's changed habits of poetic representation. A revision that indexes its own antecedents, "Valse triste et sentimentale" illusionistically mimics naturalness and spontaneity, yet this is a facade constructed over a highly intentional framework.

The changes between the 1972 and 1991 versions of "Valse triste et sentimentale" are particularly substantial in the middle sections, where a condensation from seven stanzas (varying from four to six lines in length) to five stanzas (each of five lines) occurs. The modifications render the later version more laconic, as in the second line where the remark "And what now?" stands by itself without the acerbic comment "Nice excuse" interjected in the earlier text. Other emendations replace redundant elements with symmetrical constructions, a process much like that which Enzensberger observed in Brentano's constellations. At the beginning of the second stanza, "sooner or later" in the first version becomes "with or without" in the second, reducing the number of times the term *früher* repeats in the text. Moving on through the two texts, the reader notices that the second and third stanza from the 1972 version seem to rehearse sentiments voiced in *Titanic,* especially in the lines, "You always find reasons when it's too late." Some terms (*Tour, Melancholie,* and *Hauptberuf*) vanish from the 1991 version, as does a subsequent line in the sixth stanza (the proverbial remark "The child is in the well"). Even phrases used in both poems, such as "Sometimes I already miss you," seem to force a different reading the second time, for the 1991 version is the tight-lipped meditation of a literary patriarch less worried about settling scores. Its concluding stanza performs an outburst of mock arrogance: "Me, bad conscience? I can only laugh at that."

The aesthetic assumptions of "Valse triste et sentimentale" are those of a mature and cunning writer, not a naive, personally expressive poet. Ostensibly timeless, the first-person speaker is in fact aging, as the encrypted redactions confirm. These self-references, then, teach the reader to be skeptical, to recognize that claims to order and permanence may not rule out naked disorder, which for all its ominousness turns out to be an essential element of the lyric genre that Enzensberger is intent on salvaging.

Recursion, Nature, and Poetry

Fog, clouds—comparing these elusive "disordered" phenomena with the lyric genre in "Modest Proposal," Enzensberger had argued that poetry's effects cannot be measured. The evidence given for the power of poetry in the speech was that poetic microevents do not repeat themselves and hence can never be reduced to interpretable patterns trackable by *Literaturwissenschaft*. Although Enzensberger's essays on literature repeatedly argue against interpretation, his work has nonetheless returned with noteworthy frequency to questions of voice (the role of the individual in opposition to culturally determined rhetoric, and hence the integrity of the author), proportion (how details do or do not relate to narratives of, for example, history), and aesthetics (especially whether the lyric genre exists as a static or dynamic form and transcends or is attached to reality). This continual preoccupation with questions fundamental to the lyric genre is not a mere repetition of what has come before but a reminder to readers of how contingent a poet's work remains. Never entirely new, yet never completely unchanged, poetry chaotically absorbs, appropriates, and develops in cycles.

The interest Enzensberger evinces in chaos science, which enables a reaffirmation of the literary imagination in *Der Untergang der Titanic*, proceeds in two divergent directions after the 1978 publication of the epic. For the purpose of thinking about the role which order and disorder play in Enzensberger's artistic project, I have emphasized the relevance of chaos theory to his poetry to ask how representation works in an artistic environment that involves chance, automaticity, gaming, and repetition. And we have just looked at the path that leads toward a reconnection of the lyric genre with the stuff of writerly material (the visual and aural quality of texts celebrated in *Wasserzeichen der Poesie*) and with didactic purposes (the expressed function of *Die Suche*). As fascinating as they are, however, these operations exude analytic coldness and austerity. The solutions that Enzensberger seeks in chaos science also follow a second forking path that can be traced into poems where the terminology of chaos theory, descriptions of nature, and impassioned ruminations about literature lead to engagement with emotionally charged quandaries. Here we need to look at how Enzensberger works to capture warmth and the expressive possibilities of metaphor and allegorical representation again for the lyric genre.

Describing the poet's mind as a time machine in *Der Untergang der Titanic* (1978a, 7), Enzensberger reasserts the right of the poet to call public attention to what gains voice only through the lyric genre. Without poetic expression, much of significance simply cannot be perceived, the poet contends. That idealistic conception of the lyric genre is problematized by Enzensberger's own recourse to chaos theory, which adds a self-critical element of reflection that openly acknowledges the impossibility of neutral omniscience. His ambitious reaffirmation of the lyric genre, from *Der Untergang der Titanic* on, returns poetry to one of its traditional sources — nature — and to questions about a rhetorical figure (metaphor) and a mode of representation (allegory) that had fallen out of favor in the late twentieth century. Enzensberger's late poems do not, however, simply resurrect these traditional literary instruments to make the case for the lyric genre. To do that would mean a return to the safe little world of nature verse critiqued by "In Search of the Lost Language" (1963d, 48). Instead, the poems show how emotional responses are marked as text, qualified by historical position, and expressed indirectly. Armed with this writerly self-consciousness, Enzensberger unabashedly contemplates the sublime by connecting poetry with "universal" scientific discourse and drawing analogies between nature and poetry. Beyond this stylized reflection, chaos phenomena in the recent texts create a conduit to nature that militates against intellectualized fossilization of the natural. Palpable specifics remain important in the poems, preserving the capacity of the lyric genre to revel in particulars without being reduced to mere explanatory detail. Late poems such as "Abwegiger Wunsch" ("Devious Wish") and "Seltsamer Attraktor" ("Strange Attractor") make use of this unique mimesis, for they sketch the barest outline of a scene (somewhat like the *Momentaufnahme* aesthetics before) synthesized with evocative sound patterns and logical or syntactic puzzles.

Enzensberger's reconstruction of poetry after 1980 occurred under historical circumstances that included postprotest resignation and a general search for new epistemological paradigms (of which postmodernism and chaos theory are two examples). Three trends had dominated German literature throughout the late 1970s and 1980s: New Subjectivity, a return to traditional poetic forms, and dystopian literature (Korte 1989, 144–84). These developments also conditioned reception of Enzensberger's work from the early 1980s, which was judged too pat or unpoetic in its formulations (Dietschreit and Heinze-Dietschreit 1986, 129), on the one hand, and expressive of a rejection of political obligations (Schnell 1993, 465), on the other. Considering the literary significance of nature poetry, Axel Goodbody has demonstrated that this substantial tradition in German poetry of the 1950s and 1960s was revived in the late 1970s in connection with environmental movements across Europe (1991, 375–81). Enzensberger, who had critiqued the nascent Green movement in "Zur Kritik der politischen Ökologie" ("Critique of Political Ecology" [1973]), worried nonetheless in "Zwei Randbemerkungen zum Weltuntergang" ("Two Marginal Notes on the End of the World" [1978b]) about obvious harbingers of environmental catastrophe. Moreover, as the author of "Fremder Garten," a poem published in 1957 in *Verteidigung der Wölfe* (1957b), he has been frequently cited for his early awareness of ecology issues (see R. Grimm 1984, 172–73). And alongside chaos phenomena, nature figures prominently in his late poetry, not as a site of biosphere degradation but for its cyclical processes of organic growth and decay. Although many of the descriptions of nature in Enzensberger's poems are touchingly detailed, frank recognition of the absolute indifference of the universe to humankind disabuses the poet of an emotive identification with nature under the pathetic fallacy and draws out attention to the fragile dynamics underlying the ecology of contained systems.

Several poems from the 1990s that give evidence of Enzensberger's continuing interest in chaos theory—including "Abwegiger Wunsch," "Seltsamer Attraktor," and "Zukunftsmusik"—register the separation of natural phenomena from the human perspective and refer to chaos science (all in 1991c). Numerous selections in *Zukunftsmusik* (1991c) allude to mathematical discoveries and cross over into terminology referring to organic growth. "Die Mathematiker" ("The Mathematicians"), which begins by talking about seeds, ends by evoking a litany of figures eminent in the development of the mathematical discipline, dramatically lamenting in its final lines, "Oh grief, oh Gödel, oh Mandelbrot, / in the purgatory of recursion" (27). Another poem, "In höhere Lagen gewittrige Störungen" ("In Higher Regions Stormy Disturbances"), muses upon the apparent unreconcilability of small and large phenomena, using terminology specific to chaos theory in such phrases as, "micro and macro, from intestinal flora / to the galaxies," "abracadabra of the physicists," the term "bifurcation," and "Vom Sein des Seienden" ("Of the Being of the Being"), a reference to both emergent patterns and the philosopher Heidegger. The text "Limbisches System" ("Limbic System") meditates on the significance of humankind's insignificance in the universe: "A few million cells / in the dark. The human race, / a minuscule tangle / between alpha and amnesia" (98).

"Abwegiger Wunsch" describes how an urge becomes lost in organic, fractal-form branchings. An ingenious use of vocabulary mimetically reproduces the inception, growth, and dissolution of the wish. Multiple verbs, adjectives, and adverbs sketch the organic, spiraling unfolding of something that changes color from yellow to brownish purple to a faded hue. This wish projects itself upward in tendril-like fashion, forms capsules, and then degenerates into rankness. The process, reminiscent in its particularity of Goethe's account of metamorphosis in plants, alternates between quick, unexpected transformations (*sprießt, häuft, zerspringt*) and the tension of more gradual developments ("immer schwerer, ächzt / unter seiner wuchernden Masse" ["heavier and heavier groans / beneath its proliferating mass"] and finally "langsam, / allmählich, ruhig zu versinken" ["slowly, / gradually, quietly to sink down"]). The ending—where the wish identified as "devious" in the title sinks silently into a swampy tangle (1991c, 102–3)—recapitulates the conclusion of William Carlos Williams's verse "The Widow's Lament in Springtime," which Enzensberger had translated in the 1960s. The wish itself is never articulated. It exists in the space between a primal division and the degeneration of life into nothing. The edgy regression through terms now associated with contemporary chaos science (bifurcations and branchings) to language echoing Goethe allows the poet to use an impersonal objective correlative of organic growth and decay to create distance from a personal expression of longing.

A second poem, "Seltsamer Attraktor," considers aspects of time and long-distance effects. Its materials are varying temporal intervals (minutes, hours, days), a hypnotic circling of patterns ("die helle Materie, / hypnotisch kreisend, / das glitzernde Gesicht, / in wiederkehrenden Strudeln / nie wiederkehrend" ["live matter roaring on / in hypnotic swirls, / turning in bright eddies / and glittering cycles / which never recur"] [1994b, 243]), and finally a wet something in the midst of foaming currents, a teddy bear (1991c, 112; 1994b, 243).[29] The title "Seltsamer Attraktor" refers to the points around which chaotic patterns self-organize. Here the attractor is revealed to be something seemingly trivial but intimately associated with people, a toy. This teddy bear, however, is itself odd—a child's plaything (hence a reminder of Enzensberger's insistence on the playfulness of art and the importance of play), a humanized object whose face naturally invites attachment and affection, an item whose historical origins lie in German and American history: Steiff bears and the flamboyant president Teddy Roosevelt. Jonathan Monroe reads the toy as an ironic reference to the defunct Soviet Union as represented by the Russian bear (1997, 112). The isolated, cinematic focus on this object also seems purposefully reminiscent of *Citizen Kane,* where the elusive name "Rosebud" is finally deciphered for the viewer, but not the characters in the movie, when we see the sled emblazoned with this word go up in flames. Read thus as suggestive of political symbols and the encoded, biographical mysteries surrounding famous persons, the teddy bear becomes a cipher for the blurring of private and public persona.

Indeed, throughout *Zukunftsmusik* we can see that the poems expose the vulnerabilities of the contemporary poet who tries to express personal and public concerns. The final text in the collection, itself entitled "Zukunftsmusik," predicts what the future will be in terse, abstract terms. The poem relies extensively on verbs (*erwarten* [to expect], *lehren* [to teach], *zukommen* [to come up], *gehören* [to belong], *wissen* [to know], *sagen* [to say], and *sein* [to be]) to say that the future will teach us something but that it is fundamentally indifferent (as indeed are all natural phenomena) to the world of humans. Contrasting the vastness of the unknown and the smallness of human scale, the final stanza invites the reader to join the poet in thinking the situation through to its logical conclusion. The poet admonishes all who listen (denoted by the word *uns* [us]) not to fall prey to the delusion that everything transpires for the benefit of the self, and he does so with composure and a sense of realism. This caution applies not only to life in general but to poetry and the signifying capacities of language, for the poem reveals that we know remarkably little about either. *Zukunftsmusik,* the poem tells us, does not respond to our bidding, nor even acknowledge us—if, as the poem guesses, it even exists—but we learn from it (1991c, 115). This suspension of causal relationships speculates about order that is neither predictive nor prescriptive, although always significant, as is the case for patterns in chaos theory.

The title, too, is not a mere neologism but instead an intertextual reference to Marie Luise Kaschnitz's earlier poetry collection, *Zukunftsmusik* (1950). Kaschnitz celebrated the end of wartime struggles by blending descriptions of sounds and music, biblical allusions, and expressions of hope for the future of humanity in the final poem in her book: "Do not be afraid." "Oh tones of the future, lost in euphony and discord," Kaschnitz lamented. Then, full of expectation, she concluded effusively, "Harmony she said and human dignity and freedom. / Hope she said and love, the sweetest word" (1950, 53).[30] Translating this emotion into laconic terms, Enzensberger's allusion to Kaschnitz seems to acknowledge that although direct cause and effect are unpredictable (in historical, aesthetic, or emotive terms), a kind of symmetry and order exists to the way events unfold. His reference to Kaschnitz forces an allegorical reading of the poem as a meditation on German poets' expectations after the war—bluntly, that poetry could serve a collective transformative function—and their realization as this project was replayed throughout the latter half of the twentieth century that they had little control over the future or even their own marginalization.

Far from collapsing into pessimism over this lack of efficacy, Enzensberger seems to revel in the very possibility of such lack of consequence. Several poems in Enzensberger's subsequent volume of poetry, *Kiosk* (1995b), also invite readings of their mathematical and chaos theory subjects as allegories for the work of the poet, with an emphasis on the emancipatory verve expressed by their imagery. "Von der Algebra der Gefühle" ("On the Algebra of Emotions") cleverly explores the proposition that equations could be devised for disparate emotions and bodily sensations. "Sich selbst verschluckende Sätze" ("Self-Consuming Sentences") toys with paradoxically phrased sentences that are both self-affirming and self-negating. "Bifurkationen" ("Bifurcations") responds directly to chaos science terminology as it revisits the phenomena of bifurcations and fractals, beginning in the first stanza with a detailed list of representative phenomena:

> Alles, was sich verästelt,
> verzweigt: Delta Blitz Lunge,
> Wurzeln, Synapsen, Fraktale,
> Stamm- und Entscheidungsbäume;
> alles was sich vermehrt
> und zugleich vermindert
>
> (1995b, 72)

> *All things that put out twigs,*
> *branches: delta lightning lung,*

roots, synapses, fractions,
family or decision-making trees;
all things that multiply
and at the same time diminish
                                        (1999d, 51)

Taking up the impossibility of intellectually comprehending physical reality, this poem describes how nature proliferates in varied manifestations. The real world becomes much too complex for the *Spatzenhirn* (sparrow brain) of the observer (the term most certainly a wry self-reference to Enzensberger's famous poem "Zwei Fehler" ["Two Mistakes"], which confessed to the ineffectiveness of attempts to politicize literature: "back then I shot with sparrows at canons" [1983, 306]). "Bifurkationen" concludes with the observer dissolving into a series of infinite regressions,

die sich hinter dem Rücken
dessen, der da, statt zu denken,
gedacht wird, entwickelt,
verätselt, verzweigt.
                                        (1995d, 72)

which, behind the back
of the one who instead of thinking
is thought, puts out
its twigs and branches.
                                        (1999d, 51)

This chaotic, branching complexity exploits the ability of the lyric genre to achieve poetic closure, which is here a matter of formal repetition devoid of logical resolution of the subject matter. The calculated juxtaposition of micro- and macrophenomena (from synapses to deltas), the fluid infusion of scientific terms into a poetic text (bifurcations and fractals), and the poem's acknowledgment of subjective effects correspond to the author's interest in open-ended, chaotic systems. This infinite regression celebrates the contingency of the lyric genre, which finally returns us to the question of the collective function of poetry.

Richard Rorty in *Contingency, Irony, and Solidarity* has argued that literature as a project has managed—with more effect than the work of philosophers, historians, and theorists—to fuse a sense of its own historical contingency, its origins in individual freedom, and a commitment to collective solidarity in order to promote liberal culture (1989, xiii–xvi). This hypothesis resonates with *Der Untergang der Titanic* and Enzensberger's subsequent poetry collections, where he addresses contingency by showing how logical and intuitive insights contradict, supplement, and complement each other. Engagement with the radical paradigm of chaos theory therefore coincided for Enzensberger with the recovery of literary conventions that had largely been abandoned—visual aspects of the poetic medium, didactic impulses, and source materials derived from nature and representational modes such as metaphor and allegory. With chaos theory, the poems consider behavior so complex that, to paraphrase Hayles, they thwart the usual methods for constructing a system (1991, 1). The resulting poetry challenges readers to piece together a consistent interpretation and simultaneously interpellate the notion of interpretation. Coming at a time when poetry seemed to be compromised as a vehicle for intellectual analysis or for spontaneous creativity, Enzensberger again opened the range of options available to the lyric.

As had been the case previously when Enzensberger sought out new artistic models to address social issues, a consonance exists here between his interest in chaos science and the general political climate. His tack runs counter to the general mood of complacency associated with the post-1968 decades, however. The aesthetic project accomplished by *Der Untergang der Titanic* and subsequent poems is different from that achieved earlier by his absorption of international impulses, cultivation of a revisioned relationship to the reader, or appropriation of theoretical categories to shape poetic cycles in lyrical prose. Rather than conceiving of literature as a private and very personal activity (as did New Subjectivity), or developing a model for poetry to challenge prevailing trends directly, as before, Enzensberger worked a subtle and subversive angle. As "Bescheidener Vorschlag" suggests, the aim of literature remained for him political transformation, although the efficacy of the lyric genre came to be viewed with greater skepticism. Chaos theory moved his poetry beyond mere gestures of self-effacement (as in "Sommergedicht") and toward a profoundly destabilized text in which everything, even the poem itself, becomes contingent.

Rorty, as we have seen, regards such poetic contingency as a necessary precondition for the liberal community. "Only poets, Nietzsche suspected, can truly appreciate contingency. The rest of us," Rorty writes, "are doomed to remain philosophers, to insist that there is really only one true lading-list, one true description of the human situation, one universal context of our lives. We are doomed to spend our conscious lives trying to escape from contingency rather than, like the strong poet, acknowledging and appropriating contingency" (1989, 28). Even as the poetic medium—challenged by electronic media and beset by erosion of its traditional sources in nature and the self—has increasingly found itself on the periphery, Enzensberger's late work, the product of a "strong poet" indeed, embraces this precarious condition, taking on contingency and creating space for the poet to maneuver.

5. *Et Ego*

Identity Papers and Mental Leaps

What role does authorial presence play in our reading of poems, and which means are available to contemporary German poetry for establishing who has the authority to speak in a poem? Authorial presence (and its counterpart, commitment) have been inescapable problems for Enzensberger and other poets writing in German, largely for historical reasons. This fact marks a major difference between the literary context for poets writing in German and authors of American verse. Explaining the relationship between poetry and postwar history to an American audience in 1998, the poet and anthologist Jochim Sartorius observed, "moral dilemmas were of far greater concern to postwar poets than formal and aesthetic problems, and . . . every new poem until the early Eighties had to pass a moral litmus test" (1998, 122–23). Indeed, the testing Sartorius describes has conditioned the reception of postwar German poetry by assigning roles to poets in nearly every discussion of their work.[1] Critical consideration of how Paul Celan's poetry about the Holocaust reflects biographical trauma, of why Stephan Hermlin abandoned poetry, of what impact the expatriation of Wolf Biermann had on the careers of East German authors who protested his expulsion, or of which poems by Sascha Anderson bear reinterpretation in light of his involvement with the Stasi (East German secret police) has hinged on this notion of authorial presence. Instances also exist that illustrate how writers have encountered critical dismissal when they have chosen not to be political in conventional terms. Debates about "[d]er

Sarah-Sound," as Peter Hacks termed the voice of Sarah Kirsch (Hacks 1977, 268), or the controversial popularity of Ulla Hahn's rhymed verse reflect normative expectations of political relevance.

Proposing an interpretation of how the American Robert Lowell functioned as a poet of his age, Jackson Barry argues that given the nature of speech acts, "the personhood of the author—the poet, the bard—normally contributes more meaning to his or her works than does that of the artist who works in nonlinguistic media" (1999, 87). This reasoning leads Barry to analyze Lowell's authorial presence as arising from both actual life and poetic texts. "In Lowell," he observes, "we find a very complex sign function in which a physical signifier, the man or woman so chosen, stands for a cluster of meanings attributed to but certainly not inherent in the actual person" (80). At the risk of violating the separation of biography and text, I think we should ask how this notion of authorial presence pertains to the case of Hans Magnus Enzensberger, for since the beginning of his career, critics, academics, and other readers have speculated about this author.

More often than not, Enzensberger's writings, particularly his poetry, have been treated as illustration or confirmation of political positions attributed to his person. Speculation has centered around whether he is German or international, engagé (hence dissident) or resigned, optimistic or pessimistic, utopian or dystopian, wavering or constant in his positions, an insider or an outsider. Yet for all that has been written about Enzensberger, answers to such identity questions have remained strikingly absent. Hans-Ulrich Treichel recently summed up this dilemma by resorting to a formulation from the author's monograph on Clemens Brentano to characterize Enzensberger himself. "His true being we do not know," Treichel paraphrases (1999, 367). Joachim Kaiser reaches a similar conclusion, stating that "Enzensberger's art is at all times this: to penetrate a subject, a problem thoroughly—and yet himself to remain thoroughly impenetrable" (1999, 166). Seemingly a paradox, Enzensberger is the public figure who has remained elusive.

At the start of Enzensberger's career, when he was awarded the Büchner Prize in 1963, many critiqued his political attitudes, especially his disaffection with national identity. Thus Georg Hensel was forced to ask in the poet's defense, "What should be tested there? Life history? Sentiments? Party affiliation? Religion?" (quoted in Sulzer and Kußmaul 1987, 158–59).[2] This litany of benchmarks surfaced again after Enzensberger's public renunciation of a fellowship at the Center for Advanced Studies at Wesleyan University in Connecticut to go to Cuba. That controversial departure (reexamined by Lau [1999]), shaped much of what was subsequently written about Enzensberger. The spectrum of opinion regarding this act ranged from Reinhold Grimm's meticulously documented, favorable analysis of the author's political views in "Bildnis Hans Magnus Enzensberger: Struktur, Ideologie und Vorgeschichte eines Gesellschaftskritikers" (1984, 44–96) to Christian Linder's sharp critique (1975), which disclosed that Enzensberger had first gone to Australia before traveling to Cuba. Few articles after 1968 fail to mention this biographical incident (see also Lau 1999, 227–65). Notwithstanding the relative dearth of concrete information on the Cuba episode, the concentrated attention given it steered inquiry toward political aspects of Enzensberger's work and away from other categories of analysis.

What interests me here is not to take past scholarship to task or to achieve a resolution of the writer's persona but rather to ask how this author has used authorial presence to reshape conventions available to the lyric genre. Literary criticism long ago recognized the hazards of focusing on biography and authorial intent. The interpretive route I want to take leads back into Enzensberger's work and the way in which he uses poetry to map identity issues in relation to the public and private spheres. The authorial presence constructed in his texts has clearly varied over time, much in the way the formal repertoire and subject matter have in his poetic writings.

To consider what this varying presence contributes to Enzensberger's poetry, I will concentrate on three aspects of his work. The first is the modulation of persona that occurs from the oppositional "angry young man"—a writer who defined himself against national boundaries—to poet positioned in a global context. This analysis traces authorial presence as it is constructed in texts describing the outcast expatriate, the rootless intellectuals (figured in Bakunin), and then the restless, but sited, poet of "Die Frösche von Bikini" ("The Frogs from Bikini") for whom a liberal or radically enlightened community is essential. Following this discussion, my analysis turns to the reception given Enzensberger by American authors, especially Carolyn Forché (1981; 1993), to look at divergent conventions in the United States and Germany on authorial presence. This reception raises questions about the translatability of ethical and aesthetic values in a cross-cultural context. It also sheds light on Enzensberger's project of constructing an enlightened community by means of poetry.[3] Subsequent interpretation of poems from *Kiosk* (1995b) highlights mapping practices as a device that displays Enzensberger's sensitivity to globalization and tentative affirmation of communal vision. In these works, Enzensberger's attention to the porous quality of national and cultural boundaries intersects with concern about what constitutes ethical forms of writing.[4] Finally, the chapter examines how in the 1990s Enzensberger staged a calculated effacement of individual persona. The resulting "late style," which is synthetic, prognostic, and aphoristic by design, crystallizes around the epistemological insights afforded by retrospect and ties this mode of writing to a heightened sense of mortality.

Nationalism, Global Culture, and the Author's Persona

As national boundaries have become more open, discussions of literature have directed attention to how old distinctions between the public and private spheres are being effaced in increasingly nuanced ways. The conditions of postmodernism and globalization under which this effacement is taking place have paradoxically resulted in a foregrounding of identity issues. Accordingly, Geeta Kapur analyzes the writings of Salman Rushdie and Homi K. Bhaba in terms of the new role they propose for the intellectual:

> This is a floating intelligentsia to supplant a rooted intelligentsia; the discourse of postmodernity puts rout to the notion of the "organic intellectual." Once again continents and nations recede into native habitations, and we have interpreters and translators decoding cultures across the globe. Paradoxically, if hybridity is the survivor's credo in the age of globalization, global culture, under the chasing speed of radical representation, emits a great buzz on *identity*. (Kapur 1998, 199)[5]

This formulation suggests a framework for considering questions of nationality and globalism in Enzensberger's recent poetry. Kapur contrasts a transnational intelligentsia and a rooted one, locating a tension that has also fundamentally shaped Enzensberger's work in the lyric genre, and with added intensity after *Mausoleum*. "Am I a German?" Enzensberger rhetorically queried in a 1964 article that appeared in both a special issue of *Encounter* devoted to Germany (1964b) and the influential weekly newspaper *Die Zeit* (1964c).[6] The international perspective that the author cultivated in the late 1950s and early 1960s identified the differences between global and provincial aesthetic orientations but in the end did not cast them as mutually exclusive. Always framed by Enzensberger as a product of the post-1945 context, this cosmopolitanism was not yet truly transnational in the sense we have come to understand the term since the twentieth century's last decade.

Initially Enzensberger relied on a notion of writers as social outsiders that had been a convention in Germany since the romantic period. The attraction of such a status dissolves, however, when culture's value depends on its ability to transform society. Once that occurs, writers cannot simply be weak oppositional voices. Advocating a vigorous, socially constructive function for literature, Enzensberger in effect preserved the notion of *Kulturnation* (culture-nation), which in the absence of a coherent German political state had been important since the Enlightenment. The *Kulturnation* locates identity in culture.

Enzensberger's early poetry and related prose writings touch on aspects of the citizenship of writers, belatedness, foreign relations, and German identity. "The idea of the nation state may have ceased to correspond to any concrete reality, but it lives on obstinately in the form of an illusion, and illusions on this scale deserve to be taken seriously," Enzensberger proposes in "Am I a German?" (1964b, 17). The essay cites the quirks of cold war international relations, which witnessed the burgeoning of commerce across vast distances and the concurrent isolation of the German Democratic Republic from the neighboring Federal Republic. As his position on national identity evolves, however, Enzensberger moves considerably beyond the original concept of *Kulturnation.* His heuristic textual practices of mapping take on the function of addressing complex, contemporary dilemmas related to moral responsibility, national identity, and authorial presence. The presence favored in Enzensberger's early writings is that of the poet as exile. In an important essay about the poet Nelly Sachs, who was relatively unknown at the time, "Die Steine der Freiheit" ("The Stones of Freedom" [1959c]), Enzensberger rhetorically asked, "Where do the poets live today?" His conclusion, supported by the examples of Celan, Erich Fried, and Sachs, who were living in Paris, London, and Stockholm, respectively, reads, "The few who really count live somewhere in the neighborhood of everywhere" (770). Acting as an advocate for Sachs, Enzensberger admires how her writing articulates a response to the Holocaust. His comment implicitly links poets (or intellectuals), persons of ethical integrity, and individuals in the Diaspora. This triad of elements surfaces as well in Enzensberger's remarks about his own peripatetic existence, where his own expatriate status becomes the basis for a variety of satiric texts that advocate aesthetic and intellectual autonomy. Exile becomes equated with moral integrity and freedom of thought.

Describing the malaise about Germanness as "aporias of identity," Lau presents a biography of Enzensberger's life during this period to demonstrate how deeply his views were affected by cold war political tensions, the 1961 construction of the Berlin Wall, and the conservative climate of the Adenauer era (1999, 161–98). Enzensberger's prose writings, which respond to postwar preoccupations with national identity, already declare a tension between culture and nationality in the late 1950s. "Schimpfend unter Palmen" ("Cursing under Palms"), written in 1959, voices Enzensberger's objections to German politics, society, rearmament, and territorial divisions. With youthful defiance, the author quips about the places where literati and intellectuals tend to gather: "In Düsseldorf the coffee houses don't suit me" (1960e, 25). Other texts adumbrate the impact of political conservatism on culture, hence disparage a de facto censorship of free thinking. In a 1959 review of *Mutmassungen über Jakob* (*Speculations about Jacob*) by Uwe Johnson, Enzensberger noted the frequency with which critics over the age of sixty bemoaned the lack of "German literature." "It is true that we have no plays, but we have novels, poems, stories, essays. Nonetheless we have no German literature," he continued, arguing that this was the case because so many authors had been drawn into literary escapism (1959b, 910). At fault, the text reasons, is the division of Germany into East and West.

While a note of generational conflict is sounded in both this review and "Schimpfend unter Palmen," the more consistent and pressing argument in Enzensberger's writings from the period is that political agendas insidiously limit high-quality cultural production. Occasionally this problem becomes linked to what the author identifies as Germans' uncritical nostalgia and a bourgeois taste for kitsch or comfort. Enzensberger's 1963 satirical allegory "Die Schnecken" ("The Snails"), for instance, acknowledges that it has never been easy to deal with political questions with feigned politeness, then launches into a vociferous complaint about the "irresponsible attacks of the German snail council" in matters of culture and politics. A rousing conclusion mimics political speeches in proclaiming, "We are fighting for the unconditional rights to which every German snail is entitled insofar as they swear allegiance to our free-Western persuasion. The snail question is a national question! Solidarity, not self-flagellation, is the command of the hour. One alleyway for the snails!" (1963b, 198). But, slow to move and quick to retreat into their shell—like the German intelligentsia Enzensberger assails—snails seem unlikely to promulgate revolution. The author's ironic view of his compatriots finds objective corroboration in a 1965 review for *Der Spiegel* of a collection of public opinion surveys. Here Enzensberger acerbically confirms that Germany seemed to be a nation of uninspiring stereotypes: animal lovers, early risers, stubborn moderates, and punctual conformists. A caption under one of the accompanying photographs sarcastically identifies a kitschy garden gnome as the German idol (1965b, 112).[7]

These texts view German culture through the lens of his own oppositional expatriatism; other writings by Enzensberger from the period begin to address issues of cultural belatedness and Eurocentric perspectives by adumbrating a notion of the writer-intellectual not bound by national identity. Of particular relevance to my analysis are the conditions Enzensberger sets forth as necessary for the creation of poetry and the cultural role he ascribes to the lyric genre. Initially in the 1950s and 1960s, he celebrated poetry for its capacity to transcend national boundaries, embracing the generic internationalism of the time. Such sentiment introduces a 1958 review of Saint-John Perse's verse in which Enzensberger commends poems for appealing to the ear—an appreciation that grants poetry a natural, human purpose. "Today in any case," Enzensberger continues, "poetry has created a lingua franca that blends elements of elevated style with the jargon of the masses, the linguistic refuse of civilization with the crude and beautiful vocabulary of the everyday" (1958, 511). The term "lingua franca," which is echoed in the afterword to *Museum der modernen Poesie* (1980 [ed.], 773), becomes the banner for international modernism in that collection.

"Poetry and Politics" reconnects with these issues. There Enzensberger asserts the autonomy of the lyric genre from dogma, including Marxism, for ideologies reduce it to a service "as decoration, as screen, as stagedrop for eternity" (1964f, 129), in short, make it the limited classical poetry that Roland Barthes cautioned was "an ornamental variation of prose" (1967, 43).[8] Formulations that describe national identity, hybrid cultural systems, and global media connections undergo transformation in Enzensberger's writings from the late 1960s. Gradually his scrutiny of Eurocentric attitudes from the vantage of an intellectual is supplanted by a critique of the compromised position of nomadic intellectuals themselves. Deliberations about the poet in exile, literature as a lingua franca, cultural marginalism, and the unprescriptive character of poetry represent intermediate stages in a progression that elaborates a position for the floating intelligentsia, particularly as represented in the figure of Bakunin.

Meanwhile, the division between minor and major literatures, which is implicit in the discussion given to provincial and world literatures in *Mu-*

seum der modernen Poesie, becomes slipperier as Enzensberger questions its attachment to national identity. In an article concerning twentieth-century Danish poetry, he writes about Denmark's apparently marginal literary status and state of cultural belatedness, a concept attributed to American cultural sociology (1963c, 629). He concludes that "literature doesn't live on genius; it lives from talents that can unfold themselves, from a minimum of continuity and humus and last but not least from an intrepid public" (1963c, 637). The political analysis in "Europäische Peripherie" ("European Periphery") (originally published in 1965 and later included in *Deutschland, Deutschland unter anderem* [1967d]) is less satisfied with such conclusions. Now Enzensberger reminds readers of the presumptions attached to a term like "developing" when it is used to describe so-called Third World countries in relation to industrialized nations (1967d, 158–59), and he advocates sensitivity to the rhetorical conventions of these other cultures (163–64) as well as to global power structures (166).[9]

By the late 1970s, it was clear that a naive understanding of globalism was no longer possible. The 1979 postscript to *Museum der modernen Poesie* registers not only a departure from the presumptions of a "One World" ideology (1980 [ed.], 786) but also a sense that in many respects, the function accorded poetry had changed for the better. "Poetry has," Enzensberger observed, "not only lost prestige, but also 'greatness' and 'universality,' a loss that also has its good sides" (1980 [ed.], 787). This rejection of large, totalizing systems overlaps with conclusions reached later in his writing about the emergence of ethnic conflicts and worldwide migrations. Thus the foundations for Enzensberger's provocative diagnosis of the marginal status of Germany, which he bitingly characterized as "a protectorate of the United States" (1979d, 1) in an address given in New York, already lie in his writings from the 1960s.

A parallel transformation affects the handling of national identity in Enzensberger's poetry. The trigonometric points used so effectively by him to map cold war terrains become overshadowed by the roving figure of the expatriate poet-intellectual, whose presence marks the perspective needed to evaluate public affairs.[10] *Landessprache* suggests that geographical distance allowed the poet to judge his own country. He broods passionately, "What have I lost in this land?" (1960d, 7). The poet concludes with a desire to be not in Germany, and a perpetual restlessness regardless of place:[11]

> ich hadere aber ich weiche nicht,
> da bleibe ich eine zeitlang,

bis ich von hinnen fahre zu den anderen leuten,
und ruhe aus, in einem ganz gewöhnlichen land,
hier nicht,
nicht hier.

(1960d, 12)

I grumble but do not budge,
there I shall stay for a time,
till I move on to the other people
and rest, in another country quite ordinary,
elsewhere,
not here.

(1994b, 25)

As in "Sommergedicht," whose accompanying note speaks to the ability of poetry to work from a global perspective, "Landessprache" hypothesizes that poems move dynamically through space and time. *Mausoleum* (1975) and *Der Untergang der Titanic* (1978a) enhance this temporal-geographical mapping with references to sociological distinctions and ethnic categories. The class and national origin of the ship's passengers in *Der Untergang der Titanic* are determinants of whether they survive. Many who cannot speak (the immigrant passengers who travel in steerage) perish. Ironically, figures who seem completely out of place in the epic poem—a stowaway Chinese man, anachronistic literary personages, and nomads in tents—outlive the wealthy first-class passengers. Also among the survivors is the roaming anarchist Bakunin, a famous, countryless person who shares certain traits with the nomadic, nameless intellectual who later gains voice in the "Gedankenflucht" ("Flights of Thought") texts from *Kiosk* (1995b) and similar poems.[12]

Indeed, portraits of revolutionaries such as Bakunin, Marx, or Guevara are powerful expressions of authorial presence in Enzensberger's work from this period and seem to invite comparison with his own political commitment, even though they are marked by open ambivalence.[13] Each poem about one of these figures is tinged with an admiration for principled action, then tempered by the frank recognition that individual foible or historical chance may render action futile. Thus Bakunin, whom "M.A.B. (1814–1876)" from *Mausoleum* represents as an ardent "Mohammed without Koran," is nonetheless upbraided for nomadism, foolishness and self-neglect" (1975, 94). The ballad chronicles his flights into exile through Siberia, Amur, the Pacific, and the American desert (95). Still, in the end, the poet pleads for him to return, observing that Europe still smells of police and that there will never be a monument to him (97).[14]

The portrait of Bakunin in *Der Untergang der Titanic,* where he does in fact return, is more sympathetic. Even here, however, he has no more ideological efficacy than in *Mausoleum*. Initially his identity is a riddle. He is tagged as "B. . . . a Russian emigrant" (1978a, 42), and his speeches are labeled "tirades of the Impotent" (58), a biographical detail already mentioned in *Mausoleum*. The "Fifteenth Canto" presents a dessert conversation in which the poet is asked what he is getting at with his "fairy tales about painting, Gordon Pym, Bakunin, and Dante" (53). That question at last unmistakably identifies the anarchist, aligning him with figures fascinated by other worlds or paradises. The reader watches Bakunin through a porthole in the smoking salon of the ship, a window that functions like a camera lens, permitting a voyeuristic glimpse of the anarchist's theatrical sparring. This window is also a mirror that reflects the face of the poet—an armchair anarchist—back to the audience. "Take what they have taken from you," Bakunin rants to the steerage passengers (1980b, 16). But, as the alter ego poet informs us from the other side of the looking glass, this ranting is to no avail because "[t]hey understood quite well / what he said, but they did not / understand him. His words were not their words" (17). Meanwhile, true nomads mysteriously appear on board the ship, pitch tents, and then vanish. The painter depicts a Bedouin feast on one of his canvases. Five unknown Chinese save themselves by hiding under sailcloth in the bottom of a lifeboat, only to vanish completely (1978a, 86). The artists, anarchists, nomads, and emigrants clump together—members of a diffuse, floating population that includes the intelligentsia.

This figuration of a teeming, global community of creative individuals, ethnic minorities, and social radicals draws on a paradigm of authorial presence that, like the earlier model of the expatriate writer, derives from wartime conditions. In a 1948 essay characterizing the situation of German writers throughout the twentieth century as that of nomadic intellectuals, Hannah Arendt aptly identified Bertolt Brecht as coming from one of "three lost generations." By Arendt's definition, the first generation lost consisted of Germans who experienced World War I, the second of those who lived through the devastations of the Great Depression, and the third of individuals who survived World War II. Brecht, according to Arendt, used this forced nomadism, faced stoically, to define his poetic position (Arendt 1948, 304). Her writerly celebration of the peripatetic intellectual reinscribes in positive terms the negative labeling that occurred in fascist propaganda. It rewrites vilifying images of transients, such as one found in a publication of the National Socialist German Workers Party (NSDAP or Nationalsozialistische Deutsche Arbeiterpartei) that admonished, "We are confronted . . . by an impertinent, shameless, murderous fellowship of rootless literati and Asians who poison and corrupt everything. And so we have no choice but to fight to the destruction of their spirit or ours, their way of life or ours here in Germany" (quoted in Zimmer 1988, 362). In *Der Untergang der Titanic,* written decades after the war, the persona Bakunin is problematic. He is one of Arendt's uprooted literati, but he is unable to communicate with his intended audience because he has no real connection to a place or ethnic constituency. An inhabitant of a postcolonial world, his brilliance is lost because he fails to translate, decode, or otherwise culturally transmit his ideas.

Still Bakunin is a palatable alternative to icons of nationalism. Sir Henry Morgan Stanley, who also appears in *Mausoleum,* represents by contrast the consequences of an extreme nationalism, specifically of British imperialism.[15] Despite his public reputation for empire building, Stanley turns out to be a self-serving mercenary who inhabits a world that overlaps with the space of Bakunin. The two could hardly be more different. Enzensberger maps Stanley's checkered life to reveal that no simple equation can be made between nationality and criminal acts. The borderless commerce in which Stanley is entangled follows global economic forces rather than the exchange of ideas that Bakunin seeks. In the two we witness the contest between money and ideals, a clash with new consequences in our times. Cultural historian Walter D. Mignolo identifies three stages of preglobalization, each of which was prompted by a different ideological force—Christianization (during the Spanish Empire), civilizing mission (British Empire and French colonialization), and modernization (U.S. imperialism) (1998, 36). Mignolo regards these as superseded by globalization, a term he traces to transnational corporate lingo. His analysis points out that there is a qualitative difference when world politics are driven by purely economic rather than ideological factors (32). To apply Mignolo's finding, Stanley blends some of the worst aspects of colonialism with the disadvantages of late-twentieth-century globalization, engaging in actions based solely on economic interests rather than on principle.

Stanley, of course, was British, and numerous commentative phrases point to the questionable legacy of Great Britain's colonialism. Enzensberger interjects comments about the misconstruction of hero figures ("Das falsche Bewußtsein im Tropenhelm. / Heroismus, handkoloriert"

["The false consciousness in pith helmet. / Heroism, handcolored"]), the performative aspects of propaganda used to justify expeditions ("alles Staffage ["everything mere show"]), and the spurious, voyeuristic relationship of intruders to the sites of conquest ("Tourist der Blutbäder" ["tourist of the bloodbaths"]). Stanley on his African expeditions carries *Dr Liebigs Fleischextrakt* (Dr. Liebig's flesh extract) — an item inconspicuously listed among dozens of other provisions that pointedly connects Germany with genocide (Enzensberger 1975, 106–9). A comparison of facts about the historical Stanley with the details selected for the ballad underscores the degree to which questions of nationalism and identity are at play. Stanley was a person of contradictions. As a young man, he fought in the American Civil War on the side of the Confederacy, a political affiliation that compromises his integrity in the poem. Though a successful writer, Stanley's reported discovery of Livingstone was for a time doubted. Openly racist, he helped found the Congo Free State. His expeditions, which shaped the map of Africa, resulted in numerous casualties that damaged his reputation. Attending the Berlin Conference of 1884 and 1885 on African affairs, he acted as an advisor to Americans.[16] Like other figures in *Mausoleum*, Stanley illuminates the dark aspects of humanity by obliquely mirroring German questions of guilt. His biographical terrain maps place-names that connects Africa with the power-broker nations of Britain, the United States, and Germany. His national identity is a mere pretense for mercenary opportunism justified by patriotic platitudes.

Whereas Bakunin is limited in what he can accomplish because he is the eternal exile, socially isolated, Stanley, who has the dubious distinction of being the hired nationalist, has no personal integrity. Both are individually grotesque. They are not citizens or noncitizens but pawns of larger power configurations. *Mausoleum* subtly overlays national identity with crimes against humanity. Eurocentric by design, its allusions to German political and cultural identity make Germans appear awkward, arrogant, oblivious to history, or ignorant of context. The poem about the Danish astronomer Tycho Brahe terms his German contemporary Johannes Kepler a provincial lout. The philosopher Leibniz, who commutes between provincial residences and metropolitan centers, is emotionally stunted (1975, 28). The intellectual Alexander von Humboldt, who restlessly consumes everything exotic ("Terra incognita melts like snow under his gaze" [62]), paints, travels globally, and conducts weird experiments on frogs with electrical currents. Termed ironically "our noble hero" (64), von Humboldt seems blind to the fate of native populations (64). In short, *Mausoleum* reduces

Germany's *Dichter und Denker* (thinkers and poets) to a peripheral role. Georg Büchner, Albrecht von Haller, Heinrich Heine, E. T. A. Hoffmann, Friedrich Nietzsche, and Richard Wagner are mentioned only in passing. Meanwhile, the text lavishes attention on crude, obscure figures. An alcoholic German machinist, Tobias Schmidt, fills an entire ballad section by offering Guillotin access to odd machines in his possession (52). The publications of a forgotten statistician, Johann Peter Süßmilch, concerning the lofty topic of "The Godly Order in the Changes of the Human Race," garner disproportionately large space (60).

As if following a grand, unseen flowchart, minor technologies and major criminal behaviors migrate across borders as the ballads progress. In the penultimate ballad, the British Alan Mathison Turing, who cracked the Enigma code used by the German military in World War II, dashes off across fields outside Cambridge like the maddened protagonist Woyzeck in Georg Büchner's play, yet another victim of rationalization. Behind him is left the still encoded network of rules governing nationalism, social mores, and culture represented in previous ballads. Poetry and mathematics are conjectural fields. The last ballad, about the Baudelaire-reading Che Guevara, transports readers across the globe to the margins of the Third World.

Looking at the moves in these poems as a form of mapping brings into focus the relationship between the experience that prompts a text (language, images, or political dilemmas) and the poem's capacity to signify, project, or evoke in dynamic terms—and thereby mark authorial presence. Maps can be simplifications or complex fractal designs. The references Enzensberger makes to cartographic elements in his recent writings correspond to the current understanding of mapping, which acknowledges that as a representational convention it is not a neutral practice. As James Corner observes in "The Agency of Mapping: Speculation, Critique and Invention":

> Maps present only one version of the earth's surface, an eidetic fiction constructed from factual observation. As both analogue and abstraction, then, the surface of the map functions like an operating table, a staging ground or a theater of operations upon which the mapper collects, combines, connects, marks, masks, relates and generally explores. These surfaces are massive collection, sorting and transfer sites, great fields upon which real material conditions are isolated, indexed and placed within an assortment of relational structures. (1999, 215)

Corner terms mapping "a fantastic cultural project" that creates new visions as it describes current realities (1999, 213). It is in this sense that conjectural practices in Enzensberger's poetry construct or reconstitute meaning in order to consider ethical dilemmas.[17]

Commenting with admiration on the revolutionary findings of the mathematician Kurt Gödel, Enzensberger identifies a relationship between ethical complexity and the need to recognize the artificiality of the systems we use to describe reality. Enzensberger cites Gödel's finding that no mathematical system can exist without internal contradictions, adding, "In this, he [Gödel] succeeded, once and for all, in turning on its head the deeply held conviction that mathematics alone can deliver us from the quagmire of inconsistency. Since this is quite beyond even the most refined logicians, how then can we expect to solve the ever-increasing ethical contradictions by a simple axiomatic system?" (1994a, 66).

In Enzensberger's poetry collection *Die Furie des Verschwindens* (1980a), elements that constitute a maplike organization facilitate ethical deliberations. Public forms of communication—radio broadcasts, television programs, and international consumer culture—figure in the texts as examples of a decreasing distance between the immediate and the remote. Their meditations depict the poet as thinking globally even during private moments because they contrast the chimeric exoticism of remote locations with the annoyances of bland and immediate quotidian experience. The pendulation between these extremes mirrors the mind of a poet who engages in mental journeys, not just physical ones. "Die Frösche von Bikini" ("The Frogs from Bikini"), the long poem that anchors *Die Furie des Verschwindens,* employs such cartography to a unique extent. The text, which spans forty-two stanzas, constitutes itself as a walk through Berlin that, much as in T. S. Eliot's "The Love Song of J. Alfred Prufrock," prompts its protagonist to meditate on life. Analysis reveals that this poet is an expert cartographer of ethical positions rather than a mere flaneur.

Although "Die Frösche von Bikini" presents itself as a casual, rambling monologue, it is carefully plotted to move through Berlin and its literary sites. The mind of the poet is mapped according to that city walk. Its motion opens the intimate and arguably static lyric genre to far-ranging questions of identity and ethics by allowing "Die Frösche von Bikini" to wander into reflections on ecological problems, nuclear armaments, and social reform that are near and dear to the protagonist, even as he broods about his own life. The text styles poetry as a medium with performative capacities by using cinematographic directives that pull together disparate items for the eye, ear, and mind of the reader. These elements shape the message but eschew rational deduction in favor of illusion. "Poets are born liars," Enzensberger wrote in "Poesie und Politik" (1964f, 113), that Nietzschean position echoed in *Der Untergang der Titanic*. Poets are not, as Enzensberger has frequently reminded readers, under any obligation to deliver systematic answers to political questions. "Die Frösche von Bikini" confirms that position, even as it maps out an array of ethical matters that occupy the poet.

"Die Frösche von Bikini," whose title references the South Pacific island where nuclear tests were staged, commences with the poet noticing that questions are constantly being asked. He tries to remember when he first became aware of them (1980a, 37). That beginning echoes the opening passage from *Der Untergang der Titanic*, which focuses on listening (1978a, 7), and leads to lines where the poet struggles to reclaim his own voice, wavering between the third-person subjunctive and first-person speech, both of which employ identical verb forms:

> Während ich, sagt er,
> weil mir nichts anderes übrigbleibt,
> horche auf jene Stimme,
> auf daß sie mir sage wohin,
> mit wem, wozu — *meine* Stimme,
> sagt er, die sich nicht vernehmen läßt . . .
>
> (1980a, 38)

> *While I, he says, am harkening,*
> *since I cannot help it, to the Voice,*
> *hoping to be told where to go,*
> *with whom, what for — my Voice,*
> *he says, which I cannot hear . . .*
>
> (1994b, 177)

The surrounding text — the first eleven stanzas — recounts how he has noticed a change in the climate. His antagonists admonish him to explore "paths of self-knowledge," as if suggesting that absorbed inner reflection could improve his condition (1980a, 37). During this portion of the text, he passes numerous public sites — Mariannenplatz (38), the corner of Oranienburger (38), Ansbacher Straße (38), and Droysenstraße (39). Sometime later he hears the sounds of frogs again, "in August, in out-of-the-way places" (40). His own residence is indicated generally as Friedenau (41), near Belle-Alliance Straße (46).[18]

Then he thinks of Bikini and how flora and fauna have grown back or regenerated "thirty years after the apocalypse," a reference to atomic bomb tests (1980a, 43). His attention now shifts back to matters close at hand — the cost of telephoning on Sundays and a professor writing a study of him. Four stanzas later, the poet declares that he is an observer, weary of externally imposed obligations and expectations. Sometime later, the poet announces that his penchant for *Aufmerksamkeit* (attentiveness) leads him to subject matters others ignore.[19] These topics are adumbrated in the next pair of stanzas, which mention massacres and a striking scene of people rescuing migrating frogs near a highway exit to the Bodensee. The poem announces that the protagonist has decided to be inconspicuous (*unauffällig*), knowing that he has limited effect. He threatens to record everything on tape (an apparent reference to domestic spying). After much deliberation, he resolves simply to persist.

Musing about nature, science, and accomplishments, the text reasons baroquely that all is transient:

> Nichts bleibt, wie es ist,
> glücklicherweise.
> Nicht nur der Frosch,
> auch die Froschforschung
> kann schließlich zurückblicken
> auf Errungenschaften.
> Ein ohrenbetäubendes Spektakel.
>
> (1980a, 41)

> *Nothing, fortunately,*
> *remains as it is.*
> *Not only the frogs can look back*
> *on splendid achievements.*
> *Frog ethology, too,*
> *has made great strides.*
> *Altogether a deafening show.*
>
> (1994b, 181)

The deafening spectacle is perhaps a satirical reprise of the *atemberaubendes Schauspiel* (breathtaking drama) of the iceberg in *Der Untergang der Titanic* and an allusion to Goethe's distinction between understanding the world

through the eyes or the ears.[20] Then the poem moves on to visual references. It mentions a cloud that changes shape "like certain words" (1980a,
43) and that is reminiscent of meteorological occurrences in Brecht's well-
known poem "Erinnerung an die Marie A.," Hans Arp's *Wolkenpumpe*
series, and the mushroom clouds caused by nuclear testing.

"Die Frösche von Bikini" also references "Dr. Benn," a resident of Berlin (1980a, 46), a gesture that underscores Enzensberger's indebtedness to
Gottfried Benn's adroit use of colloquial diction. Here the poem specifically evokes T. S. Eliot's famous "The Love Song of J. Alfred Prufrock,"
whose lines muse, "I am no prophet—and here's no great matter; / I have
seen the moment of my greatness flicker, / And I have seen the eternal
Footman hold my coat, and snicker, / And in short, I was afraid" (1980
[ed.], 72). Inverting the syntax slightly and rephrasing matters to assert
boldness rather than withdrawal, Enzensberger writes,

> Er sei kein Prophet,
> über manches rede er nicht,
> er deute nur an, warte, und seine Stimme
> lasse er nur deshalb erschallen,
> weil sonst keine Stimme zu hören sei,
> keine Angst, keine Tränen,
> er sei ja da, er bleibe.
>
> (1980a, 51–52)

> *He'd not qualify as a prophet.*
> *There were things he'd rather not talk about.*
> *He'd just drop a hint every now and then,*
> *only because there was no other voice*
> *to be heard, no panic, no tears.*
> *He was here to stay.*
>
> (1994b, 195)

This echoing of Eliot's lines makes clear that Enzensberger plots no retreat
into the purely aesthetic, self-indulgent mode of German New Subjectivity
or the nomadic disquiet of Bakunin. In its perambulations, the poem maps
out a cityscape in which ethical issues cannot be avoided. Here the poet
asks, "Utopias? Yes, but where? / We do not see them. We only feel them /
like the knife in the back" (1980a, 46).[21]

"Die Frösche von Bikini" carves out a position for the writer that is
distinct from that of the historian, social analyst, and politician, yet not

wholly detached from actions in the real world or from a remembrance of the past that is embedded in the city. Neither the "angry young man" nor the nomadic intellectual, and also not utopian or dystopian, this poet contributes to society by flexibly engaging with his surroundings while using the eidetic tools of the lyric genre.[22] Jonathan Monroe has suggested that the questions of identity addressed by Enzensberger have become more pressing since German reunification. "Interweaving critical reflections on the past, present, and future in ways that refuse to allow memory to fade," Monroe observes, "Enzensberger's recent writing calls us to look carefully into who 'we' are and want to be, who 'we' includes and who the future of poetry will be of, by, and for, in the wake of 1989" (1997, 74).[23] The modes of presentation Enzensberger devised to address present dilemmas and to project the future return us to the unfinished project that had been urged on German literature, the project of truly mapping a past that witnessed crimes against humanity—a German question, but also one that transcends national boundaries.

Hybrid Culture: Forché on Enzensberger

We might be tempted to assume that culture operates freely across national borders when no discernible physical barriers exist to the dissemination of texts, ideas, and ethical values, but this isomorphism is patently not the case. In a world where everything can actually be translated and instantaneously sent to the most remote corners of the earth in hypermedia form (thereby surpassing even Walter Benjamin's projections about the reproducibility of art and Enzensberger's nightmare in "Die babylonische Bibliothek" [1960b]), poetry should be able to escape sheer material limitations on cultural reproduction. That greater cultural openness has not been achieved appears related to the persistence of modernist biases that have naturalized ethnocentric values. Although after 1945, Germans had turned to modernism as an antidote to provincialism, even at the close of the twentieth century, modernist sensibilities appeared to have subtly tempered globalism.

According to the indices Christopher Beach uses in *Poetic Culture: Contemporary American Poetry between Community and Institution* (1999) to measure literary impact, it would seem that Enzensberger has enjoyed relative success as a foreign author in the United States. His works have appeared in the dominant print media Beach cites (commercial venues, newspapers, and general audience magazines [23]) and even received attention in book reviews and a wide range of scholarly articles. Enzensberger began publishing in the United States in 1956, when "Cultivate Your Garden" appeared in *Poetry* magazine. Since then, his poetry and essays appeared regularly in *Harper's*. In addition, other texts have reached print in the *American Poetry Review, Evergreen Review, Literary Review, Midwest Quarterly, New York Times Book Review, Partisan Review, World Literature Today,* and *Times Literary Supplement*. Occasionally Enzensberger has been cited by Americans in relationship to Adorno's pronouncement about poetry after Auschwitz, especially in connection with the philosopher's essay "Commitment," which acknowledges Enzensberger for arguing that poets should continue to write.[24] His major works are abundantly represented in English translation (see R. Wieland 1999, 249–341). A prodigious experimenter with new technologies, Enzensberger was surely one of the first authors to mention e-mail in a German poem (in "Die Glasglocke" from *Die Furie des Verschwindens* [1980a]), and he is well represented on the Internet. Erk Grimm's essay examining the effects of electronic media on recent German poetry (1997) concludes that Enzensberger, unlike younger authors, is skeptical of these current developments.[25] All the same, it is clear that his poetry has not been isolated from cybernetic content or dissemination.

The sustained interest Enzensberger has demonstrated in American verse might appear to dispose his work to good reception in the United States, especially because he has been in contact with major writers. Yet this fact seems to have had little impact, for Enzensberger remains better known for his media analysis and political essays than for his poetry. His important role as a Continental mediator of American poetry and his recent translations of Wallace Stevens and Charles Simic underscore his ongoing fascination with the U.S. verse scene.[26] Brief remarks printed on the dust jacket of the Simic translations, *Ein Buch von Göttern und Teufeln* (Enzensberger 1993 [trans.]), distinguish Simic from the German trends and echo the words Enzensberger had used to describe Williams: "His [Simic's] poetry is thoroughly saturated with American daily life, with the sadness and glory of the street. . . . But are those elements metaphors or are they simply observations?" Continuing in this vein, Enzensberger concludes "that the commonplace appears simultaneously as the mysterious."[27]

Reciprocal acknowledgments of Enzensberger by American writers remain for the most part sketchy.[28] Monroe summarizes the situation as follows: "That his work remains less well known in the United States than it deserves to be is all the more regrettable in light of the fact that Enzensberger's work has demonstrated from the very beginning a truly international character that has always extended well beyond the confines of more narrowly German concerns" (1997, 42). Australian John Tranter, a poet translated by Enzensberger, similarly commented in a 1995 interview, "I've discovered with some dismay that few American poets have heard of Enzensberger. He has a profoundly ironic and richly political view of things; that's a dimension sometimes lacking in the US, I suspect" (1995). This assumption that American poets are inherently less political than European ones is frequently voiced, as in a recent special issue of *Poetry* (173, no. 1 [1998]), titled *Contemporary German Poetry* and devoted to contemporary German verse, but it bears closer scrutiny. The exception to this obscurity is Enzensberger's essay collection *The Consciousness Industry*, which became the subject of an article by Stanley Aronowitz (1976). Cited by Fredric Jameson in his essay "Aesthetics and Politics" (1992), the book received broader attention than Enzensberger's other works and eventually came to bear on the work of an American poet, Carolyn Forché. Enzensberger's reception by Forché can be traced in a series of publications that reference his views on poetry.[29]

Foregrounding Enzensberger's discussion of poetry in *The Consciousness Industry* (1974a) for a 1981 article published in the *American Poetry Review*, the American poet Carolyn Forché commented that "the impulse to witness confronted the prevailing poetic" and led her to write political poetry (1981, 7). The essay by Forché, which appeared one year after *Die Furie des Verschwindens* (Enzensberger 1980a), embraces Enzensberger's description of poetry as a medium of conscience. Her reaction to his work sheds light on the persuasiveness of the ethical positions Enzensberger had been formulating for the lyric genre, yet it also reveals critical areas in which authorial presence and cultural context become essential co-determinants of a text. Forché's understanding of his poetic theory filters out—perhaps inevitably—elements particular to the German context that inhere in Enzensberger's statements. Arguably more than any other German poet, Enzensberger has sought connection with international literature and a large audience. His project for the lyric genre has always been connected with the notion that poetry is part of a liberal community, an undertaking that should theoretically transcend chauvinism. Nonetheless, in the United States—the site of much of his mediative activity and Forché's own work—reception of his poetic writings has been conditioned by expectations about German writers. Forché is not the only American who has displayed interest in Enzensberger's work, but her response reveals as much about the conventions governing discussions of postwar German poetry as about our tastes for international literature. Indeed, the tenor of her remarks complicates current definitions of globalism and hybrid culture, for it shows an area in which cultural boundaries are less porous than might be expected.

Forché, whose work Kevin Stein regards as blurring distinctions among ethical, moral, aesthetic, and political matters (1996, 148), quotes from Enzensberger's *The Consciousness Industry* in her *American Poetry Review* article, "El Salvador: An Aide Memoire," which appeared in 1981. The citations, which play a pivotal role in her argument, provide confirmation for Forché's reflections on the possibility of creating a form of writing that is committed to instigating political change. The essay relates her own turn from poetry based on experience to a form of literature that attempts to give witness to crimes against humanity. Quoting Enzensberger, she takes up his argument against the constraints of bourgeois aesthetics, which concludes, "For a political quarantine placed on poetry in the name of eternal values, itself serves political ends" (quoted in Forché 1981, 6).

When Forché writes about her own decision to create political poetry, however, she amends Enzensberger's statement in two ways. First, she overlooks a rather specific reference to New Subjectivity, his statement that "[t]oo often the champions of inwardness and sensibility are reactionaries" (quoted in Forché 1981, 6). This is an understandable oversight, because *Neue Subjektivität* would not have been well known to a general audience of American readers. Second, and more significantly, she extrapolates on Enzensberger's references to "vulgar Marxism" and "high aspirations and eternal values." In the German context, these terms are linked to arguments that date back to fascist rhetoric about what kind of art is appropriate. Forché, describing how poets work from an inherited tradition and yet must invent new, authentic language, transforms Enzensberger's specifically internal, national reference into a sweeping generalization:

> All language then is political; vision is always ideologically charged; perceptions are shaped *a priori* by our assumptions and sensibility formed by consciousness at once social, historical and aesthetic. There is no such thing as non-political poetry. (Forché 1981, 6)

While this formulation is reminiscent of Enzensberger's own *Museum der modernen Poesie* (1980 [ed.]), it goes beyond the kind of position he took. Forché's celebration of political verse and her reception of Enzensberger here appear to engage with a phase in moral reasoning that he had passed through in the late 1950s. It is one thing to assert that all poetry is political, as Enzensberger did circa 1960 in contemplating the relationship of poetry and politics in the immediate post-Holocaust German context.[30] It is a different matter when Forché generalizes to make the statement that all poetry is political, particularly in the wake of activist disillusionment after 1968.

The gaze of a witness to history entails both a sense of guilt and of insight. When Enzensberger evokes an ocular perspective, he focuses attention on an ethical problem, but does so as an individual who has himself fallen under the scrutiny of others' watchful eyes. His open letter "On Leaving America" (1968b) noted that as an author, he realized he could not separate himself from other Germans. The self-conscious person experiences the incriminating looks of others. Enzensberger reflects, "The fact is that most Americans have no idea of what they and their country look like to the outside world. I have seen the glance that follows them. . . . It is a terrible look, because it makes no distinction, and no allowances. I will tell you why I recognize this look. It is because I am a German. It is because I have felt it on myself" (1968b, 32). Forché, by contrast, stands in the position of a witness in order to represent distant events to her fellow compatriots. She reports to Americans outside El Salvador about atrocities committed within that country (and to a certain extent about how actions by the United States have contributed to the violence), but she also addresses a sympathetic, if small, audience. While Forché acknowledges that she has less authority as a U.S. citizen speaking about Central America, her sense of the scrutinizing gaze of the external world community is paler than Enzensberger's. Where her evocation of Enzensberger is an affective response to an excruciating situation, his position is reasoned, contextualized diagnosis. Enzensberger qualifies and limits his statements; Forché enlarges hers. As in translation, the transmission of ideas from one context to another disperses the specificity of the original statement. It is not the case that Forché has in some fundamental way misunderstood Enzensberger. On the contrary, she has grasped his general intention quite well, but she connects with his ethical position by extension, reformulating it in her own terms.

Given Forché's enthusiasm for Enzensberger in this essay, it is curious that her subsequent anthology *Against Forgetting: Twentieth-Century Poetry of Witness* (1993) neither mentions nor includes him, while many other Germans do appear in the collection. Adorno is cited for his statement on poetry after Auschwitz. Celan and Eich receive mention in Forché's introductory remarks as well. The collection itself includes Benn, Georg Trakl, Brecht, Fried, Grass, Sachs, Gertrud Kolmar, Peter Huchel, Johannes Bobrowski, and Sarah Kirsch. The works of these authors readily conform to the categories used to organize the anthology. Perhaps Enzensberger's poetry, political as it is, is omitted because it does not fit Forché's arrangement of poems by historical epochs: the two world wars, the Holocaust, and oppression in Eastern Europe.

The comments Forché makes in the introduction nonetheless parallel Enzensberger's poetic project. In advocating a respect for otherness and for the function of poetry of witness as she defines it, Forché acknowledges that American literary criticism has long presumed an opposition between "man" and "society" (1993, 46). The poetry of witness that she proposes—more concrete than the type presupposed in Adorno's observation in "Commitment" that political poetry has infiltrated unexpected recesses of expression—depends on the notion of community, especially since the traces of witnessing surface in unconventional media. "Postcards, letters, and reports on the news—all these are communal forms," Forché observes, "ways of writing that stress the interpersonal aspects of poetry, the public side of literature. They underline the collective urgency that propels a literature of the social" (36). Further, she explains, poetry of witness requires sensitivity to the fact that it is often difficult to speak about social matters, let alone for the situations of others (37). The difficulty in achieving authorized expression of social concern, then, requires respect for all individuals. "The gap between self and other," Forché continues, "opens up the problem of relativism that has bedeviled modern philosophy, politics, and poetry. Respect for otherness seems always to release the specter of an infinite regress" (37).

Enzensberger overcomes the hazard of relativism that concerns Forché by means of authorial presence. For the sake of honesty, he openly questions the validity of the poet's autonomy through rhetorical gestures of self-effacement, reflexive contradiction, and protean change. Rhetorically, at least, these gestures of vanishing, qualification, and oscillation maintain ethical integrity since they acknowledge, unlike Forché, that he is *speaking as* an observer rather than *speaking for* someone else. This principle assumes that poets who diagnose a social flaw should acknowledge that their own view may be partial. Moreover, the collective urgency sensed in poetry of witness, which Forché locates in interpersonal, communal forms of writing, inheres in Enzensberger's cartographic practices. His mappings involve impersonal, public discourse, but they capture and stabilize for the lyric genre the public use of language as a tool for communication. Enzensberger references various forms of quasi-public communicative writing (telegrams, form letters, and electronic information). Some poems even equate dynamic poetry with our dependence on messaging media that quickly traverse time and space. The personal urgency and shared public purpose of these forms of discourse make the otherwise antithetical trajectories of personal and public exchanges mutually reinforcing.

For Forché in *Against Forgetting,* the distinction between communal subject matter (the events observed by poetry of witness) and the poem can prompt reading audiences to seek communal vision. She emphasizes the voicing of expression that reveals interpersonal, hence ultimately intimate, communication. Hers is a memory project to keep from losing what poetry can witness. By contrast, Enzensberger pursues a planned, intellectual regimen that stages poetry in a public arena in which the lyric genre's dynamic properties give it ethical value. His recent deliberations on ethnic tensions in Europe exemplify this practice.

In the opening section of "The Great Migration," Enzensberger notes the limitations of cartography in portraying complex phenomena. "A map of the world. Swarms of blue and red arrows condense into eddies before scattering in opposite directions again. . . . Such a weather chart looks pretty, but it cannot be accurately interpreted without previous knowledge," he writes. "It is abstract. It has to represent a dynamic process by static means. Only a film could show what is really going on. The normal state of the atmosphere is turbulence. The same is true of the settlement of the earth by human beings" (1994a, 103). Even prior to this work, Enzensberger had experimented with an amalgamation of cinematic and cartographic constructions for poetry. *Der Untergang der Titanic* (1978a), which includes one filmlike segment complete with directions for camera shots, contained disparate geographical sites, multicultural elements, and diachronic perspective. Later, the film-inspired documentary images, instructions for aural production, and quick splicings of text in "Die Frösche von Bikini" ("The Frogs from Bikini") served to question the ability of poetry as a linear medium to reflect dynamic events. Diagramming its city walk to overcome conventions of sequence, "Die Frösche von Bikini" connected introspective, private reflections with an external gaze across the globe. The more recent prose essays of *Civil Wars,* by contrast, analyze population movements and ethnic tensions as consisting of fundamentally unpredictable individual events (as in chaos theory). Viewed as a series of molecular mass movements in which "[c]apital tears down national barriers" (1994a, 111), the most powerful global force is economics rather than ideology, which now seems weakened.

In *Kiosk* (1995b), then, distinctions marked by time and space dissolve as the poet engages in what James Rolleston terms interpretive narrations (1987). The poem "Eine Begegnung der anderen Art" ("An Encounter of Another Kind") echoes selections in *Blindenschrift* (1964d), notably "Küchenzettel" and "Abendnachrichten," as the poet records disconnected bits of news:

> Die Gründe für das Massaker sind im 13. Jahrhundert zu suchen.
> Das las ich heute morgen beim Frühstück.
> Daß die Bienen nicht taub sind, sondern mit den Fühlern hören,
> verlautete aus Stanford in Kalifornien.
> Die Krawatten werden neuerdings wieder etwas breiter getragen;
> das bewies mir eine Postwurfsendung aus 33102 Paderborn.
>
> (1995b, 110)

> *The reasons for the massacre must be looked for in the 13th century.*
> *That's what I read this morning at breakfast.*
>
> *That bees are not deaf but hear with their antennae,*
> *was made known in Stanford, California.*
>
> *Neckties are now worn again a little wider;*
> *this was proved to me by a junk mail missive from 33102 Paderborn.*
>
> (1999d, 76)

This familiar triad—an anonymous land, America, and Germany—now maps the author's consciousness about where massacres are likely to occur, namely, everywhere. Awareness of these atrocities clashes with the mundane concerns that intrude on the thoughts of the poet. "Time," Enzensberger continues, quoting someone identified as a philosopher friend, "is not a parameter, but an operator." Limits are hence not constraining but indicate where dynamic possibilities or alternate visions exist. As if to illustrate this, a nearby cat seems to live in another universe (*ein anderes Universum*) than the poet. The poem ends with a gesture that acknowledges that his and the cat's worlds may occupy the same space, yet remain fundamentally unfathomable, "like the gods" (1995b, 111). That domestic vignette sums up a dilemma that had troubled German poets since the mid–twentieth century: How is it possible to write about things that matter when the poet is caught between responding to small or seemingly insignificant immediate experiences and large or distant events? Enzensberger's poetry from the 1990s provisionally attempts to find vision by mapping trajectories with movement across time and space.

Four poems in *Kiosk* (1995b) carry the title "Gedankenflucht," flights of thought (or perhaps fancy). Monologues of sorts in which the poet talks back and forth, with or without a separate interlocutor, the texts replay conversations, bemusedly ponder ideas, forget details, or lose the thread and grasp at tentative summaries.[31] Reminiscences, old causes, counterarguments, and memory lapses move the texts in unexpected directions. The first of the poems drifts from Helsinki and Las Palmas to Juba, Lubango, and Phnom Penh and voices a longing for continued oscillation (1999d, 127). The second broods on the desire for stability and the porous quality of thought (61). "Gedankenflucht (III)" uses a quotation to remind the reader that " 'the concept of totality exists in theory, not in life' " (1999d, 86). The poet, apparently talking to himself, decides,

> Du ziehst um, fliehst,
> vermischt dich mit dem,
> was der Fall ist.
>
> Auf Weiterungen
> heißt es gefaßt sein.
> Bei uns bleibt es nicht.[32]
> (1995b, 88)

> *You move house, flee,*
> *Mix with that which is the case.*
>
> *You'd better be prepared*
> *For complications.*
> *We don't remain what we are.*
> (1999d, 61)

Such preoccupations with constancy and change, consolidation and extension, with the subjective over and against the objective continue to motivate many of Enzensberger's poems from the 1980s and 1990s and into the twenty-first century. Thus, poetry, as Enzensberger handles it in his recent lyric work, is a dynamic medium that traverses immense geographical and temporal spaces, a medium in which the irresolution of content nestles in the containment that the brevity of verse form prescribes. His texts use free indirect discourse that combines mimesis and literariness. They carry readers through public and private spaces with a kind of cartographic force, a geographic display of rapid turns of thought.[33] This cognitive mapping affirms the author's presence by displaying his intellectual investments.

Enzensberger's recent poetry also attests that the lyric genre has again become the location where certain shared concerns of writers and intellectuals can be expressed; it shows as well that art must operate in more complex terms than the utopian/dystopian models of the 1970s and 1980s. Steeped in convention, the lyric genre in particular needs a pliable framework for addressing such matters as globalism, postmodernism, and identity. More than ever, poetry depends on the community in which the poet participates. Enzensberger's work in the lyric genre from the 1990s suggests that the poem need not move in the direction of either explicit politics or esoteric speech to achieve such grounding. While German poetry, like its American counterpart, has been substantially changed by experimental verse and language poetry in the 1990s,[34] Enzensberger's recent exploration of the writerly medium is directed toward making it accessible to readers through the response intellect and senses make to poetical texts.

Modes of Reflection: Toward a Poetics of Postmodernism and Late Style

At one time Enzensberger's penchant for movement, withdrawal, disappearance, and radical change (which Karla Lydia Schultz has perceptively analyzed in his works through the 1980s) seemed to celebrate dystopian anarchy (Schultz 1986, 202). His gestures of effacement take on different significance in the 1990s. Even Enzensberger has openly identified with the perception that he is protean. "Der fliegende Robert," the penultimate text in *Die Furie des Verschwindens* (1980a), builds on this persona. The title *Der Fliegende Robert* further graced a collection of Enzensberger's poetry and prose pieces, whose book jacket depicts the painting *Liberty or Death* by Jean-Baptiste Regnault, a winged figure advancing through the clouds between a female and a black-cloaked skeleton. In *Zukunftsmusik* (1991c), *Kiosk* (1995b), and *Leichter als Luft* (1999e), it is not just physical changes of position or conceptual leaps that are recorded in the poems but also lapses in memory. Here the perambulations are characteristic of a late style of writing in which quirks of recollection, and even mental gaps, become a virtue, for this forgetfulness creates opportunities for reexamining subjects from multiple perspectives.[35]

The wandering mind gains the freedom simply to discard logic if illogical thinking goes to the heart of the matter. Aphoristic wisdom can be dispensed along with casual observations. Disjunctures perceived between old ways and newfangled inventions—including communally operant novel media—open up space for the poet to comment about life in general terms. As the provocative title of a 1995 interview suggests ("I don't want to be the rag for cleaning the world"), Enzensberger has lately avoided bald pronouncements about political affairs;[36] yet this practice has by no means eviscerated his poems of their ethical force. Instead of labeling this stance resignation, we can ask whether these modes reflect a kind of late style where a connection exists between a diffuse handling of language and the drive toward a late-style aesthetic.

The notion of late style, which was elaborated by Theodor W. Adorno in writings about the music of Beethoven, focuses on shifts in the work of artists who have enjoyed long careers. Declaring that late style (*Spätstil*) is not the mere fact that a work has been produced late in life (a *Spätwerk*), Adorno discerns in Beethoven's advanced compositions a neutralization of cultural norms and a tendency toward fragmentation. "The power of subjectivity in late works," Adorno reasons, "is their ability to depart from art and shed its appearance (*Schein*)" (1994, 183). Linking the concept of late style to human life, he comments, "in other words, late style is self-consciousness of the triviality of the individual existence. Therein lies the relationship of the late style to death" (1994, 233). Rudolf Arnheim enlarges on Adorno's concept by pointing to the significance of late style in the visual arts. Arnheim observes, "One might say that the artist, from whose initiative all activity in the work ultimately springs, has delegated his resources of energy to the agents of his composition. And these agents behave as though they were acting on their own inherent impulses" (1978, 154–55). Further, Edward Said relates late style to the problem of exile (see Lawrence 1997, 15–24). The abandonment of cultural conventions, the dispersion of artistic energy into the medium itself, and the contemplation of exilelike detachment noted by Adorno, Arnheim, and Said with respect to late-style works—such characteristics mark Enzensberger's recent poetry.

"Die Verwechselung" ("The Mix-Up") from *Zukunftsmusik* exemplifies senility-like forgetfulness (1991c, 68–69). The reader encounters in this rambling monologue poem a speaker who starts off by reminding her interlocutor of a time they stayed in Prague. The woman tries to place her memories relative to history, flitting through time frames from the autumn when the Berlin Wall came down (1989) to a crisis in the Gulf (circa 1990), complaining to her listener of the period's humidity, so intense it almost chilled her. She reminisces that they watched ice-skaters and, on another occasion, that she needed to get medicine at a pharmacy on a Sunday in July. Seemingly random elements of the hotel decor (the scent of hay, stag antlers in the hall) punctuate the poem. Outbursts of anger toward her listener pepper the text ("betrogen hast du mich"; "faß mich bloß nicht an"; "du verwechselst mich wohl"; and "laß mich wenigstens ausreden" ["you've deceived me"; "don't touch me"; "you're mixing me up"; and "at least let me finish talking"]). As in Williams's "Last Words of My English Grandmother," the poem concludes with a curt dismissal, the declaration that the relationship has ended. It is a bitter finale, yet one that shows a respect for the endearing if irascible woman instead of an antagonistic parody, as was often the case for eccentric protagonists in Enzensberger's early verse.

One memory lapse from "Die Verwechslung" foregrounds especially well the radical synthesis of personal, literary, and political elements that occurs in the poem. The protagonist has great difficulty in recalling the name of the Prague hotel where they stayed. "Orlik, Horlik, something with *k*," she mutters. Finally, she stumbles on the name, exclaiming, "I've got it, it was called Odradek, / what, the hotel" (1991c, 68–69). That hotel has a label identical to that of a thing in Franz Kafka's short story "Die Sorge des Hausvaters" ("The Cares of a Family Man"). Odradek— Kafka opens his narrative with a futile etymology of the word—is an object come alive whose mode of existence the author finds difficult to determine. Something like a star-shaped bobbin, Kafka's Odradek is exceedingly mobile: it moves from the attic to the stairway or entry hall; sometimes it even disappears for months at a time, but it always returns (Kafka 1974, 139). Finally, Kafka's exasperated narrator asks whether Odradek will always be with him, and indeed with generations to come, outliving him, a painful thought (1974, 140). In Enzensberger's "Die Verwechslung," Odradek— associated with perpetual instability, with memory, and ultimately with writing or history—is something vaguely remembered. And in the final lines, the speaker returns to this name with a vengeance directed against the poet/listener:

> . . . Herrgottnochmal,
> hör endlich auf damit, mit deinem Heu und deinem Gedächtnis,
> von wegen Odradek, jetzt, wo es zu spät ist, ja, meinetwegen,
> ja, du hast recht, das war damals, das ist vorbei.
>
> (Enzensberger 1991c, 69)

. . . For God's sake,
cut it out already, with your hay and your memory,
and that bit about Odradek, now, when it's too late, sure, for all I care,
yes, you're right, that was then, it's all past.

Though confusion overcomes this woman, her wild ramblings connect mental tangents, merging Kafka's and Enzensberger's Odradek.

Such artful conflation blurs historical dates, brackets the poem's ramblings between the prewar Prague of Kafka and the post–cold war world, and sums up nearly a century of events. While the female protagonist has lost her grasp of chronology, "Die Verwechselung" finds its own moorings in the frame of twentieth-century European history, suggesting that even at the start of the twenty-first century we have not yet left the past behind. In much the same way, "Zukunftsmusik," the final piece in the collection, reminds readers of the postwar epoch through the reference we have already noted in chapter 4 to *Zunkuftsmusik* (1950) by Maria Luise Kaschnitz. For Kaschnitz, hope existed for a better world; Enzensberger's formulation of futurity in *Zunkuftsmusik* is spare, indeed postapocalyptic (cf. Berger 1999). Seemingly distanced from political and physical realities, Enzensberger's poem holds up for us a sort of black-and-white postwar image to prove the future's ambiguity and adumbrate the contingency of the poet in relation to time.

This late-style diachronic webbing continues in *Kiosk* (1995b), where wandering thought (associated with the mental ramblings of the elderly that we observed in *Zukunftsmusik*) helps describe a transnational, postmodern culture dominated by new media and consumerism. Juxtapositions of remote events with immediate observer perceptions connect the far and near in *Kiosk,* producing both unconventional mental associations that facilitate insight and a map of the poet's very restless mind. "Abgesehen davon" ("Aside from That"; originally published in *Monatshefte* in 1982), for example, describes a scene in the Washington Square area of New York City from different vantage points to contrast the perspectives gained. The text briefly portrays "the limping caretaker" (who works at an institute for medieval manuscripts and reportedly has suspicious origins in Bukowina), "the pregnant black woman" (who wears earphones), and "the gallbladder patient" (who is looking for a three-room apartment for his butterfly collection). These grotesques are locked in self-isolating behaviors. "If you can't see beyond that, / you're no theoretician," the poem comments. But then, contemplating the space opened by distance, the poem notices that the larger the perspective, the smaller everything becomes (1995b, 52). It concludes with the caution that explanations detached from actual motivations, especially from the question of where the "I" or ego is, resemble the motions of an ungainly Goodyear blimp rising above a water tank located on the roof of a nearby building. Resisting the impulse to privilege either the micro- or macroscopic perspective, the poem asks how capricious details expose the need for explanations—and how explanations potentially suppress illuminating particulars.[37]

"Altes Europa" ("Old Europe") compares and contrasts among three figures—"a fat magician from Guinea," "a small wiry dealer in gigantic sneakers," and "the old Bosnian woman." These geographically marked personages represent a new multicultural society mapped onto a terrain of tradition. Old European elements decorate the places the protagonists haunt: a bakery identified by its warm scent and gold pretzel sign, the Graubrüdergasse and wall near the Church of the Holy Spirit. The observer seems to have forgotten the significance of these sites. The poem asks parenthetically "(Who were the Grey Brothers?)" and even puzzles "(Who was the Holy Ghost?)" (1995b, 17). The woman from Bosnia sits on a bench near the "Portal of the House of the Elephant, built 1639." The name deftly alludes to the venerated Hotel Elephant in Weimar, a location visited by Goethe and other famous German writers. This writerly sleight of hand ironically insinuates that the vagaries of contemporary European identity feed nostalgia for a stable, historical past. The rhetorical questions that punctuate the text remind us that the old order has become unintelligible to many who inhabit the present.

Other poems in *Kiosk* similarly reflect on German immigration issues. "Privilegierte Tatbestände" ("Privileged Facts") uses anaphoric construction to condemn acts of racist violence. With formal restraint, the text lists acts that are forbidden, adding each element to a core sentence, "Es ist verboten, Personen in Brand zu stecken" (1995b, 10), or "It is forbidden to set persons on fire." Legalistically restating German laws, the poem censures neoconservative arson attacks on foreign residents. A note about the text instructs readers that all translations of the text shall be modified to include the relevant national laws of the audience and a footnote acknowledging the author's wishes (11).

This tense, legalistic language also shapes "Der Krieg, wie" ("The War, Like"), which shows transnationalism in terms of communication, commerce, and technology. War, the text tells us, glitters like a broken beer bottle at the bus stop next to the home for the aged, rustles like a ghost-written speech at a peace conference, or flickers like a television screen across somnambulistic faces. These images evocatively mirror other historical events from the twentieth century — the beer hall birth of Nazism, the oft-repeated futility of intellectualized posturing about peace, and the horrifying nightly news. Lest the reader assume that war is something distant and metaphoric, the poem constructs three tight stanzas that compare immediate events in Germany and distant conflicts:

> Er riecht wie der Stahl der Maschinen im Fitness-Studio
> wie der Atem des Leibwächters auf dem Flughafen
>
> Er röhrt wie die Rede des Vorsitzenden
> Er bläht sich wie die Fatwa im Munde des Ajatollah
>
> Er zirpt wie das Videospiel auf der Diskette des Schülers
> Er funkelt wie der Chip im Rechenzentrum der Bank
> (1995b, 8)

> *It smells like the steel of the apparatus in fitness clubs*
> *like the bodyguard's breath at the airport*
>
> *It blows like the chairman's speech*
> *It inflates like the fatwa in the Ayatollah's mouth*
>
> *It chirps like the video game on the schoolboy's disk*
> *It sparkles like the chips at the bank's computer centre*
> (1999d, 4)

Each case argues that the borderless commerce that has fed luxurious standards of living has brought war all the closer to our own backyards. Airline flight, media reporting, and electronic technologies have collapsed the borders that once neatly divided peace from conflict, political discourse from religious fervor, and children's games from financial speculation. What threatens us is no longer an unidentifiable substance that gradually leeches out into the world like the dangerous element in Enzensberger's "An Alle Fernsprechteilnehmer" from *Landessprache* (1960d). That hazard mercifully required an occasion of contact for infection to occur, which kept it just outside the cozy world of readers. Now, Enzensberger shows us that writing and global community operate instantaneously; mankind has leveled distinctions among the languages of public speech (rhetoric), video games (play), and data banks (information), but we have lost reassuring safety. The poem "Kiosk" takes the reader into the street, past all the sites in a teeming, urban setting to a newsstand where three sisters "offer . . . murder poison war to their nice customers for breakfast." Acknowledging life's vicissitudes, the poet admits that he, too, likes to shop at the Fates' (1999d, 7).

Then in *Leichter als Luft* (1999e), Enzensberger registers the interpretation of these linguistic-economic, transnational forces. "Länderlexikon" ("Atlas") tersely catalogs guerrilla wars and greets their casualties with feigned indifference. "Weltmarkt" ("World Market") broods on the flow of souvenirs, killer bees, and car bombs in our borderless, insatiable, consumer-driven world. Enzensberger looks back at the Vietnam era—when world politics became so murky—to call Richard Nixon "the plague-sick man" ("Nach dem Rücktritt des Präsidenten R.M.N." [1999e, 13]), flies across the globe ("Hong Kong 1997," "Terminal B, Abflughalle," "Albedo," "Hotel Caesar Palace," and "Die Verspätung"), and pauses with "In Jerusalem" to think about a bloody, insurmountable conflict over apparently ordinary stones.

Moving into the domain of eschatology, the poet in *Leichter als Luft* embraces mortality in "Abschiedsgruß an die Astronauten" ("Farewell to the Astronauts"), where he resolves to hold himself to promises that are more certain than fantastic intergalactic adventures: "Earth to earth / and dust to dust" (1999e, 113). "Arme Kassandra" ("Poor Cassandra") mixes a fatalism with gallows humor to comment that now we can see in the late night news that the prophetess was right with her dire predictions (30). "Das Kleingedruckte" ("The Fine Print") ironically reminds readers that the fine print on product packaging always exempts manufacturers from warranty guarantees in cases determined to be "an Act of God" (78). The eponymous "Leichter als Luft" comments that many things—helium, smoke, zeppelins, and what remains of us after death—are lighter than air (37–38). Its sagacious moralizing accepts mortality with composure.

"Die Grablegung" ("The Entombment") from *Kiosk* seems to sum up many feelings about fatedness, both fateful encounters that prompt insight and the awareness of mortality bound up in the notion of fate. Its title emulates that of the penultimate scene in Goethe's *Faust* and Hamletesque monologue; the poem enjoys moments of irony as it broods about the shortness of life. Asking what our mortal shell is, it delivers its own serious and witty rejoinders, answering that the individual is "the human personality, according to the Human Resources chiefs" (1999d, 129). Finally the text waxes poetic on the subject of what essence transcends the fragile body and tries to account for the psyche, id, ego, and superego:

Der Schmetterling,
der sich aus diesem Gedrängel
erheben soll,
gehört einer Art an,
von der wir nichts wissen.

(1995b, 129)

The butterfly which is to rise
from this very mixed lot
belongs to a species
about which nothing is known.

(1999d, 88)

The butterfly seems to echo "Selige Sehnsucht" by Goethe, which compares the longing of the lover with the drivenness of a winged creature (*Schmetterling*) attracted to a candle. Goethe's poem commands the butterfly to pursue its yearnings, urging, "And as long as you do not have this / this: "die and become!" / You are only a sad guest on the dark earth" (Goethe 1994, 24–25)[38]

Mapping the contours of the psyche and personality, Enzensberger hints at the existence of a utopian vision with a symbol of the soul, a hypothetical butterfly. In the end this vision is withheld not through a dystopian gesture but through speculation that leaves this last element of identity in a place yet to be imagined. "All perceiving is also thinking, all reasoning is also intuition, all observation is also intention," Rudolf Arnheim writes in *Art and Visual Perception* (1954, vii). Both *Kiosk* and *Leichter als Luft* practice "Geschichtsklitterung" (a biased account of history that combines perception and intention), as the title of a section from *Kiosk* calls it. In Enzensberger's late poetry, which is rich in palpable late-style signs of individual subjectivity and openly acknowledged mortality, the capacities to notice, think, and experience become the language that creates the identity that the poet uses to meet the ethical complexity of the contemporary world. The afterword to his literary anthology *Eine literarische Landkarte* (*A Literary Map*) speaks about how the gradual formation of a network of names, projects, languages, and places constitutes his work as an author (1999 [ed.], 388–89). Enzensberger characterizes this map as intensely personal: "More than a map of my interests, my predilections, my sympathies, I do not have to offer" (389).

Conclusion

At the end of the twentieth century, poetry, Enzensberger reminds us, appears perhaps to be an old and perhaps marginalized medium. Poised between public and private domains, the lyric genre seems at best a paradoxical thing, in ways that are eloquently adumbrated in "Altes Medium" ("Old Medium") from Enzensberger's recent collection of poems, *Kiosk:*

> Was Sie vor Augen haben,
> meine Damen und Herren,
> dieses Gewimmel,
> das sind Buchstaben.
> Entschuldigen Sie.
> Entschuldigen Sie.
> Schwer zu entziffern,
> ich weiß, ich weiß.
> Eine Zumutung.
> Sie hätten es lieber audiovisuell,
> digital und in Farbe.
>
> Aber wem es wirklich ernst ist
> mit *virtual reality,*
> sagen wir mal:
> Füllest wieder Busch und Tal,
> oder: Einsamer nie
> als im August, oder auch:

Die Nacht schwingt ihre Fahn,
der kommt mit wenig aus.

Sechsundzwanzig
dieser schwarz-weißen Tänzer,
ganz ohne Graphik-Display
und CD-ROM,
als Hardware ein Bleistiftstummel—
das ist alles.

Entschuldigen Sie.
Entschuldigen Sie bitte.
Ich wollte Ihnen nicht zu nahe treten.
Aber Sie wissen ja, wie das ist:
Manche verlernen es nie.

(1995b, 96–97)

What you see in front of you,
ladies and gentlemen,
this swarm
is letters.
Please bear with me.
Please bear with me.
Hard to decipher,
I know, I know.
Too much to ask.
You'd rather have it audio-visual,
digital and in colour.

But anyone really serious about
virtual reality,
for instance:
Shall I compare thee . . .
or: April is the cruelest
month, or else:
He that is down needs fear no fall,
can make do with very little.

Twenty-six
of these black-on-white dancers,
quite without graphic display

and CD-ROM,
for hardware the stub of a pencil—
that's all.

My apologies.
Accept them, please.
The last thing I wanted was to make excessive demands.
But you know how it is:
some of us never learn—or unlearn.

(1999d, 67)

The opening lines of the text cast the poem as a public lecture delivered in didactic tone—a slightly embarrassing circumstance for the author, who repeatedly apologizes for appearing too forward. This self-deprecating gesture sets up a careful alternation between the advances of the speaker and his withdrawal from any confrontation with the audience. That ironic pattern of affirmation by effacement builds to the final line in "Altes Medium," where the verb *verlernen* (to unlearn) underscores by negation the pedagogical, hence enlightening, intentions of the text.

For while the poet confesses that he cannot renounce his old habit, the reader is taught in spite of himself or herself to appreciate poetry. Already in the first stanza, this process of education begins with a highly sensual yet rudimentary description of the print media. The black and white letters that comprise words are represented as a difficult-to-decipher throng of shapes that the poet contrasts with the crisp presentation of materials in electronic, Technicolor formats (cf. Eich 1981, 13). Such symmetrical oppositions provide "Altes Medium" with a deceptively simple structure of dichotomies: old versus new, analogical language versus digitally displayed information bits, and monochrome verses synesthetic presentation. This is the rhetoric of aporia, which hesitates between two incompatible alternatives that, as we will see, are not as stable as they initially appear.

Already in the second stanza, the sharp dichotomies begin to blur. Here the distinction between the tools or medium used to present a message and the message itself is critical, for the poet asserts that the best means to achieve virtual reality is, not surprisingly, poetry. The examples from Johann Wolfgang Goethe, Gottfried Benn, and Andreas Gryphius applaud the semantic richness of poetic language and allude to a literary heritage important for Enzensberger. All three authors are included in *Das Wasserzeichen der Poesie* (1985). Goethe, elsewhere quoted abundantly in Enzensberger's poetry, figures in *Nieder mit Goethe: Eine Liebeserklärung* (*Down with Goethe: A Declaration of Love* [1995c]). Benn, to whom Enzensberger was indebted in his early career for direction in handling colloquial language and conceptualizing the poetic process, surfaces again as a referent after *Die Furie des Verschwindens* (1980a). For Gryphius, Enzensberger penned an afterword for a 1962 edition of poems (Gryphius 1962).

Representing influences that cut across Enzensberger's career, the passages quoted also set forth alternate foundational clusters for poetry. "An den Mond" by Goethe (1974), one of the most famous poems written in the German language, evokes a profound experience of nature as a sublime force that animates tactile and auditory senses. Written in rhymed verse, its intensely rhythmical language has attracted several composers to set this poem to music as an art song. Benn's much anthologized "Einsamer nie" (1960a), likewise a rhymed composition, broods on the relationship between art and solitude. This subject matter foregrounds the affective sources of poetry. Finally, the lines quoted from "Abend" by Gryphius (1980, 118) appear in a sonnet that contemplates mortality, where they are made more urgent by other phrases that acknowledge the fleetingness of life ("Der schnelle Tag ist hin" and "diß Leben kommt mir als eine renne bahn"). Whereas the poem by Gryphius culminates in a prayerful request for God's help, the phrase quoted by Enzensberger seems to beg for the modern interpretation that the night brings intense psychological activity and that flags are political symbols. Artful rhetoric combined with the text's mention of elements from the natural world connect the entire stanza with a conception of poetry as a private response to experience and of the lyric genre as aesthetically pure.

As such, poetry is profoundly incompatible with the electronic hardware mentioned in the next stanza. A startling, postmodern collision results between what can be expressed and the inexpressible, the messily interactive computer and the pristine poem, and above all between the trivial and the sublime. For while a few small handwritten letters may seem less promising than glittering technology, they are for Enzensberger the reliable tools for counterfeiting, far more capable than their electronic cousins of representing the world. True language is not programmed, predictable, or automatic; rather, like a dancer, it performs, moves, and lives. Thus the obsequious apologies in the first and last stanza are belied by the sheer existence of the poem, its ostensible representation of itself as a speech, not to mention the stature of Enzensberger as a poet. Self-effacing, the text repositions poetry as a still-viable form of art.

In examining poems by Enzensberger, I have sought to discern ways in which contemporary poetry can be read in connection with historical context, intellectual debates, and aesthetic conventions without making poems mere illustrations for trends. Clearly Enzensberger devises solutions that respond to the particularly contested status of the lyric genre in the German setting, where it has had variable cultural value since 1945. At times promoted as a malleable art form that could respond to ideological or aesthetically programmatic demands, poetry there just as frequently languished when it was perceived to be ineffective. Enzensberger reminds us, however, that the lyric genre is always both a public and a private medium, an art that should ultimately transcend tendentious demands.

My premise has been that when Enzensberger's poetic texts display a shift in position or technique, this move reflects an intentional coming to terms with the extraliterary context that gives rise to poems. This fact does not make the lyric genre a compensatory art that only follows the lead of other disciplines. Instead of a model of secondariness, I have proposed that German poetry since World War II has maintained its vitality through a symbiotic relationship with companion discourses. For Enzensberger, debate about the lyric genre's demise signals a rejuvenation that occurs when values shift or problems are displaced into alternate forums. To read such developments in his work, and that of other contemporary poets, we need to open poetry analysis—to a greater extent than has yet occurred in studies of German literature—to parallel discourses and heuristic, craft-related practices developed by poets as they engage with such discussions.

Rejecting the notion of originality as a delusion of modernism (1999c, 392), Enzensberger has employed some of the most brilliant inventions of the modernist avant-garde to develop forms of expression to address these poets' issues. His work has grown increasingly complex and postmodern in character and more focused on the implications of such concepts as voice, intellect, spontaneity, and sitedness for the lyric genre. Changes in the style, and hence voice, of Enzensberger's early poems were related to his openness to international poetry in both ideological and aesthetic terms. Critical theory shaped his poetic response to fundamental changes in the social and cultural fields. This theoretical bent was gradually augmented, amended, and tempered through Enzensberger's interest in chaos theory and creative spontaneity. His newest poetic texts foreground the relationships between authorial presence and questions of ethical integrity, national identity, and heightened globalization. As the specific interpretations show, Enzensberger's shifts in position are prepared for by long phases of gestation; his poetic techniques are both more introspectively self-referential and extrovertedly directed toward shaping the response of readers than has generally been assumed. That reader response always reshapes the text as well. After the ocean liner has sunk in *Der Untergang der Titanic,* the survivors rejoice at the prospect that they will finally be able to set the record straight and to edit the text of the now dead poet (1978a, 110).

Nature itself makes revisions in "Vom Leben nach dem Tode" (1995b, 128). After the collapse of "civilization," life begins to regenerate itself from tiny insects, sores, and seeds that start to patch over the wreckage. "A strangely sublime spectacle," the poet comments, "but far and wide there is no Piranesi to populate this Angkor Wat with shepherds and cavaliers" (128). Man-made work, the poem tells us, is different from organic life. A work's continued existence cannot be assumed but must always be reasserted, however "natural" it seems to a committed modernist that a particular kind of art exist. This sense of art's contingency and of its possible renewal has characterized Enzensberger's poetic work from the outset, authorizing many of the poetic maneuvers he has made. Such continual reflection upon the status of his own work insistently reminds the reader in many ways that "[a] poem intended to be, and to remain, open must make the critique of itself as part of its movement. It participates in the twilight of which it speaks and must finally vanish in it if it is not to give itself the lie" (Enzensberger 1994b, 89).

Notes

Introduction

1. An overview of the author's work can be gained from Lau 1999, which was preceded by Falkenstein 1977. The major collections of reviews, critical essays, and documentation about Enzensberger's career are Schickel 1970; R. Grimm 1984; Dietschreit and Heinze-Dietschreit 1986; and R. Wieland 1999.

2. The concept of the consciousness industry is detailed in Enzensberger 1964e.

3. For a description of the major American poetry schools, see, in particular, Hoffman 1979.

4. These studies include Fredman 1990 and Monroe 1987.

Chapter I

The title of this chapter echoes the subtitle of Jonathan Monroe's *A Poverty of Objects: The Prose Poem and the Politics of Genre* (1987). The lucid discussion Monroe supplies of the socioaesthetic tensions at work in the formation of this genre have helped me refine my analysis of Enzensberger's poetic project.

1. Examples of triads are to be found throughout Enzensberger's poetry and essays, although the poem "Trigonometrischer Punkt" from *Blindenschrift* (1964d) draws attention most explicitly to the existence of the device in its title. Enzensberger makes varied use of this formula, which derives from both the rhetorical tradition and its contemporary variants. Wilpert (1969) explains threefold expressions in relation to rhetorical figuration and sacred conventions as conveying particular pathos (191) and further identifies the rhetorical device of *Trikolon* as an effect cultivated widely during the baroque period (802–3). While in Enzensberger's essays the triads do often serve to focus the emotive qualities of an argument, in his lyric poetry their chief virtue lies in their effectiveness in mapping out the breadth of subject matter treated in the text. The most immediate contemporary model for the triadic structure in *Blindenschrift* is the poetry of Günter Eich. Eich adumbrates the trigonal construction in his poem "Der große Lübbe-See" from *Zu den Akten* (1964), which speaks of "the scaffolding of the trigonometric point" created by lines of migrating birds from whom the poet seeks orientation (quoted in Eich 1981, 37). Enzensberger more recently has evoked triadic concepts in his children's book *Der Zahlenteufel* (1997a), where his discussion of mathematics in terms approachable to younger audiences coins the term "triangle numbers" to illustrate regularities in special numerical sequences.

2. For a discussion of texts by Enzensberger that focus on controversy in political and literary forums, see R. Grimm 1984, 148–68. In addition, Enzensberger's

"Die Schnecken" (1963b, 195–98) and the poems "Einunddreissigster Gesang" in *Der Untergang* (1978a, 107–12), "Die Frösche von Bikini" in *Die Furie* (1980a, 37–52), and "Der und der hat das gesagt" in *Zukunftsmusik* (1991c, 20–21) depict intellectual infighting.

3. In selecting examples for analysis, I have purposely reserved treatment of Enzensberger's essay "Gemeinplätze" (1968a), and the slogan "death of literature" that became associated with it, for chapter 3 in order to support a discussion of the context it shares with *Mausoleum* (1975).

4. While the lyric genre in its traditional form claims only a small portion of the publishing market in both the United States and Europe, quite a different picture emerges when the broad spectrum of texts, workshops, publications, and performances related to poetry is taken into account. Poetry slams, a proliferation of Internet sites for poems, and special festivals or events (such as the celebration of Poetry Month in April in the United States) have burgeoned since the early 1990s.

5. My consideration of poetic canon is informed by the work of Guillory (1993) and Golding (1995). Guillory identifies three types of matrices (the compositional, generic, and linguistic) as significant in the formation of canon (1993, 87–92). The focus in this chapter is the generic matrix, which defines the institutional context surrounding literary works. Golding draws attention to the different roles poets, anthologies, and the academy have played in determining poetic canon in the United States. While aware of the structural differences that characterize the literary industry in its broadest sense in the United States and Germany, I have found it useful to incorporate evidence of developments in these three areas into my analysis of Enzensberger's poetry because his activities have not been confined to one or another of these fields.

6. See Zimmer 1988 and Schnell 1993, 1–65.

7. Discussion of time is, of course, by no means confined to the postwar. Staiger is preceded in this respect by philosopher Martin Heidegger's *Sein und Zeit* (1927).

8. "The three concepts past, present, future are far from adequate since they obviously contain a traditional prejudice against time" (Staiger 1991, 190).

9. Emphasizing the role context plays in later understandings of programmatic statements about literature, Zimmer cites a noteworthy statement made by Johannes R. Becher during the war years. Becher's words taken at face value seem only to long for traditional verse; as Zimmer points out, however, his audience was comprised of writers in exile in the Soviet Union, for whom the remarks would have been a general appeal for the autonomy of poetry rather than a blueprint for aesthetic conservatism.

10. When Kayser asserts that poets need to learn *Handwerkliches* (1946, 7), he means that they must acquire formal techniques.

11. See Enzensberger 1961, 119–27. Scholarly investigations of the relation between this dissertation and the author's poetry have concluded that Enzensberger's account of Brentano closely reflects his own writerly practices. An overview of

critical literature on this subject and a lengthy discussion of the dissertation are provided by Dietschreit and Heinze-Dietschreit (1986, 1–8). Further details about Enzensberger's selection of Brentano as a dissertation topic (he reportedly wished to investigate Hitler's rhetoric) and affinities in the construction of poetic identity between the two authors are offered by Lau (1999, 29–33). While previous scholarship (Schwab-Felisch 1963; Bohrer 1970; Linder 1975; Korte 1989) has focused on Enzensberger's use of the concept *Entstellung* (a montage technique of "deformation"), coined in his interpretation of Brentano's poetic language and on his affinities to romantic poetry, my analysis centers on aspects of the dissertation that express Enzensberger's disagreement with academic treatments of the lyric genre. In a later chapter, I return to the dissertation to elucidate Enzensberger's discussion of image complexes as a facet of Brentano's work and to explore his own cultivation of this technique.

12. Enzensberger defines *Entstellung* as "recourse from the already formed and prepared language to possibilities of the word not previously used. We call this procedure 'deformation' (*Entstellung*), because the word is wrested from the common arrangement in order to make it poetically newly available" (1961, 28).

13. The distinction between private and public forms of memory resembles the quarrel Adorno establishes between Valéry and Proust in his essay "Valéry Proust Museum." According to Adorno, Proust happily visited museums, which he regarded as a site for contemplation, while Valéry was made miserable by dead visions of the past. "For Valéry art is lost," Adorno observes, "when it has relinquished its place in the immediacy of life, in its functional context; for him the ultimate question is that of the possible use of the work of art" (1967b, 180). Thus Valéry has no interest in cultural conservation, Adorno argues, which after all has much to do with illusionistically preserving a constructed past. Proust, the connoisseur, was by contrast invigorated by his contemplative consumption of the past as well as moved to write fiction by his personal memories (Adorno 1967b, 180).

14. See Ledanff 1981 and Braun 1986 for the literary context of this aesthetic discussion and Melin 1992 concerning the transference of *Momentaufnahme* style to poetry by Brinkmann, Born, Sarah Kirsch, and other postwar poets.

15. Walter Höllerer traces the history of imagism in postwar German poetry to American origins in "Gedichte in den sechziger Jahren." Höllerer remarks, "He [Axel Schmidt, a poet] sees correctly that the blink-of-an-eye theories and moment poems by Pound and Hulme are among the foundations from which this development of the long poem in America took its starting point. The Whitman tradition of the unconcerned grand trajectory of speech was influenced and modified by them. Epiphany elements, elements of 'glimpses,' of the 'blinkings of an eye,' the 'fleeting glance' (in the theory of William Carlos Williams) create important prerequisites for the long poem" (1966, 379).

16. See also Braun 1986, 23–28.

17. Compare also the acclaimed photographic collection by Burri, *Die*

Deutschen, which in the most recent revised edition (1999) pairs images with poems by Enzensberger.

18. For further discussion, see Melin 1992, 86–89.

19. Poetry translation, which as a postwar literary phenomenon had a lasting influence on the evolution of German literature in the latter half of the twentieth century, will be discussed in further detail in the next chapter. For confirmation of the significance of efforts to legitimate German literature either through reliance on foreign models or by theoretical statements, see Wellershoff 1997. Wellershoff observes, "German postwar literature stood under a quite definite requirement to legitimate itself, it had to deal with Nazi injustice, the war, and for that reason it was, in a certain respect, a strongly moralizing, pathetic and didactic literature, which did not interest me at all."

20. The texts to be considered here document these trends as evidenced in major literary journals and monographs that appeared between 1945 and 1980. These materials include statements by poets and translators about their craft. The closing date for the discussion is based on the assessment that by the 1980s, translation had assumed a more neutral position in the context of literary debates, hence that statements after that point would have to be read in terms other than those applied in this analysis to elicit references to artistic autonomy that express postwar efforts to legitimate cultural production.

21. Discussion of *Museum der modernen Poesie* continues in the following chapter.

22. It lies beyond the scope of the present analysis to consider the nature of postwar reeducation programs in relation to the formation of attitudes about foreign literary works and translations. Concerning reeducation programs, see Schnell 1993, 84, and Schonauer 1969.

23. Schwedhelm 1947, 14–15. Schwedhelm's categories are not tied to a specific national context but rather address approaches taken by translators. As such, they closely resemble the discussion of this issue in a contemporary essay by McFarlane (1953).

24. Schwedhelm writes, "A people (*Volk*) whose intellectual life for over a decade circles only around itself in a forced hermetic enclosure, now feels the task and necessity of making up for the intellectual property that had eluded them by making it their own" (1947, 14).

25. Likewise, Bab justifies the selection criteria used to create his anthology of recent American verse as a matter of choosing "exclusively pieces that strongly addressed me on a personal level and thereby set into motion a force that is akin to the poetic one" (1953, 9).

26. For additional perspectives on translation from the vantage of poets who have worked as translators, see Honig 1985, Rabassa 1987, Weissbort 1989, and Belitt 1995. Systematic studies of translation theory and practice include Kloepfer

1967, Levy 1969, Wuthenow 1969, Holmes et al. 1970, Holmes 1978, Biguenet and Schulte 1989, Lefevere 1992, Schulte and Biguenet 1992, and Nägele 1997.

27. Enzensberger's contributions to the Hebrew and German edition of *David Rokeah* are another example of this kind of poetic translation. A further instance is found in the work of Kruntorad, one of the translators for *Museum*, who was in one case mistakenly identified as a translator of works from the Hungarian. As a result, he later became involved in a collaborative translation project for which he worked with someone who could supply a rendering of the original text into German that formed the basis of his work. His comments concerning this experience appear in Kruntorad 1969.

28. Prominent poet-translators included but were not limited to Erich Arendt, Bachmann, Bobrowski, Volker Braun, Celan, Domin, Fried, Hagelstange, Heissenbüttel, Hermlin, Rühmkorf, and Sachs.

29. "In the process of translation I feel as if two beings approach each other: as I open myself, the foreign being meets me and takes off its visor. It strips itself of its visible body and reveals the body of its soul, its inner, invisible form. This I seize and carry in a waking dream through the twilight of no-man's land, were the metamorphosis occurs, over into the visiblity of my own language domain" (Meyer-Clason 1966, 166).

30. See also Kirsch's publications in Jähnichen et al. 1973 and Kirsch 1979.

31. The significance of Friedrich's theories in relation to Enzensberger's work receives further discussion in the next chapter.

32. Evidence of the renaissance in German poetry includes Stephan 1998 and the publication of *Luchterhand Jahrbuch der Lyrik, Frankfurter Anthologie, ProE, Das Gedicht,* and *manuskripte.* See H. Hartung 1991 and Enzensberger 1999c.

33. Compare also Enzensberger 1971c. Enzensberger comments, "It is a superstition that writers have to compose their own texts. I really regard that as a bourgeois superstition. Behind it there lurks a presumption about originality that I find extremely questionable" (76).

34. It is not clear why Enzensberger chose to publish under the pseudonym of Andreas Thalmayr. For further discussion of *Das Wasserzeichen der Poesie,* however, see chapter 4.

35. For bibliographies of Enzensberger's translations, see Estermann 1984, Dietschreit and Heinze-Dietschreit 1986, and R. Wieland 1999.

36. The dialogue maintains the repartee by using parlando tone, as in this exchange between antagonists concerning the merits of a sonnet that Alceste presents as his own, which is actually Friedrich Rückert's "Amaryllis" from *Ein Sommer auf dem Lande* (1812):

> *Oronte:* Ein bißchen bieder, und ein bißchen out!
> *Alceste:* An Ihrer Stelle wär ich nicht so laut.

Oronte: Auf jeden Fall hat mein Gedicht mehr power.
Alceste: Ihr Eigenlob steht fest wie eine Mauer.
(Enzensberger 1979[ed.], 29–30)

37. The most comprehensive overviews of German poetry in the latter half of the twentieth century are Rühmkorf 1962, Wodtke 1968, Demetz 1970, Theobaldy and Züricher 1976, Knörrich 1978, Drews 1980, Emmerich 1981, and Schäfer 1981. See also Schumacher 1981b, Weissenberger 1981, Ryan 1982, Demetz 1986, Wittstock 1989, and Korte 1989.

38. The phrase "death of literature" is associated with Enzensberger's essay "Gemeinplätze" (1968a).

39. Schödlbauer's chronology of modern poetry follows the lead established by Friedrich and Enzensberger in stating that "modern lyric poetry is Baudelaire's invention" (171).

40. It should be noted that Rutschky places his recollection of these events before they actually occurred, following "Gemeinplätze, die Neueste Literatur betreffend," which appeared in 1968.

41. Hartung's assessment must be regarded in part as a reflection of his own considerable contributions as a mediator of poetry, including the important anthology *Luftfracht* (1991), which he edited.

42. The quip can be read as a backhanded remark on the author's own status among these readerships, for despite his many visits to the United States and his fascination with that country, Enzensberger's reception there has remained less than the proportions commensurate with his international stature.

43. This formulation reiterates Enzensberger's statement in *Das Wasserzeichen* (1985), "If the number of producers determined things, poetry would be a mass medium" (V).

44. One such shift is registered in Enzensberger's 1962 essay, "Die Aporien der Avantgarde" (1976b, 113–80), which critiques aesthetic models of antagonistic revolt and delivers a plea for genuine innovation.

45. This is the effect, for example, of "Wieviel Literatur im Leben, wieviel Politik in der Poesie?" (1992).

46. This is not to say, however, that these recent monumental collections have been accepted without reservation. Stephan, for example, wryly pokes fun at the new aestheticism, as in "Lyrische Visite" (10), where he disparages the posturing self-irony of Schrott and other poets, quipping, "And so, one would like to add with a sigh, we awaken again in the arms of Hans Magnus Enzensberger" (1998, 154).

47. Although the literary relations depicted in the foregoing analysis have been somewhat one-sided in nature, it is interesting to note the number of Anglo-American poets—especially those associated with avant-garde experimentalism— with German connections, including Rosmarie Waldrop (a trained Germanist),

Tom Raworth (who had helped edit a posthumously published tribute to Gerhardt), Robert Creeley and Charles Olson (who corresponded with Gerhardt), Rita Dove (married to German author Fred Viebahn), and Jerome Rothenberg (one of the translators of Enzensberger's work). Contact among Fluxus artists also extended to poets. The absorption and questioning of American verse conventions (such as colloquial diction, techniques for the handling of line, and content areas) creates favorable conditions for the reception of German poetry on this side of the Atlantic.

48. Oleschinski's admonishment that poetry not be expected to function as a public performance may also be read as a reaction against the penchant of experimental authors for "text as event" aesthetics—in other words, a display of linguistic acrobatics. For a discussion of this, see Geist 1993. Compare further Hahn's "Meine Damen und Herren" from *Unerhörte Nähe,* a poem that positions the poet squarely in front of an audience, whom she provocatively and wittily addresses by declaring, "The poem, Madame, is not eau de cologne / for cold compresses to the heart, is not deodorant against the sweaty smell of angst" (1988, 64).

49. This piece, the subject of further analysis in the fourth chapter, was originally delivered as a speech to a meeting of the American Association of Teachers of German, a context that heightens the purpose of Enzensberger's remarks.

50. It should be noted that German scholars were initially reluctant to embrace the notion of postmodernism as relevant to aesthetic developments in German-speaking countries, although it has gained currency in the past decade. Writers, on the other hand, have appeared to be more receptive to this term, and, indeed, many examples of arguably postmodern literary techniques (fragmented narratives, pastiche, and temporal juxtapositions) surface in works written in German dating from the late 1970s.

51. This list does not include authors who experimented with rhyme such as Gerhardt, Hahn, Krolow, and Rühmkorf.

52. For a discussion of new media and poetry see E. Grimm 1997.

53. For a discussion of the critique Adorno supplies of poetry's communicative potential, see further Hohendahl 1995, 235–36.

Chapter 2

1. In using the terms "plain style" and "discursive mode," I am relying on Pinsky's discussion of Modern American poetry in *The Situation of Poetry* (1976). Pinsky identifies two competing approaches to the craft of verse in American poetry, plain and rhetorical style, the latter of which he aligns with the discursive mode. These concepts elucidate Enzensberger's poetry because they address his absorption of a particularly American style. Plain or unembellished style, as Pinsky observes, reduces language to its essentials with the intention of achieving more

authentic representation: "Strictly speaking, the ultimate goal of the nominalist poem is logically impossible. Language is absolutely abstract, a web of concepts and patterns; and if one believes experience to consist of unique, ungeneralizable moments, then the gap between language and experience is absolute. But the pursuit of the goal, or the effort to make the gap seem less than absolute, has produced some of the most remarkable and moving poetry in the language" (1976, 59). Discursive poetry, by contrast, he defines as "primarily neither ironic nor ecstatic. It is speech, organized by its meaning, avoiding the distances and complications of irony on one side and the ecstatic fusion of speaker, meaning, and subject on the other. The idea is to have all the virtues of prose, in addition to those qualities and degrees of precision which can be called poetic" (134).

2. Enzensberger, quite mindful of the precarious nature of his project of cultural renewal, pokes fun at it in a translation of a limerick by Edward Lear, writing about a critical man from Kaufbeuern who sardonically protests, "er wolle mitnichten / mit seinen Gedichten / das Bildungswesen erneuern" (1977 [trans.], 323).

3. For other discussions of Enzensberger's poetry, see Gutmann 1970, Reinhold 1971, Lohner 1978, Gutzat 1977, Zimmermann 1977, Stoffer-Heibel 1981, Colombat 1994, and Korte 1997. Dissertations on Enzensberger's poetry include Buckley 1975, Innerhofer 1980, Murphy 1992, Kolb 1993, and Hauptmann 1997.

4. See Trommler 1971, 1970, 1977; Korte 1989, 1–29; Schnell 1993, 67–70.

5. Consult further Höllerer 1959; Schonauer 1969, which discussed the attention given literature in newspapers, weekend supplements, reviews, and radio broadcasts in conjunction with the discovery of American literature; and Zuther 1965 for additional documentation concerning the role American literature played.

6. Quoted in Schnell 1993 is an editorial announcement from an early issue of the journal *Ulenspiegel* that states, "We request that our contributors please not send us any more poems. Or come look for us. We are almost lost, the poems have flooded us. Write prose instead of poetry!" (90).

7. The most authoritative accounts of German-American literary relations for the lyric genre are supplied by Galinsky (1972). Concerning this phase of reception, see also Höllerer 1959, L. Price 1966, Fleischmann 1973, and Schmitt-Kaufhold 1977. In a recent study that grew out of her dissertation, Mueller productively reexamines a wealth of materials related to the German postwar reception of American verse. Mueller concludes that a delayed interest in American verse became significant only after German audiences developed a need to explore these writings, following the mediative efforts of Gerhardt, Enzensberger, Höllerer, and Brinkmann. See Mueller 1999. My own analysis suggests that the reception accorded American verse was important already in the postwar years but strongly influenced by conditions affecting the lyric genre and poetic canon formation in general. This early reception, which occurred in part without the benefit of translations, was different in character and purpose from the reception that occurred after the mid-1950s, when well-crafted translations of poetry became more avail-

able. Mueller's interview with Enzensberger supports this analysis as the author comments, "I read a lot in the original English" (Mueller 1997, 205). In addition, I argue for an understanding of the later reception in relation to discourses about cultural and national identity that took hold around 1960. Concerning this phase of reception see also Jordan 1984 and H. Hartung 1994.

8. Of further note are the literary contacts established by Höllerer, who taught in the United States and initiated a series of literary colloquia in Germany, and Rose Ausländer's contacts with the American poet Marianne Moore during the war years. For a discussion of exchanges among Gerhardt, Olson, and Creeley, see Knape 1995, 11–15.

9. Note also that the American literary scene was at the same time being re-shaped by the expansion of universities and the appearance of numerous translations, according to Perloff (1998, 95).

10. The translations from *Museum* are my own and rely on the 1980 reprint edition; the 1960 edition's original afterword appears under the title "Nachwort."

11. Compare the oscillation between literary and intellectual cultures cited as characteristic of Enzensberger by Roberts (1996).

12. See Bender 1961, Holthusen 1970, R. Hartung 1960, Horst 1961, Krolow 1960, and Schmied 1961.

13. Lau correctly suggests that this poem is a fictive conversation with Benn and Williams (Lau 1999, 54).

14. The tone of this rhetoric comes through in the English translation, *Oswald Spengler's Today and Destiny: Vital Excerpts from the Decline of the West*, chapter 2, "The Life of Estates and Classes": "Cosmopolitanism is a mere waking-consciousness association of intelligentsias. In it there is a hatred of Destiny, and above all history as the expression of Destiny. . . . *Cosmopolitanism is literature* and remains literature—very strong in reasons; very weak in defending them otherwise than with more reasons, in defending them with the blood" (Spengler 1940, 233).

15. Comparable language appears in an article by Heuss (the then president of the Federal Republic of Germany), "German Character and History": "There are fools in Germany who have criticized this receptiveness toward foreign writers as a sign of wavering patriotism (whereas foreigners are always charging the Germans with excessive nationalism). In fact, it is a sign of active curiosity about the world and of a desire for intellectual enrichment" (1957, 108).

16. Working under the most dire of circumstances in a city that had been devastated by wartime bombings, Gerhardt founded a literary magazine, envisioned an ambitious series of translation volumes, kept up an active correspondence with American poets Robert Creeley and Charles Olson, and produced innovative experimental verse. Knape reads in Enzensberger's afterword to *Museum* an acknowledgment of Gerhardt's projects in his discussion of how poets should actively use the presented texts, although, as will be seen, the formulation likely had other sources as well. The unrealized publishing plan developed by Gerhardt before his

death incorporated more experimental poetry than came to be included in *Museum* (Knape 1995, 181). That the Freiburg circle was held in high regard by German poets can further be construed from a remark by Benn that poetry as an institution appeared moribund after the war, yet the few innovators included "several young Germans from the Freiburg circle" (1950, 202).

17. The piece is reminiscent of the story by Jorge Luis Borges known in English as "The Library of Babel"; Enzensberger was involved as an editor with publication of this work in Norwegian for the Borges edition *Labyrinter* (1964 [ed.]). Also thematically similar, however, is Canetti's description of the library in *Die Blendung* (1935). Finally, the notion of reproducibility brings to mind Benjamin's famous essay, "Das Kunstwerk im Zeitalter seiner technischen Reproduzierbarkeit" (1974a).

18. Concerning its importance see H. Hartung 1991, 4–5. Sartorius in "Schmuggler, Torwächter, Virtuose" adds, "I remember how in 1986 and 1987 I traveled frequently to East Berlin and heard from many young poets in the *Prenzlauer Berg* circle what a decisive impact *Museum* still had there, even 35 and 40 years after its appearance in the West" (1999, 207).

19. Enzensberger's remarks for the 1980 edition critique the Eurocentrism of his own anthology, as well as the "One World" outlook, which he attributes to American postwar ideology (1980b [ed.], 786).

20. Enzensberger's canon is followed by Lamping (1991) in *Moderne Lyrik,* whose account largely detaches a discussion of modern poetry from the political and social specifics that in part prompted the development of "modernism." It is thus seen as an aesthetic rather than a social formation.

21. See Huyssen 1995, 105–6. For further discussion of Friedrich's assumptions in relationship to Enzensberger, see R. Grimm 1998a.

22. It is interesting to note that Gadamer's *Wahrheit und Methode* also appears in 1960.

23. Enzensberger's approach to translation (both his techniques and choice of subjects) invites comparison with the efforts of Pound to transform poetry by looking to older or culturally remote literatures. See Perloff 1990, which summarizes Pound's legacy as the drive toward precise use of words, free-verse line, and "translation as the invention of the desired other" (122).

24. For an analysis of the literary sources for Benn's essay, see R. Grimm 1967.

25. The ambivalent attitude Enzensberger has toward Benn in this essay is characteristic of the response of German postwar authors who were at once attracted to Benn's brilliant poetic innovations and repulsed by his association with fascism. See Holbeche 1981 and Ryan 1980.

26. Compare Trommler's remark that Enzensberger objected to "faulen Traditionalismus" (lazy traditionalism) and sought a more constructive approach (1971, 60).

27. See R. Grimm 1984, 45. A further intriguing use of this trope exists in

Ransom 1968. The essay, which originally appeared in a 1938 collection, chastises scholars who show little feeling for literary works because they are chiefly concerned with historical studies: "The professors so engaged are properly curators, and the museum of which they have the care is furnished with the cherished literary masterpieces, just as another museum might be filled with paintings" (Ransom 1968, 339). With the advent of postmodernism, the notion of a museum has come to be associated with a store of dead artifacts placed at the disposal of culture. Habermas critiques the entombment of art in museums in *Legitimation* (1975, 85). For a discussion of the relation between pastiche and the museum, see Huyssen's comments on Jameson's definition of postmodernism in *Twilight Memories* (Huyssen 1995, 164).

28. This argument is nonetheless framed in general terms, thus it still reflects its origins in the modernist sensibility of the 1950s and early 1960s.

29. Compare also discussion of the term *techne* in the writings of Aristotle and Gadamer in Haney 1999. Haney remarks on the inseparability of creation and meaning in the work of art as described by Gadamer. Enzensberger's account similarly emphasizes the indivisibility of these terms.

30. Enzensberger's insistence on a metaphor for writing that conveys instrumentality—the comparison of a poem to a machine, a trope which goes back to Valéry—also represents a point of connection with Williams. In 1964, Enzensberger again chose a strikingly similar antiaesthetic metaphor, "means of production," to describe poetry. This industrial terminology is conspicuous and functions as a refutation of Benn: "Poems are not consumer goods but means of production, with the help of which the reader can succeed in producing the truth" (Enzensberger 1964i, 146–47).

31. For further discussion of Enzensberger's relation to Adorno, see Schultz 1984. R. Grimm terms Adorno Enzensberger's mentor (1984, 48).

32. Compare Trommler's conclusion that definitions of literature during the postwar era tended to draw on the perceptions of younger authors whose attitudes were shaped by their own youthful rebellions against their elders (1977, 168–78).

33. Further elaboration of this concept occurs in *Einzelheiten I* (Enzensberger 1964e).

34. Enzensberger comments, "The two translators battle heroically . . . with the rubbish" (1959a, 759).

35. The claims Enzensberger sees as characteristic of this group are its false valorization of unlimited freedom, youth culture, spontaneity, rebellion, protest against the machine age, rejection of mass culture, and an indulgence in cult beliefs. Compare also the discussion of Enzensberger in the context of generational conflicts and 1950s youth culture in Lau 1999, 50–54.

36. Given Enzensberger's influence as an anthologist on canon formation, it is instructive to compare analytical categories outlined by Golding (1995). Golding notes that anthologies may have the function of articulating oppositional stances,

serve as teaching tools or as revisionist compilations, represent the formation of canonical tradition by either poets or academics, and in their scope also intersect with expressions of national identity. These factors may also be considered to have affected the character of *Museum*. Essmann and Frank (1991) outline areas in which the creators of translation anthologies have particular influence in shaping the canon.

37. Compare also the neutralized generalization of the term "provincial" to deflect an association between it and unacceptable attitudes in Heuss: "The German has never been aloof from the world. To the extent that he is 'provincial,' he is no more so than other peoples" (1957, 108).

38. This recasting of the dichotomy reverses the contrast of world-city and province in the work of Spengler (1940, 120–21). Spengler associates the metropolis with the mass and the province with rootedness and vitality.

39. This muting occurs on the level of word choice. For example, instances of eye-dialect are relatively rare in the translations, although there are a few examples: *möcht* instead of *möchte, gen* instead of *gegen,* or *was andres* for *etwas anderes.* Neologisms appear largely as cognate formations (*Seeschnecken* for *Meerschnecken* as the translation for sea snails).

40. The reception of Williams's work in Germany is detailed in Galinsky 1968. Enzensberger's interest in Williams receives mention in Bridgwater 1967–68. Sewell 1979 outlines philosophical affinities between the two poets, while the influence Enzensberger's mediation had on postwar German poetry is pursued in Melin 1992 and 1990. Lamping (1987) revisits the subject of Williams reception in connection with Enzensberger, without acknowledging the studies of Sewell and Melin. See also Bonheim and Nischik 1978, which relies largely on Galinsky's discussion.

41. The question of how class values play into this equation lies beyond the scope of the present interpretation, although the contrast between "higher" purpose and "lower" consumerism clearly invites such an analysis. Enzensberger's admiration of American modernists, however, clearly is attached to a sense that their work is political. This sense is confirmed by his remarks in a recent interview that "American authors like Williams most certainly had a fundamentally different conception of politics — a completely different form of politics dominates in the USA, too; it is much more oriented to everyday concerns" (Mueller 1997, 208).

42. Similar questions of representation arise as well in debate about the lyric genre as detailed in the previous chapter in connection with the work of Staiger.

43. Despite having been imprisoned after the war for treasonous actions, Pound was well known in Germany, where many of his works were published in the 1950s. Zuther's bibliography lists some twenty-four items by or about Pound, the earliest of which appeared in 1949, including the "ABC of Reading," poems, and cantos (Zuther 1965, 103–5). Hesse's translations of Pound began to appear in 1953 (Pound

1953), and Schirmer's comprehensive study (1954) included a chapter on Eliot and Pound.

44. Compare also Pound 1956, "Ballad of the Goodly Fere": "Aye lover he was of brawny men, / O' ships and the Open sea" (9), and "Canto I": "And then went down to the ship, / Set keel to breakers, forth on the godly sea" (96).

45. This tense, teasing relationship to the reader distinguishes Enzensberger's work from that of many of his contemporaries and invites comparison with Perloff's reading of American and European poetry in the 1950s, which summarizes the contrasting styles that dominated the literary scene: " 'Counterculture' poetics of the 1950s is thus a far cry from the avant-garde of the early century. . . . [T]he 'oppositional' poetry of the fifties was cool . . . rather than hot, mordant and witty performance rather than its more contemplative, engaged, and analytical European postwar counterpart, as found in, say, the lyric of Paul Celan or Ingeborg Bachmann" (Perloff 1998, 114).

46. Enzensberger's use of imperatives relies on modes of authorized language discussed in Bourdieu 1991, 107–16. The commands Enzensberger uses already presume both the authority of the speaker to determine what the reader will do and confidence in the illocutionary force of language.

47. The likely source for this image is Rembrandt. Lau supplies details concerning a 1963 writer's conference trip Enzensberger attended in the Soviet Union, which culminated in a visit to Chrutchow's summer home (1999, 154–59). Compare also the discussion of "Küchenzettel" in Nägele 1984, esp. 215–17. Enzensberger frequently uses the physical geometry of a house or room to mark the space of the writer. In an interview with Hulse, the author relates an anecdote from his childhood that seems to shed light on this trope. Enzensberger tells that he once received as a Christmas present a playhouse that his father had built: "Strangely enough, he had not furnished it in traditional doll's house style but with writing equipment, so that it looked almost like an office: sheaves of paper, pencils, india rubbers—marvelous! It was just the thing for me" (Enzensberger 1991b, 4). Finally, the book jacket of *Kiosk* (1995b) matches this thematic cluster by displaying five small, white paper gazebos set in a backdrop of lush green leaves.

48. Knape 1995 details Gerhardt's career. Galinsky, who cites Gerhardt's importance as an early postwar mediator of American verse, dates the reception of work by Williams from the 1930s, although two poems appeared in the literary journal *Der Querschnitt* in 1924 (Melin 1992, 90)

49. For an overview of Eliot reception in German through 1970, see Fink 1971 and Zuther 1965.

50. See R. Grimm 1984, 28–29. Enzensberger's adroit handling of rhetorical conventions likewise contributes to his parodies. Compare further Hinderer 1984.

51. See Schnell 1993, 242–43 and 310–20. Schnell connects the so-called legitimation crisis in literature with political events: "These economic and political

data and facts did not exercise a direct effect on the development of literature in the 1960s. If they find mention here it is because of their indirect consequences. For they did produce consequences in the form of a politically-grounded culture crisis. They shook the self-understanding of a society whose belief in the political potency of the West and in its own economic growth had until then been completely free of doubt" (311).

52. See Enzensberger 1999f, 102–3, wherein he reports having received a Fulbright Foundation stipend to visit the United States in 1953.

53. Early reviewers of Enzensberger's poetry noted the affinities of his work to many German authors and to those he translated as well. His debt to Brecht, Benn, and Schiller has been particularly well detailed by scholars (Bridgwater 1967–68; R. Grimm 1984, 129–47). Like Deschner (1964), some have regarded this eclectic tendency on the part of Enzensberger as dilettantishly derivative and all but plagiarism, while others, Bridgwater in particular, have mentioned other poets as a constructive point of comparison. Bridgwater, very accurately characterizing both the weaknesses and the strengths of Enzensberger's early work, offered a long list of authors from whom the young poet probably learned, ranging from Brecht and Benn to Auden, Ginsberg, Gregory Corso, Eich, Williams, Fried, and Celan. While it remains undisputed that Enzensberger has broad familiarity with literature, his own pronouncements about the nature of these influences have been consistently reserved. See Deschner 1964.

54. A further comparison of the handling of syntax and lineation in the Williams translations with Enzensberger's poetry is suggested by the attention he devotes to the nature of poetry writing as a recursive practice that proceeds line by line in "Die Entstehung eines Gedichts" (1962b), which appeared in various versions starting in 1960–61.

55. For example, Enzensberger renders the phrase "Kingdom of death" from Eliot's "The Hollow Men" as "des Todes Reich" (1980 [ed.], 635). The technique seems more awkward in "Sparrow among Dry Leaves" by Williams, where "and love's / obscure and insatiable / appetite" becomes "und der Liebe / dunklem unersättlichen / Appetit" (Enzensberger 1962b [trans.], 125).

56. Enzensberger's selection of Williams's poems has been criticized for representing only a positive image of the poet. See Bonheim and Nischik 1978, 15. This assessment overlooks the representative nature of Enzensberger's selection, which spans two volumes of poetry, *The Collected Earlier Poems* and *The Collected Later Poems* by Williams. Enzensberger does include a number of rather unpoetic selections ("Time the Hangman," "A Portrait of the Times," and "Pastoral"), emphasizes the pragmatic aspects of Williams in his introduction, and occasionally approaches the translations in a way that heightens the bluntness of Williams's language.

57. See Rimmon-Kenan's discussion of this as "grammatically and mimetically intermediate between indirect and direct discourse" (1983, 110).

58. Compare also the conclusion of "Süße kleine . . ." from *Leichter als Luft* (1999e, 93–94), which again echoes the poem by Cummings.

59. Cummings, perhaps due to the formally experimental character of his poetry, was less known than other American poets. Fewer than a dozen Cummings poems appeared in German translation in the 1940s and 1950s (in such literary journals as *Wort und Wahrheit, Perspektiven,* and *Deutsche Universitätszeitung,* in addition to Hesse's translations for *Gedichte* [Cummings 1958]).

60. Bloom suggests that the impulse to elaborate upon antecedents may well be an American trait, for he asserts, "It seems true that British poets swerve from their precursors, while American poets labor rather to 'complete' their fathers" (1973, 68).

61. This stylistic development invites comparison with the work of American poets as described by Pinsky: "For many contemporary poets, the effective practice seems to be based upon a particular kind of voice: enigmatic, slangy, fey, tough, idiosyncratic, darting between the plain and the daffy with a mock-naive, teenage sort of detachment. That detachment, a knowing, ironic superiority to parts of one's own mind and experience—the 'cool' of high school in the early sixties or late fifties—defines the manner for me better than references to surrealism or location in California or New York" (1976, 3–4). Pinsky traces development of this voice to the work of modernists, including Stevens and Williams.

62. The similarity of these poems and the cyclical construction *Blindenschrift* displays is characteristic of Enzensberger's poetic work and will be explored at length in the fourth chapter of this study.

63. Enzensberger uses this form again in other, later poems, such as "Beschreibung eines Dickichts" and "Die Macht der Gewohnheit," which are collected in Enzensberger 1983.

64. For a discussion of representational degrees see Rimmon-Kenan 1983, 109–10.

65. Compare also Perloff 1991: " 'Making strange' now occurs at the level of phrasal and sentence structure rather than at the level of the image cluster so that poetic language cannot be absorbed into the discourse of the media" (78).

66. Rolleston (1981, 81) has interpreted Enzensberger's poetic work as opposing 1950s aesthetic values by resisting the synthesis represented by the work of Benn and Brecht. My reading suggests a modification of this view to acknowledge that Enzensberger works with and against these norms to enlarge the poetic repertoire.

67. In important respects this questioning of language, authenticity, and authority anticipates Enzensberger's essays in the mid- to late 1960s, which cast doubt on the efficacy of literature as a tool to effect social change.

68. Little scholarly attention has been directed toward the relation between the *Hörspiel* (radio play) and lyric poetry in postwar Germany. The importance of performativity, aural quality, and silence (as both a topos and an aspect of the poetic medium) in verse of this period, however, suggests that further investigation of

this subject is needed, such as of the relationship between Gerhardt's broadcasts about poetry in 1952 to 1954 and interest in international poetry (Knape 1995, 76–79).

Chapter 3

1. At the risk of abridging the highly nuanced analysis in *Self*, I mention these premises to Altieri's approach in order to foreground methodological consider-ations for my chapter. Altieri details his own interpretive procedures in terms of seven complex, interrelated questions having to do with the empirical formula-tions of craft, signs of internal contradictions within poetry, and the status of critical principles that need elaboration when we interpret the lyric genre.

2. This is not strictly true, however, if one considers his publications in Ameri-can little magazines. Compare the Estermann bibliography (1984, 207) concerning poems that appeared in *Luchterhand Loseblatt Lyrik* and in English, and the dis-cussion in Dietschreit and Heinze-Dietschreit 1986, 90–92, concerning *Gedichte 1955–1970* (Enzensberger 1971b).

3. In addition to the new poems in *Gedichte 1955–1970* (1971b), Enzensberger published poems in other sources; see 1963f, 1966a, 1967a, 1967b, 1967e, 1968d, 1970a, 1970b, and 1971a.

4. For a discussion of agitprop poetry, consult Hahn 1978.

5. See especially Holthusen's critical appraisal of *Mausoleum* and *Der Untergang* (1982); Holthusen 1980a; Dujmic 1996; Parkes 1986; Koepke 1980; and Reinhold 1981. The incisive discussion of Enzensberger's political views in the 1990s avail-able is the essay collection edited by Fischer (1996), which substantially corrects limitations of earlier scholarship on this subject.

6. This poem and the accompanying "Note" first appeared in an English trans-lation by Hamburger (in Enzensberger 1968c); English citations are referenced to Enzensberger 1994b. Interestingly, the later German publication of "Sommer-gedicht" (in *Gedichte 1955–1970* [1971b]) is not accompanied by an explanatory essay.

7. Compare also the allusion to Marilyn Monroe in Frank O'Hara's poem "A Step Away from Them," as discussed in Perloff 1998, 105–10.

8. Golding categorizes anthologies as teaching and revisionist collections (1995, 30). I apply the latter term to Enzensberger's presentation of Williams because it diverges from the canon of the 1960s.

9. This was an unauthorized quotation from Olson, as noted by Bollobás (1992, 21–22).

10. By contrast, Enzensberger negatively evaluates the use of netlike intercon-nections of language in news media journalism, as his analysis of *Der Spiegel* in *Einzelheiten I* indicates (1964e, 81). Here he connects the creation of news stories

by the loose association of details with a manipulation of the reader, who as a sort of tabula rasa is supposed to be gullibly inclined to accept anything.

11. According to Lau, Enzensberger's father worked on elaborate maps and charts (1999, 14). This pastime invites comparison with Enzensberger's poetical interest in maps, timetables, and statistical charting.

12. While it is not possible to establish a single source for this text, Adorno comments on the dynamic interaction of parts and whole in works of art: "For traditional aesthetics, and to a large extent for traditional art as well, the determination of the totality of the artwork is its determination as a nexus of meaning. The reciprocal relation of whole and parts is supposed to shape the work as something meaningful to such an extent that the quintessence of this meaning coincides with the metaphysical content. Because the nexus of meaning is constituted by the relation of elements—and not in atomistic fashion in something given that is sensual—what can justly be called the spirit of artworks should be comprehensible in that nexus" (1970, 152).

13. In coining the term "translative," I wish to draw attention to the capacities translations have for mediating the artistic vocabulary of different cultures, compensating for temporal disjunctures between original and contemporary verbiage, and producing richly textured forms of discourse through the application of original source features to another language.

14. The asphodel figures in the poetry of Benn and is associated with the elysian fields.

15. German poets who make use of the stepped-down line form and montage technique include Brinkmann, Becker, and Krechel.

16. Enzensberger asks about more esoteric writers (specifically Pound and Raymond Chandler), "wer aber wird sie lesen?" or "who will read them?" (1964e, 164).

17. This poem, first published in 1959, lent its title to one of the sections in *Landessprache* (1960d) and the later translated collection of the author's work, *Poems for People Who Don't Read Poems* (1968c).

18. See also "Journalismus als Eiertanz" and "Scherbenwelt" in Enzensberger 1964e.

19. In his 1979 "Nachbemerkung" for the reprinted edition of *Museum,* Enzensberger rejects "one world" ideology of the restoration period after 1945 as based on false solidarity (1980 [ed.], 786).

20. Schultz 1984 details Enzensberger's connection to Adorno.

21. Compare with Habermas's discussion of nonreflexive and reflexive learning: "*Non-reflexive* learning takes place in action contexts in which implicitly raised theoretical and practical validity claims are naively taken for granted and accepted or rejected without discursive consideration. *Reflexive learning* takes place through discourses in which we thematize practical validity claims that have become problematic or have been rendered problematic through institutionalized doubt, and redeem or dismiss them on the basis of arguments" (1975, 15).

22. See Witting 1981, Gnüg 1979, Novak 1975, and Petersdorff 1996. Novak, herself a ballad author, expresses puzzlement over why Enzensberger terms his poems ballads: some are lyrical poetry, some prose poems; others blend these two genres. For a comprehensive overview of the European prose poem, see Monroe 1987. Documentation concerning prose poem texts in Germany is to be found in Fülleborn 1976 and Fritz 1970.

23. See further Volckmann 1979.

24. Montage techniques previously used by Enzensberger are described in both R. Grimm 1984, 21–43 and Wunberg 1964. Enzensberger's renewed interest in montage at the end of the 1960s is strongly connected to his experimentation with documentary forms of literature as a matter of principle. His introduction to *Gespräche mit Marx und Engels* observes that it is considered by some the most advanced technique of literature in the twentieth century (1973 [ed.], V).

25. Compare Habermas: "Output crises have the form of a *rationality crisis* in which the administrative system does not succeed in reconciling and fulfilling the imperatives received from the economic system. Input crises have the form of a *legitimation crisis;* the legitimizing system does not succeed in maintaining the requisite level of mass loyalty while the steering imperatives taken over from the economic system are carried through" (1975, 46).

26. Franz (1984) has related the collection to the documentary literature promulgated by the New Left and to critiques of consumer culture by Marx and Adorno.

27. It is beyond the scope of the present analysis to consider all references in this densely intertextual collection. Parallels, however, also exist between Enzensberger's project and the work of Benjamin. Compare especially the discussion of Benjamin's writerly practices in Sieburth 1989. Further, Enzensberger in his advocacy on behalf of dynamic art mirrors the analysis of problematized artistic autonomy set forth by Bürger (1974).

28. Øhrgaard (1978, 428) draws the connection to Kenner. Both books include discussions of the inventors Turing, Vaucauson, Babbage, and Guillotin, for example.

29. Because it self-consciously makes use of and alters canon, *Mausoleum* also requires a reading sensitive to the caution articulated by Guillory that in evaluating canon formation, one should not seek direct signs of individual intentions, positions, and creations but rather recognize that certain "effects of ideology" seem to be "generated about the conceptualization of literature itself" (Guillory 1993, 135).

30. See Witting 1981, 438, for a discussion of how Habermas's analysis of *Öffentlichkeit* and *Subjektivität* pertains to Enzensberger's work.

31. On the visual aspects of poems, see Levenston 1992, 107–23.

32. The original publication provided only the initials of the historical personages described, estranging them and compelling the reader to look up the full names in the book's index, a process designed to prompt further reflection. To

make the content of the ballads more transparent here, however, I use full names. This is the presentational convention used in cases in which the poems have been published as individual texts or incorporated into collections of other work by the author.

33. A number of scholars have examined how Enzensberger's nuanced handling of themes in *Mausoleum* systematically shapes the collection and engages with contemporary issues. Øhrgaard's essay (1978) focuses on Enzensberger's presentation of time (celestial, human, and mechanical), reason and madness, and the living and the dead, and directs attention to how these elements define a new world shaped by technology. Witting (1981) centers his interpretation around Bakunin and Machiavelli (whom he sees as the antitheses of spontaneity and rationality), raising the question of how poetry intersects with political dogma and social activism, an eminently contemporary problem. Compare also Melin 1989.

34. Dante also figures in Enzensberger's *Der Untergang der Titanic* (1978a).

35. These sections should be read in relation to Enzensberger's "Blumenfest," based on an Aztec text (1983, 118–19), and to his introduction to *Bartolomé de las Casas* (1966 [ed.]).

36. Compare with Foucault's analysis of how language use is related to the control of social structures, sexuality, and mores in *The Order of Things* (1970) and *The Archaeology of Knowledge* (1972).

37. For a discussion of speech representation, see Rimmon-Kenan 1983, 106–16.

38. It should be noted that Enzensberger seems to follow the lead of Kenner, who extrapolates the notion of the "Turing Machine" or "Turing Game" by provocatively asking readers to imagine that a man-made device could be capable of producing the work of Shakespeare, Donne, Dante, or Herman Wouk if sufficiently programmed (Kenner 1968, 120).

39. Witting questions whether such complex reading is not too demanding of readers (1981, 450).

40. See also Øhrgaard 1978, 423–27, concerning this contrast.

41. Compare also Habermas on the role of critical analysis: "The level of learning which a social formation makes possible could depend upon whether the organizational principle of the society permits (a) differentiation between theoretical and practical questions and (b) transition from non-reflexive (prescientific) to reflexive learning" (1975, 15).

Chapter 4

1. Compare also the title of Celan's collection *Atemwende* (1967). This discussion of free verse in relation to physical breath invites comparison with the account of free verse in Perloff 1998, 151–53. Perloff notes as salient features of this poetic form its rhythmical variability, organization around images, and speech-based syn-

tax, which generally involves complete sentences, linear character, and unobtrusive sound patterning. She cites Ginsberg and Creeley, who had been well known in Germany since the 1950s.

2. That predicament was, of course, not new to the lyric genre. Barthes in *Writing Degree Zero* in 1953 had warned against the reduction of nature to linguistic fragments, because then "there is no humanism of modern poetry. This erect discourse is full of terror, that is to say, it related man not to other men, but to the most inhuman images in Nature: heaven, hell, holiness, childhood, madness, pure matter, etc." (1967, 50).

3. Gleick reports on a series of publications that drew scientific attention to chaos theory in 1975–1976 (1987, 329–30). Mitchel Feigenbaum publicized his findings on chaos theory at a New Hampshire conference in August 1976 (reported in Gleick 1987, 183). Also of note are Mandelbrot 1975 and Schwenk 1976.

4. Lyotard refers to Mandelbrot, one of the founders of what became the science of chaos, in *The Postmodern Condition* (Lyotard 1984, 58). Both Huyssen (1993) and Jameson (1992) refer to Enzensberger as a postmodern thinker. Compare also the critical studies on the connection between literature and chaos theory by Paulson (1988) and the reservations expressed by Riebling (1993).

5. The type of jagged shapes known as fractals include those of snowflakes, coastlines, and computer-generated patterns. Similar formations are found throughout the physical world and include patterning characteristic of both inanimate objects (watershed or crystalline structures) and organic things (plant branchings or arterial formations). Enzensberger's interest in fractals parallels the publication by Springer Verlag in Berlin beginning in the 1970s of several important works in the field of chaos theory, including the lushly illustrated book *The Beauty of Fractals* by Heinz-Otto Peitgen and Peter H. Richter (1986).

6. Enzensberger's essay on Williams gives further evidence of this focus on the scientific by emphasizing both scientific descriptions of poetry and Williams's career as a physician.

7. Turing (1912–1954) is credited with cracking the German Enigma code.

8. Gleick points out that fractals apply to phenomena regardless of size and can account for the microscopic patterns of snowflakes and vast shoreline formations (118).

9. In poetry, of course, ships traditionally stand for poetry, as in the simile by Emily Dickinson, "There is no frigate like a book / To take us lands away," which appears in the Louis Untermeyer–edited anthology *A Treasury of Great Poems* (Dickinson 1942) that Enzensberger likely read in the 1940s (1999f, 100). Enzensberger had begun his first poetry collection, *Verteidigung,* with lines that described the power of poetry to transport the reader as if on a ship (1957b, 9).

10. Lehmann 1984 provides analysis of major themes. An account of Enzensberger's literary allusions and the topic of ice ages in German literature of the late

1970s and 1980s is supplied by R. Grimm 1984, 174–217. See further Bohrer 1978; Holthusen 1980c; Goetz 1981; Seeba 1981; H. Hartung 1985; Sorg 1985; Kiermeier-Debre 1986; and Lamping 1987.

11. For a discussion of the lore surrounding the *Titanic,* see Biel 1996. Concerning Hardy, see R. Grimm 1984, 199. The poem by Bishop appears in her *Complete Poems* (1969, 4).

12. Conceptually related to the "butterfly effect" is the Lorenz attractor, named for Edward Lorenz, who researched the meteorological occurrences associated with the "butterfly effect" and devised equations for representing chaotic phenomena. The Lorenz attractor produces visual patterns used to show the relationship of three variables. The pattern that results has overlapping tracings that resemble the shape of butterfly wings (Gleick 1987, 11–31).

13. In the radio play version of the text, produced by Vollmer (1979b), the barely perceptible noises eventually crescendo into a fortissimo of ripping canvas.

14. The title imitates Brecht's poem "Verlustliste" ("List of Losses"), which cataloged compatriot writers lost during the Third Reich (1967a, 829).

15. Enzensberger's choice of the name Solomon Pollock hardly seems coincidental, for it causes the reader to associate that surname with Jackson Pollock, the abstract expressionist painter best known for using random, accidental techniques to create moving "epic" abstractions. In suggesting this correspondence, I do not wish to exclude the possibility that this surname echoes that of other individuals, as, for example, the social theorist Friedrich Pollock. For a discussion of how the apparent randomness of these paintings depends on controlled and defined structures, see Rohn 1987.

16. Lettau 1967, 160. See also Lau 1999, 145. For a discussion of the references to paintings, see Künzel 1980. Künzel's discussion, which notes allusions to Bruegel the Elder, Bosch, and Veronese, does not consider the turtle. Compare also Melin 1991.

17. Michel reads the turtle merely as an Enzensbergian irony (1999, 153).

18. Compare *Der Untergang* (1978a, 61–62) with Eliot's "The Hollow Men" and its translation in *Museum* (1980 [ed.], 634–41). For discussion of this poem as an expression of doubt about language, see Lau 1999, 311.

19. It is beyond the scope of the present analysis to explore the sexual implications of the term *Orgasmus.* For a discussion of the interface between desire and radical politics, see Herzog 1998. For discussion of the positions of Weiss (certainly alluded to here through Dante, who appeared in *Ästhetik des Widerstands*) and Enzensberger, see Teraoka 1996 as well as R. Grimm 1984 [ed.], 90–105. Compare also Derrida on Rousseau: "imagination, origin of différence between power and desire is determined as *difference:* of or within presence or pleasure" (1998, 186).

20. Given the literary figures who populate Enzensberger's epic, it is worth noting that Pound and Eliot figure in a song by Bob Dylan, where they are de-

scribed as being on board the *Titanic* and "fighting in the tower." See "Desolation Row" (Dylan 1965). During the interview Mueller conducted with Enzensberger, he noted the importance of Dylan in Germany in the 1960s (Mueller 1997, 285).

21. For a discussion of the implications of this time and space after a cataclysmic event occurs, see Berger 1999. Note that under Gödel's principle of indeterminacy, such openness is a given, whereas Turing sought an endpoint for mathematical calculations.

22. One of these, "Nearer, My God to Thee," is quoted by Enzensberger in "Chicago-Ballade" ("Chicago Ballad"), in *Politik und Verbrechen* (1964h, 137). Several Enzensberger musical pieces overlap with the composition of *Der Untergang: El cimarrón* with Henze in 1971, Henze's setting for "Hommage à Gödel" ("Homage to Gödel") in 1973, and poems for Ingrid Caven in 1980 (all in Enzensberger 1983), including one about the end of the world, "In zehn Sekunden ist alles vorbei" ("In Ten Seconds Everything Is Over") (340–41).

23. Compare the description of the iceberg as a "sublime spectacle" with C. M. Wieland's "Die Aeronauten," a text indexed in "Sommergedicht": He describes early airships as "ein so wunderbares Schauspiel" (such a marvelous drama or spectacle [Enzensberger 1983, 111]).

24. Janson compares this painting with Turner's depiction of the wreck of the *Hope* (1991, 646).

25. *Die Suche* includes a photograph of a man that bears a resemblance to the book jacket photograph of Enzensberger for the American edition of *The Sinking of the Titanic* (1976c).

26. Enzensberger asserts that passages in Brentano's poems can be understood only by keeping in mind his work as a whole (1961, 81).

27. Gerhardt's work appeared in the journal *Work* (1965/66). This magazine, a tribute to Gerhardt, was edited by Tom Raworth, who acknowledged the assistance of poets Creeley, Hollo, Jonathan Williams, and Cid Corman in assembling the materials (Gerhardt 1965/66, 1).

28. The phrasing of both versions is reminiscent of "Letztwillige Verfügung" from *Verteidigung* ("Lebt wohl. / Im Nachttisch sind noch ein paar Zigaretten" ["Farewell. / In the night table there are still a few cigarettes"] [1957b, 34]) and his translation of "The Last Words of My English Grandmother" by Williams ("Geht, / ich will nichts mehr davon wissen, / und drehte den Kopf weg" ["Go, / I don't want to know any more about it, / and turned her head away"] [Enzensberger 1985, 22]).

29. This liquidity resembles subjects in earlier poems by Enzensberger that considered threats to the environment and nuclear destruction. These include "Rätsel," which begins "Dort ist es immer dunkel und naß, / dort quillt eine heiße Flut" ("There it is always dark and damp, / there gushes a hot flood"), from *Verteidigung der Wölfe* (1957b, 41), and the circumlocution from *Landessprache,* "An Alle Fernsprechteilnehmer" (1960d, 26): "etwas, das keine farbe hat, etwas, / das

nach nichts riecht, . . . etwas zähes, davor der salm stirbt, / in die flüsse, und sickert, farblos, / und tötet den butt auf den bänken" ("something that has no color, something / that smells like nothing, . . . viscous that kills the salmon, / into the rivers, and trickling, colorless, / and kills the flatfish on the banks").

30. The title *Zukunftsmusik* also suggests the use of this term by Hofmannsthal and Richard Wagner. Compare the discussion in Thomasberger 1994, 152.

Chapter 5

1. Compare also the category of "oppositional voices," which Ryan effectively uses to examine German poetry written after historical turning points (1997, 40).

2. Public interrogation of authorial identity characterized many postwar discussions of German literature, and Hensel's reaction invites comparison with the satirical response given by Enzensberger to a survey of authors: "I have quite a few professions: editor, radio writer, essayist, author of poems, father of a family, translator. Which is the main one, I even ask myself from time to time. Then there's the answering of numerous polls, which is a profession in and of itself" (Enzensberger 1960a, 13).

3. Compare also Enzensberger's remarks concerning Aristotle, who warned that poets were capable of "collecting, even inventing, collective feelings" (1997c, 100).

4. While acknowledging the continuities that exist in postwar German literature, I distinguish here between the ethical imperatives confronting poetry in the immediate postwar period and the embedded, more fluid political critique that characterizes recent verse written in German.

5. The term "organic intellectual" comes from Gramsci, according to Mignolo (1998, 44).

6. For a discussion of the author's national identity, see Goodbody 1990.

7. Enzensberger's critique of bourgeois tendencies resurfaces in 1997c, 143–61.

8. Lau discerns similarities between Enzensberger's thinking and Barthes's writings about mythology (Lau 1999, 95) and cites as significant *Kursbuch* 5 (1966), which was devoted to structuralism—including the work of Barthes—and appeared just as attention was being turned to French theory by West German academics (222). Further, it should be noted that during the period 1949–54, Enzensberger spent time in Paris at the Sorbonne.

9. For further discussion of Enzensberger's position see Teraoka 1996 and Sadji 1984. The relationship between central and marginal cultures assumes a prominent role in Enzensberger's writings beginning the late 1960s. His afterword to Nirumand's *Iran: The New Imperialism in Action* (Enzensberger 1969a), for example, seeks to identify European misperceptions of Iran that are based on cultural stereotypes. Following this rationale, "Revolutions-Tourismus" in *Palaver* (1974b) delivers a plea for greater sensitivity among leftists to Third World issues.

Enzensberger criticizes as superficial and economically unproductive the emerging practice of politically inspired junkets to developing nations. Later prose points to some of the paradoxes of marginality and globalization, especially *Svensk Höst* (1982) and *Norsk utakt* (1984b). More recently, *Die große Wanderung* (1992a), *Aussichten auf den Bürgerkrieg* (1993), and *Zickzack* (1997c) have generated discussion of the relation between global and ethnic politics. See Fischer 1996.

10. Compare the discussion of "Trigonometrischer Punkt" from *Blindenschrift* (1964d) in chapter 4.

11. See also Enzensberger, "Das langsame Verschwinden" (1984a), and the account of the poet's restlessness by Ritter-Santini (1984). Bohn (1986) sums up the author's career as a tension between anarchic and traditional tendencies. Pabisch (1993) supplies an extended analysis of "Landessprache."

12. For a detailed discussion of the textual sources of the Bakunin text in *Mausoleum,* see Witting 1981. Arguing that farcical elements in the presentation of the anarchist prompt the reader to respond critically to the text, Witting reads Bakunin as a figure whose spontaneity contrasts favorably with the rationalizing control of Machiavelli. Müller (1977) analyzes Enzensberger's political views in relation to the ballad about Bakunin.

13. Compare also Enzensberger's documentary novel *Der kurze Sommer der Anarchie* (1972a).

14. In this discussion of *Mausoleum* and *Der Untergang der Titanic,* I use my own translations when a more literal rendering of the text better foregrounds elements significant to the interpretation I am pursuing. Where the available English translations sufficiently convey the meaning of the original text, I refer to those published sources.

15. Note that Stanley's name is actually Henry Morten Stanley. The slippage from "Morton" to "Morgan" Stanley suggests a play on the name of the financial firm of the same name.

16. *Encyclopaedia Britannica,* 1965 ed., s. v. "Stanley, Sir Henry Morton."

17. Jameson proposes that postmodern cognitive mapping offers the potential to imagine a global totality: "Cognitive mapping will be a matter of form . . . an integral part of a socialist politics" (1999, 167).

18. The English versions not referenced to published translations are mine and are used to point to specific phrasings that support the interpretation I am proposing.

19. Enzensberger writes: "Seine Lieblingsdroge / sei die Aufmerksamkeit. / Auf die tägliche Prise / von ideologischem Kokain / könne er notfalls verzichten" (1980a, 47) ("His favourite drug, he maintains, / is alertness, the daily dose / of ideological cocaine / he'd just as well do without" [1994b, 189]).

20. These observations occur throughout Goethe 1970. Compare also Enzensberger's remarks from 1979 in Kesting 1984, 131: "But the mind of an author is always a radio head, full of voices and echoes. One always writes, if one writes,

a dictation or a paraphrase. In that sense, literature is a collective task in which everyone else who is working on it is always present; whether they've been dead for two hundred years or are sitting in the next room is not important."

21. For a discussion of the "Messer im Rücken" motif see R. Grimm 1984, 148–68.

22. Stavropoulos (1996) delivers a forceful critique of Enzensberger's recent political essays, arguing that as an author he has become engaged in rationalizing his position, which she sees as disconnecting individuals from their social context. Her keen analysis raises the question of whether it is ethical for an author who works creatively to circumscribe limits for writing by remaining relativistic when pragmatic solutions to political problems are needed. Stavropoulos regards Enzensberger's blurring of aesthetic and political matters as both a strength and weakness but considers the appeal of his writing to intuitive faculties ultimately problematic (1996, 86). For further discussion of Enzensberger as a quixotic thinker, see Parkes 1986.

23. Elaborating on the evolution of the concept of engagé writing in postwar European literature, Monroe reads Enzensberger's recent verse as moving from cold war dichotomies toward open-endedness that enlarges on the categories proposed by Jean-Paul Sartre (1997, 63). This model was embraced but also already modified by Enzensberger in "Poesie und Politik" (1964f). As has been seen, this movement toward openness commences with the formal innovations of "Sommergedicht" in the mid-1960s.

24. On Enzensberger's rejoinder to Adorno, see Kumar 1997, 895.

25. Enzensberger has also worked on pop-poster format poems (published in the series *Luchterhand Loseblattlyrik*), film, and musical productions, all enumerated in Estermann 1984, as well as a hologram ("Hologram/Hologramm") cited in R. Wieland's bibliography (1999, 249–341). See further Perloff 1998, 354, concerning the Hanhardt collection of video, which includes a piece by Enzensberger. Internet sites include Glossen (Stollmann, "Ein fiktives Interview mit Hans Magnus Enzensberger über seine neuesten politischen Essays"), *Die Zeit,* and Projekt EWALD.

26. See also Stevens 1995 and Enzensberger's translation of a poem by Gregory Corso about Al Capone in *Politik und Verbrechen* (1964h, 137).

27. Compare also the poem Simic dedicated to Enzensberger, "Das Leben der Alchimisten" (1999, 128). Enzensberger's significance to the literary scene in Europe and South America is documented in a special issue of the cultural magazine *Du.*

28. Enzensberger's efforts to connect with international writers suggest interesting literary exchanges that merit investigation of archival materials. For now, however, most of these ties remain sketchy. Existing bibliographies and records provide some evidence of literary connections. Experimental poet Rothenberg translated Enzensberger (e.g., Enzensberger 1967a, 1968c). See also a satirical poem

by Robert Peters that places him among poetic innovators of the twentieth century. Spoofing Olson's poetry, Peters proclaims, "I want to drink from Neruda's pitcher, Enzensberger's / blue bottle . . . !" (1981, 297).

29. Since the late 1960s, Enzensberger's reputation as a social critic seems to have overshadowed his poetry, as in the citation of *Civil Wars* in Ehrlich et al. 1995, 259. The author has participated in U.S. conferences that have furthered this reputation. See, for example, the proceedings from a conference at Rutgers on social change in Central and Eastern Europe (Enzensberger 1992b). Compare the Italian film *Caro Diario* by Nanni Moretti (1994) in which one of the main characters attempts to show that he is socially progressive by repeatedly asking his counterpart whether he knows Enzensberger's writings and then stating that he agrees with him.

30. This formulation, of course, has its origins in Aristotle.

31. These flights of fancy are anticipated in "Drift I" and "Drift II" in *Verteidigung* (1957b), the long poem forms discussed in chapter 3, and the interlude "Die Ruhe" in *Der Untergang* (1978a).

32. The terms *Weiterungen* and *weiter* in the *Gedankenflucht* texts hark back to the poem "Weiterung" from *Blindenschrift* (1964d), which, as we have seen, intricately reworked language of Cummings and Brecht to comment on two world wars and the prospect of a contemporary nuclear apocalypse. Compare the discussion of Enzensberger's poem "Weiterung" and his translation of E. E. Cummings's "My sweet old etcetera" in chapter 2.

33. For a discussion of discourse modes, see Rimmon-Kenan 1983, 106–16. She points out that speech register marks a text's literariness and that when a work mimics common speech, this everyday register undermines the privileged status of literature.

34. Awareness of the relationship between language and ideology has been especially intense in the work of younger GDR authors, including Elke Erb, Uwe Kolbe, Stefan Döring, Bert Papenfuß-Gorek, and other authors of the Prenzlauer Berg group. For a discussion of how linguistic experimentation in their work is related to an interrogation of power see Leeder 1996, 144–77. The importance of textuality in recent poetry finds further analysis in Ryan 1997 and Schnell's discussion of Pastior, Thomas Kling, and Prenzlauer Berg poets (1993, 469–72).

35. Indeed, in his review of *Zukunftsmusik,* fellow poet Rühmkorf praised the subversive playfulness of the collection (1962, 170).

36. See Enzensberger's interview with Müller (Enzensberger 1995a). This sentiment is echoed in an interview with Kluge (Enzensberger 1999b).

37. For the sake of pointing out specific details in the *Kiosk* poems, I again use my own translations, unless otherwise noted in the text.

38. Ziebritzski (1997) has interpreted the butterfly as a reference to ancient Greek representations of the soul and Christian imagery dating from the fourth century that equates metamorphosis with resurrection, a motif continued in the

work of Lessing and burial symbolism of the nineteenth century. To read the image as multiply referential and, hence, to acknowledge its speculative closure, it is necessary to recognize the allusion it generates to modern psychology and also to European responses to East-West relations. This indexing symmetrically returns the poet and reader to the political questions of ethnicity that opened *Kiosk* (Enzensberger 1995b).

References

Adorno, Theodor W. 1955a. "Kulturkritik und Gesellschaft." In *Prismen,* 7–31. Berlin: Suhrkamp.

———. 1955b. "Valéry Proust Museum." In *Prismen,* 215–31. Berlin: Suhrkamp.

———. 1967a. "Cultural Theory and Society." In *Prisms.* Trans. Samuel and Shierry Weber, 19–34. London: Neville Spearman.

———. 1967b. "Valéry Proust Museum." In *Prisms.* Trans. Samuel and Shierry Weber, 173–85. London: Neville Spearman.

———. 1970. *Ästhetische Theorie.* Ed. Gretel Adorno and Rolf Tiedemann. Frankfurt am Main: Suhrkamp.

———. 1974a. *Minima Moralia.* Trans. E. F. N. Jephcott. London: Verso.

———. 1974b. "Rede über Lyrik und Gesellschaft." In *Noten zur Literatur.* Ed. Rolf Tiedemann, 49–68. Frankfurt am Main: Suhrkamp.

———. 1991a. "Commitment." In *Notes to Literature.* Vol. 2. Ed. Rolf Tiedemann. Trans. Shierry Weber Nicholsen, 76–94. New York: Columbia University Press.

———. 1991b. "On Lyric Poetry and Society." In *Notes to Literature.* Vol. 1. Ed. Rolf Tiedemann. Trans. Shierry Weber Nicholsen, 37–54. New York: Columbia University Press.

———. 1994. *Beethoven: Philosophie der Musik.* Ed. Rolf Tiedemann. Frankfurt am Main: Suhrkamp.

———. 1997. *Aesthetic Theory.* Ed. Gretel Adorno and Rolf Tiedemann. Trans. Robert Hullot-Kentor. Minneapolis: University of Minnesota Press.

Altieri, Charles. 1979. *Enlarging the Temple: New Directions in American Poetry during the 1960s.* Lewisburg, Penn.: Bucknell University Press.

———. 1984. *Self and Sensibility in Contemporary American Poetry.* Cambridge: Cambridge University Press.

Andersch, Alfred. 1948. *Deutsche Literatur in der Entscheidung.* Karlsruhe: Verlag Volk und Zeit.

———. 1965. "Dort ist ein Feuer." *Merkur* 202:83–84.

Andrews, Bruce. 1996. *Paradise and Method: Poetics and Practice.* Evanston, Ill.: Northwestern University Press.

Arendt, Hannah. 1948. "Beyond Personal Frustration: The Poetry of Bertolt Brecht." *Kenyon Review* 10, no. 2 (spring): 304–12.

Arnheim, Rudolf. 1954. *Art and Visual Perception.* Berkeley and Los Angeles: University of California Press.

———. 1978. "On the Late Style of Life and Art." *Michigan Quarterly Review* 17, no.2:149–56.

Aronowitz, Stanley. 1976. "Enzensberger on Mass Culture: A Review Essay." *Minnesota Review* 7 (1976): 90–99.

Bab, Julius, ed. 1953. *Amerikas neuere Lyrik*. Bad Nauheim: Christian-Verlag, 1953.

Bachmann, Ingeborg. 1978. *Sämtliche Gedichte*. Munich: Piper.

———. 1980. *Frankfurter Vorlesungen: Probleme zeitgenössisscher Dichtung.* Munich: Piper.

Barry, Jackson. 1999. "The Meaning of the Author: Robert Lowell as Image of an Age." In *Art, Culture, and the Semiotics of Meaning,* 77–87. New York: St. Martin's.

Barthes, Roland. 1967. *Writing Degree Zero and Elements of Semiology.* Trans. Annette Lavers and Colin Smith. Boston: Beacon.

Bassnett-McGuire, Susan. 1980. *Translation Studies.* London: Methuen.

Beach, Christopher. 1999. *Poetic Culture: Contemporary American Poetry between Community and Institution.* Evanston, Ill.: Northwestern University Press.

Belitt, Ben. 1995. *The Forgèd Feature.* New York: Fordham University Press.

Bender, Hans. 1961. "Die Weisheit der unausgesprochenen Worte." *Merkur* 15:178–90.

———. 1972. "Letter from Germany: The Myth of Kahlschlag." *Dimensions* 5, no. 3:395–401.

Benjamin, Walter. 1968. "The Task of the Translator." In *Illuminations.* Trans. Harry Zohn, 69–82. New York: Harcourt, Brace & World.

———. 1974a. "Das Kunstwerk im Zeitalter seiner technischen Reproduzierbarkeit." In *Illuminationen: Ausgewählte Schriften,* 136–69. Frankfurt am Main: Suhrkamp.

———. 1974b. "Die Aufgabe des Übersetzers." In *Illuminationen: Ausgewählte Schriften,* 50–62. Frankfurt am Main: Suhrkamp.

Benn, Gottfried. 1950. *Doppelleben: Zwei Selbstdarstellungen.* Wiesbaden: Limes.

———. 1951. *Probleme der Lyrik.* Wiesbaden: Limes.

———. 1960a. "Einsamer nie." In *Gedichte.* Vol. 3, *Gesammelte Werke,* edited by Dieter Wellershoff, 140. Wiesbaden: Limes.

———. 1960b. "Valse Triste." In *Gedichte.* Vol. 3, *Gesammelte Werke,* edited by Dieter Wellershoff, 72–73. Wiesbaden: Limes.

Bennett, Benjamin. 1993. "The Politics of the Mörike-Debate and Its Object." *Germanic Review* 67, no. 2 (1993): 60–68.

Berger, James. 1999. *After the End: Representations of Post-Apocalypse.* Minneapolis: University of Minnesota Press.

Biel, Steven. 1996. *Down with the Old Canoe: A Cultural History of the Titanic Disaster.* New York: W. W. Norton.

Biguenet, John, and Rainer Schulte, eds. 1989. *The Craft of Translation.* Chicago: University of Chicago Press.

Bishop, Elizabeth. 1969. "The Imaginary Iceberg." In *The Complete Poems,* 4. New York: Farrar, Straus and Giroux.

Bloom, Harold. 1973. *The Anxiety of Influence: A Theory of Poetry*. London: Oxford University Press.

Bohn, Volker. 1986. "*Die Furie des Verschwindens*. Zu Hans Magnus Enzensbergers Poetik." *Neue Rundschau* 1: 97–108.

Bohrer, Karl Heinz. 1970. "Revolution als Metapher." In *Die gefährdete Phantasie, oder Surrealismus und Terror*, 89–105. Munich: Hanser.

———. 1978. "Betarnte Anarchie." *Merkur* 12:1275–79.

Bollobás, Eniko. 1992. *Charles Olson*. New York: Twayne.

Bonheim, Helmut, and Reingard Nischik. 1978. "William Carlos Williams in Germany." *William Carlos Williams Newsletter* 4, no. 1:14–18.

Bourdieu, Pierre. 1991. *Language and Symbolic Power*. Trans. Gino Raymond and Matthew Adamson. Cambridge, Mass.: Harvard University Press.

———. 1993. *The Field of Cultural Production: Essays on Art and Literature*. Ed. Randal Johnson. New York: Columbia University Press.

Braun, Michael. 1986. *Der poetische Augenblick: Essays zur Gegenwartsliteratur*. Berlin: Vis-à-Vis.

Brecht, Bertolt. 1967a. *Gesammelte Gedichte*. Vol. 1. Frankfurt am Main: Suhrkamp.

———. 1967b. *Schriften: Zur Literatur und Kunst 2. 1934–1941*. Frankfurt am Main: Suhrkamp.

Bridgwater, Patrick. 1966. "Hans Magnus Enzensberger." *Essays on Contemporary German Literature: German Men of Letters*. Vol. 4. Ed. Brian Keith-Smith, 239–58. London: Oswald Wolff.

———. 1967–68. "The Making of a Poet: H. M. Enzensberger." *German Life and Letters* 1:27–44.

Buck, Theo. 1976. "Enzensberger und Brecht." *Text + Kritik* 49:5–16.

Buckley, Michael Travers. 1975. "Art Is Not Enough: Hans Magnus Enzensberger and the Politics of Poetry." Ph.D. diss., University of Massachusetts.

Buell, Fredrick. 1974. *National Culture and the New Global System*. Baltimore: Johns Hopkins University Press.

Bürger, Peter. 1974. *Theorie der Avantgarde*. Frankfurt am Main: Suhrkamp.

Burri, René. 1999. *Die Deutschen: Photographien 1957–1997. Mit einer Einführung von Hans-Michael Koetzle und Gedichten von Hans Magnus Enzensberger*. Munich: Schirmer/Mosel.

Canetti, Elias. 1993. *Die Blendung*. Munich: C. Hanser.

Celan, Paul. 1968. "Ansprache anläßlich der Entgegennahme des Literaturpreises der Freien Hansestadt Bremen." In *Ausgewählte Gedichte*, 127–29. Frankfurt am Main: Suhrkamp.

———. 1967. *Atemwende*. Frankfurt am Main: Suhrkamp.

———. 1972. "Der Meridian." In *Ausgewählte Gedichte*, 133–48. Frankfurt am Main: Suhrkamp.

———. 1975. *Gedichte I*. Frankfurt am Main: Suhrkamp.

———. 1999a. "The Meridian." In *Collected Prose*. Trans. Rosmarie Waldrop, 37–55. Manchester: Carcanet.

———. 1999b. "Speech on the Occasion of Receiving the Literature Prize of the Free Hanseatic City of Bremen." In *Collected Prose*. Trans. Rosmarie Waldrop, 33–35. Manchester: Carcanet.

Colombat, Rémy. 1994. "Quelques avatars de l'existence poétique: Continuités et ruptures dans le lyrisme de Hans Magnus Enzensberger." *Études Germaniques* 49:29–52.

Corner, James. 1999. "The Agency of Mapping." In *Mappings*. Ed. Denis Cosgrove, 213–52. London: Reaktion Books.

Cummings, E. E. 1958. *Gedichte: Deutsch von Eva Hesse*. Trans. Eva Hesse. Munich: Langewiesche-Brandt.

Demetz, Peter. 1970. *Postwar German Literature: A Critical Introduction*. New York: Pegasus.

———. 1986. *After the Fires*. San Diego: Harcourt Brace Jovanovich.

Derrida, Jacques. 1998. *Of Grammatology*. Trans. Gayatri Chakravorty Spivak. Baltimore: Johns Hopkins University Press.

Deschner, Karlheinz. 1964. "H. M. Enzensberger: Lyrik und Kritik." In *Talente, Dichter, Dilettanten: Überschätzte und unterschätzte Werke in der deutschen Literatur der Gegenwart*, 269–383. Wiesbaden: Limes.

Dickinson, Emily. 1942. "There is no frigate like a book." In *A Treasury of Great Poems*. Ed. Louis Untermeyer, 948. New York: Simon and Schuster.

Dietschreit, Frank, and Barbara Heinze-Dietschreit. 1986. *Hans Magnus Enzensberger*. Stuttgart: Metzler.

Domin, Hilde. 1966. *Doppelinterpretationen: Das zeitgenössische deutsche Gedicht zwischen Autor und Leser*. Frankfurt am Main: Athenäum.

———. 1968. "Ein Drehpunkt der Lyrikinterpretation. Zu Hugo Friedrichs 'Struktur der modernen Lyrik.'" *Der Monat* 20, no. 242:57–65.

Drews, Jörg. 1980. *Vom "Kahlschlag" zu "movens": Über das langsame Auftauchen experimenteller Schreibweisen in der westdeutschen Literatur der fünfziger Jahre*. Munich: Edition Text + Kritik.

———. 1995. *Das bleibt: Deutsche Gedichte 1945–1995*. Leipzig: Reclam.

Dujmiać, Daniela. 1996. *Literatur zwischen Autonomie und Engagement: Zur Poetik von H. M. Enzensberger, Peter Handke und Dieter Wellershoff*. Konstanz: Hartung-Gorre.

DuPlessis, Rachel Blau. 1994. "'Corpses of Poesy': Some Modern Poets and Some Gender Ideologies of Lyric." In *Feminist Measures: Soundings in Poetry and Theory*. Ed. Lynn Keller and Cristanne Miller, 69–95. Ann Arbor: University of Michigan Press.

Dylan, Bob. 1965. "Desolation Row," On *Bob Dylan: Highway 61 Revisited*. Columbia CL 2389.

Easthope, Anthony. 1983. *Poetry as Discourse*. London: Methuen.

Easthope, Anthony, and John O. Thompson, eds. 1991. *Contemporary Poetry Meets Modern Theory*. New York: Harvester Wheatsheaf.

Ehrlich, Paul R., Anne H. Ehrlich, and Gretchen C. Daily. 1995. *The Stork and the Plow: The Equity Answer to the Human Dilemma*. New York: Putnam's.

Eich, Günter. 1981. *Ein Lesebuch*. Frankfurt am Main: Suhrkamp.

Eliot, Thomas Stearns. 1948. "Aschermittwoch." *Deutsche Universitätszeitung* 3:v, 3.

———. 1972. *Gesammelte Gedichte 1909–1962*. Ed. Eva Hesse. Trans. Eva Hesse et al. Frankfurt am Main: Suhrkamp.

Emmerich, Wolfgang. 1981. *Kleine Literaturgeschichte der DDR*. Darmstadt: Luchterhand.

Enzensberger, Hans Magnus. 1956. "Cultivate Your Garden." *Poetry* 88, no. 4:250–51.

———. 1957a. "Genie als Karikatur," *Texte und Zeichen* 5:87–91.

———. 1957b. *Verteidigung der Wölfe*. Frankfurt am Main: Suhrkamp.

———. 1958. "Reine Sprache des Exils." *Frankfurter Hefte* 13:511–13.

———. 1959a. "Die Dummheit Unterwegs." *Neue Deutsche Hefte* 64 (November): 158–59.

———. 1959b. "Die große Ausnahme." Review of *Mutmassungen über Jakob*, by Uwe Johnson. *Frankfurter Hefte* 14:910–12.

———. 1959c. "Die Steine der Freiheit." *Merkur* 138, no. 8:770–75.

———. 1960a. "Antwort auf eine Konkret-Umfrage, die soziale Situation der deutschen Schriftsteller betreffend," *Konkret* 6, no. 21:13.

———. 1960b. "Die babylonische Bibliothek." *Magnum* 33:37–38.

———. 1960c. "Die Weltsprache der modernen Poesie." *Süddeutsche Zeitung*, 29 October.

———. 1960d. *Landessprache*. Frankfurt am Main: Suhrkamp.

———. 1960e. "Schimpfend unter Palmen." In *Ich lebe in der Bundesrepublik*. Ed. Wolfgang Weyrauch, 24–31. Munich: List.

———. 1961. *Brentanos Poetik*. Munich: Hanser.

———. 1962a. "Beat: Eine Anthologie." *Der Spiegel* 45:118–19.

———. 1962b. "Die Entstehung eines Gedichts." In *Gedichte: Die Entstehung eines Gedichts*, 37–54. Frankfurt am Main: Suhrkamp.

———. 1962c. "Ein Gedicht ist eine Maschine." *Die Zeit* 18 January.

———. 1963a. "Carson McCullers, *Uhr Ohne Zeiger*," *Der Spiegel* 10:65–66.

———. 1963b. "Die Schnecken." In *Club Voltaire*, 195–98. Munich: Szczesny.

———. 1963c. "Gulliver in Kopenhagen." *Akzente* 6:628–48.

———. 1963d. "In Search of the Lost Language." *Encounter* 21, no. 3:44–51.

———. 1963e. "Mein Gedicht ist eine Maschine." *Süddeutsche Zeitung*, 6 March.

———. 1963f. "Zum Andenken an William Carlos Williams." *Die Zeit*, 15 March.

———. 1964a. Afterword to *Krepsens vendekrets* [*Tropic of Cancer*], by Henry Miller. Trans. Axel Jensen. Oslo: Cappelen.

———. 1964b. "Am I a German?" *Encounter* 127:16–18.

———. 1964c. "Bin ich ein Deutscher?" *Die Zeit,* 5 June.

———. 1964d. *Blindenschrift*. Frankfurt am Main: Suhrkamp.

———. 1964e. *Einzelheiten I: Bewußtseins-Industrie*. Frankfurt am Main: Suhrkamp.

———. 1964f. *Einzelheiten II: Poesie und Politik*. Frankfurt am Main: Suhrkamp.

———. 1964g. *Mein Gedicht ist mein Messer*. Ed. Hans Bender. Munich: List.

———. 1964h. *Politik und Verbrechen: Neun Beiträge*. Frankfurt am Main: Suhrkamp.

———. 1964i. "Scherenschleifer und Poeten." In *Mein Gedicht ist mein Messer*. Ed. Hans Bender, 144–48. Munich: List.

———. 1965a. Afterword to *Winesburg Ohio,* by Sherwood Anderson. Trans. Gerd Hoff. Oslo: J. W. Cappelens.

———. 1965b. "Orakel vom Bodensee." Review of *Jahrbuch der öffentlichen Meinung 1958–64. Der Spiegel* 57:112–13.

———. 1966a. "Soziale Marktwirtschaft." *Luchterhands Loseblattlyrik* 1:2.

———. 1966b. "Wie entsteht ein Gedicht?" In *Ars Poetica*. Ed. Beda Allemann, 5–9. Darmstadt: Wissenschaftliche Buchgesellschaft.

———. 1967a. "Autobiography." Trans. Jerome Rothenberg. *Partisan Review* 4:49.

———. 1967b. "Berliner Modell 1967," "Gedicht über die Zukunft," "Illustrierte Geschichte der deutschen Revolution," "Lied von denen auf die alles zutrifft und die alles schon wissen," and "Vorschlag zur Strafrechtsreform." *Kursbuch* 10:140–49.

———. 1967c. "Der Heizer Hieronymus und die Kultur." *Deutsche Volkszeitung,* 31 March.

———. 1967d. *Deutschland, Deutschland unter anderem*. Frankfurt am Main: Suhrkamp.

———. 1967e. "Dickicht." *Luchterhands Loseblattlyrik* 7:3.

———. 1967f. "Nürnberger Rede." *Tribüne* 6, no. 22:2367–73.

———. 1967/68a. "Innenleben." Trans. Ingo Seidler. *Mundus Artium* 3:92–93.

———. 1967/68b. "Notstandsgesetz." Trans. Ingo Seidler. *Mundus Artium* 3:94–95.

———. 1968a. "Gemeinplätze, die Neueste Literatur betreffend." *Kursbuch* 15:187–97.

———. 1968b. "On Leaving America." *New York Review of Books,* 29 February.

———. 1968c. *Poems for People Who Don't Read Poems*. Trans. Michael Hamburger, Jerome Rothenberg, and H. M. Enzensberger. New York: Atheneum.

————. 1968d. "Vorschlag zur Strafrechtsreform." In *Lesebuch: Deutsche Literature der sechziger Jahre*, 144–46. Ed. Klaus Wagenbach. Berlin: K. Wagenbach.

————. 1969a. Afterword to *Iran: The New Imperialism in Action*, by Bahman Nirumand. New York: Monthly Review Press.

————. 1969b. "The Industrialization of the Mind." *Partisan Review* 36, no. 1:100–1.

————. 1970a. "Black and White Drawing," "Celestial Machine," "Paper Turkey," and "Riddle." Trans. H. M. Enzensberger. *Kayak* 23:3–7.

————. 1970b. "Die Scheiße." *Luchterhands Loseblattlyrik* 26:3.

————. 1971a. "Die Macht der Gewohnheit." *Tintenfisch* 4:11–12.

————. 1971b. *Gedichte 1955–1970*. Frankfurt am Main: Suhrkamp.

————. 1971c. "Interview mit Hans Magnus Enzensberger." Interview by Ursula Reinhold. *Weimarer Beiträge* 17, no. 5:73–93.

————. 1972a. *Der kurze Sommer der Anarchie. Buenaventura Durrutis Leben und Tod*. Frankfurt am Main: Suhrkamp.

————. 1972b. "Valse triste et sentimentale." *Literarische Hefte* 41:4–5.

————. 1973. "Zur Kritik der politischen Ökologie." *Kursbuch* 33:43–52.

————. 1974a. *The Consciousness Industry: On Literature, Politics and the Media*. Trans. Michael Roloff. New York: Seabury.

————. 1974b. *Palaver: Politische Überlegungen, 1967–73*. Frankfurt am Main: Suhrkamp.

————. 1975. *Mausoleum: Siebenunddreißig Balladen aus der Geschichte des Fortschritts*. Frankfurt am Main: Suhrkamp.

————. 1976a. "Bescheidener Vorschlag zum Schutze der Jugend vor den Erzeugnissen der Poesie." *German Quarterly* 49, no. 4:425–37.

————. 1976b. "Die Aporien der Avantgarde." In *Einzelheiten II: Poesie und Politik*, 50–80. Frankfurt am Main: Suhrkamp.

————. 1976c. *Mausoleum: Thirty-seven Ballads from the History of Progress*. Trans. Joachim Neugroschel. New York: Urizen.

————. 1978a. *Der Untergang der Titanic: Eine Kömodie*. Frankfurt am Main: Suhrkamp.

————. 1978b. "Zwei Randbemerkungen zum Weltuntergang." *Kursbuch* 52:1–8.

————. 1979a. "Autor und Wirklichkeit." *Theater der Zeit* 9:20.

————. 1979b. *Der Untergang der Titanic*. Radio-play version by Horst H. Vollmer. 1987. Stuttgart: Klett. Cottas Hörbuhne Audiocassette 76131.

————. 1979c. "Die Literatur nach dem Tod der Literatur: Ein Gespräch." Interview by Alfred Andersch. In *Nach dem Protest: Literatur im Umbruch*. Ed. W. Martin Lüdke, 85–102. Frankfurt am Main: Suhrkamp.

————. 1979d. "Unentwegter Versuch, einem New Yorker Publikum die

Geheimnisse der deutschen Demokratie zu erklären." *Kursbuch* 56 (June): 1–14.

———. 1980a. *Die Furie des Verschwindens: Gedichte.* Frankfurt am Main: Suhrkamp.

———. 1980b. *The Sinking of the Titanic: A Poem.* Trans. H. M. Enzensberger. Boston: Houghton Mifflin.

———. 1982. *Svensk Höst.* Trans. Madeleine Gustafsson. Stockholm: Dagens Nyheter.

———. 1983. *Die Gedichte.* Frankfurt am Main: Suhrkamp.

———. 1984a. "Das langsame Verschwinden der Personen." In *Hans Magnus Enzensberger.* Ed. Reinhold Grimm, 15–17. Frankfurt am Main: Suhrkamp.

———. 1984b. *Norsk utakt.* Trans. Lasse Tømte. Oslo: Universitetsforlaget.

———[Andreas Thalmayr, pseud.]. 1985. *Das Wasserzeichen der Poesie, oder, Die Kunst und das Vergnügen, Gedichte zu lesen, in Hundertvierundsechzig Spielarten vorgeführt.* Nördlingen: Greno.

———. 1989a. *Der Fliegende Robert: Gedichte, Szenen, Essays.* Frankfurt am Main: Suhrkamp.

———. 1989b. *Mittelmaß und Wahn: Gesammelte Zerstreuungen.* Frankfurt am Main: Suhrkamp.

———. 1991a. "Hans Magnus Enzensberger in Conversation with Michael Hulse." Interview by Michael Hulse. *Poetry Review* 81, no. 3:4–9.

———. 1991b. *Zukunftsmusik.* Frankfurt am Main: Suhrkamp.

———. 1992a. *Die große Wanderung: Dreiunddreißig Markierungen. Mit einer Fußnote "Über einige Besonderheiten bei der Menschenjagd."* Frankfurt am Main: Suhrkamp.

———. 1992b. "Intellectuals as Leaders." *Partisan Review* 59, no. 4:666–700.

———. 1993a. *Aussichten auf den Bürgerkrieg.* Frankfurt am Main: Suhrkamp.

———. 1993b. "Carry on, Gutenberg! Two Cheers for a Minority." In *The Situation of High-Quality Literature.* Ed. Sture Allén, 33–46. Stockholm: Swedish Academy.

———. 1994a. *Civil Wars: From L.A. to Bosnia.* New York: New Press.

———. 1994b. *Selected Poems.* Trans. Michael Hamburger and H. M. Enzensberger. Newcastle upon Tyne: Bloodaxe.

———. 1995a. "Ich will nicht der Lappen sein, mit dem man die Welt putzt." Interview by André Müller. *Die Zeit,* 20 January.

———. 1995b. *Kiosk: Neue Gedichte.* Frankfurt am Main: Suhrkamp.

———. 1995c. *Nieder mit Goethe: Eine Liebeserklärung/Requiem für eine romantische Frau: ein Liebeskampf in sieben Sätzen.* Frankfurt am Main: Verlag der Autoren.

———. 1997a. *Der Zahlenteufel: Ein Kopfkissenbuch für alle, die Angst vor der Mathematik haben.* Compiled and with illustrations provided by Rotraut Susanne Berner. Munich: Hanser.

————. 1997b. *The Number Devil: A Mathematical Adventure.* Trans. Michael Henry Heim. New York: Metropolitan Books.

————. 1997c. *Zickzack: Aufsätze.* Frankfurt am Main: Suhrkamp.

————. 1999a. "Das Haus in der Burggasse: Ein Fluchtversuch." In *Der Zorn altert, die Ironie ist unsterblich: Über Hans Magnus Enzensberger.* Ed. Rainer Wieland, 118–21. Frankfurt am Main: Suhrkamp.

————. 1999b. "Deutscher sein ist kein Beruf." Interview by Alexander Kluge. *Hans Magnus Enzensberger: Der Raum des Intellektuellen.* Special issue of *Du* 699, no. 9:2–3.

————. 1999c. *Geisterstimmen: Übersetzungen und Imitationen.* Frankfurt am Main: Suhrkamp.

————. 1999d. *Kiosk.* Trans. Michael Hamburger and Hans Magnus Enzensberger. Riverdale-on-Hudson, New York: Sheep Meadow Press.

————. 1999e. *Leichter als Luft: Moralische Gedichte.* Frankfurt am Main: Suhrkamp.

————. 1999f. "Wie ich fünfzig Jahre lang versuchte, Amerika zu entdecken." In *Der Zorn altert, die Ironie ist unsterblich: Über Hans Magnus Enzensberger.* Ed. Rainer Wieland, 96–111. Frankfurt am Main: Suhrkamp.

————. 2000. *Einladung zu einem Poesie-Automaten.* Frankfurt am Main: Suhrkamp.

————, ed. 1964. *Labyrinter,* by Jorge Luis Borges. Trans. Finn Aasen. Oslo: Cappelen.

————. 1966. *Bartolomé de las Casas: Kurzgefaßter Bericht von der Verwüstung der Westindischen Länder.* Trans. D. W. Andreä. Frankfurt am Main: Insel.

————. 1973. *Gespräche mit Marx und Engels.* Frankfurt am Main: Insel.

————. 1980. *Museum der modernen Poesie.* Frankfurt am Main: Suhrkamp.

————. 1999. *Eine literarische Landkarte.* Munich: Goldmann.

————, trans. 1962a. *David Rokeah: Poesie,* by David Rokeah. Frankfurt am Main: Suhrkamp.

————. 1962b. *William Carlos Williams: Gedichte,* by William Carlos Williams. Frankfurt am Main: Suhrkamp.

————. 1977. *Edward Lears Kompletter Nonsens,* by Edward Lear. Frankfurt am Main: Insel.

————. 1979b. *Der Menschenfeind.* Frankfurt am Main: Insel.

————. 1984. "Der falsche Atlas," by John Tranter. *Akzente* 5:466–74.

————. 1993. *Ein Buch von Göttern und Teufeln: Gedichte,* by Charles Simic. Munich: Hanser.

Enzensberger, Hans Magnus, and Volker Eisman. 1993. *Die Suche: Das andere Lehrwerk für Deutsch als Fremdsprache.* Berlin: Langenscheidt.

Enzensberger, Hans Magnus, Reinhold Grimm, and Bruce Armstrong. 1982. *Critical Essays.* New York: Continuum.

Enzensberger, Hans Magnus, and Raoul Schrott. 1999. *Mutmassungen über die*

Poesie: Lesungen und ein Gespräch mit Hans Magnus Enzensberger und Raoul Schrott. Ed. Denis Scheck and Hubert Winkels. Berlin: Eichborn.

Er. 1955. "Zwischenbilanz des Buches." *Neue Deutsche Hefte* 10:799–800.

Essmann, Helga, and Armin Paul Frank. 1991. "Translation Anthologies: An Invitation to the Curious and a Case Study." *Target* 3, no. 1:65–90.

Estermann, Alfred. 1984. "Hans Magnus Enzensberger: Eine Bibliographie." In *Über Hans Magnus Enzensberger.* Ed. Reinhold Grimm, 343–435. Frankfurt am Main: Suhrkamp.

Even-Zohar, Itamar. 1978. "The Position of Translated Literature within the Literary Polysystem." In *Literature and Translation: New Perspectives in Literary Studies with a Basic Bibliography of Books on Translation Studies.* Ed. James S. Holmes, José Lambert, and Raymond van den Broeck, 117–27. Leuven, Belgium: Acco.

Falkenstein, Henning. 1977. *Hans Magnus Enzensberger.* Berlin: Colloquium.

Falkner, Gerhard. 1993. *Über den Unwert des Gedichts: Fragmente und Reflexionen.* Berlin: Aufbau.

Ferber, Christian. 1952. "Die Legende vom Kahlschlag." *Die Literatur* 6:1–2.

Fink, Ernst O. 1971. *Die übersetzerische Rezeption des lyrischen Werkes von T. S. Eliot im deutschsprachigen Raum.* Bamberg: Bamberger Fotodruck.

Fischer, Gerhard, ed. 1996. *Debating Enzensberger: Great Migration and Civil War.* Tübingen: Stauffenburg.

Fleischmann, Wolfgang B. 1962. "Translation Problems Related to Rendering the Work of Certain Contemporary American Poets into German." *Jahrbuch für Amerikastudien* 7:176–82.

———. 1973. "Amerikanische Dichtkunst und deutsche, 1945–1965." In *Nordamerikanische Literatur im deutschen Sprachraum seit 1945: Beiträge zu ihrer Rezeption.* Ed. Horst Frenz and Hans-Joachim Lang, 65–78. Munich: Winkler.

Forché, Carolyn, ed. 1981. "El Salvador: An Aide Memoire." *American Poetry Review* (July/August): 6–7.

———. 1993. *Against Forgetting: Twentieth-Century Poetry of Witness.* New York: W. W. Norton.

Foucault, Michel. 1965. *Madness and Civilization: A History of Insanity in the Age of Reason.* Trans. Richard Howard. New York: Vintage.

———. 1970. *The Order of Things.* London: Tavistock.

———. 1972. *The Archaeology of Knowledge and the Discourse on Language.* Trans. A. M. Sheridan Smith. New York: Pantheon.

Franz, Michael. 1984. "Hans Magnus Enzensberger: *Mausoleum.*" In *Hans Magnus Enzensberger.* Ed. Reinhold Grimm, 294–311. Frankfurt am Main: Suhrkamp.

Fredman, Stephen. 1990. *Poet's Prose: The Crisis in American Verse.* Cambridge: Cambridge University Press.

Frey, John R. 1953–54. "America and Her Literature Reviewed by Postwar Germany." *American German Review* 20, no. 5:4–6, 31.

———. 1954–55. "Postwar Germany: Enter American Literature." *American German Review* 21, no. 1:9–12.

Fried, Erich. 1957. "e. e. cummings oder Die Sprache, in der man nicht lügen kann." *Texte und Zeichen* 3:496–511.

———. 1969. "Wie ich Shakespeare übersetze." *Theater heute* 10, no. 6:25–26.

———. 1978. "Neue Subjektivität." *Lyrik-Katalog Bundesrepublik: Gedichte, Biographien, Statements*. Ed. Jan Hans, Uwe Herms, and Ralf Thenior, 115–16. Munich: Goldmann.

Friedrich, Hugo. 1958. *Die Struktur der modernen Lyrik*. Reinbek: Rowohlt.

———. 1974. *The Structure of Modern Poetry: From the Mid-Nineteenth to the Mid-Twentieth Century*. Trans. Joachim Neugroschel. Evanston, Ill.: Northwestern University Press.

Frischmuth, Barbara. 1969. "Rede anlässlich einer Lesung im Collegium Hungaricum Wien 1969." *Literatur und Kritik* 35:257–58.

Fritz, Walter H. 1969. *Bemerkungen zu einer Gegend: Prosa*. Frankfurt am Main: Fischer.

———. 1970. *Möglichkeiten des Prosagedichts anhand einiger französischer Beispiele*. Mainz: Verlag der Akademie der Wissenschaften und der Literatur.

Fülleborn, Ulrich, ed. 1976. *Deutsche Prosagedichte des 20. Jahrhunderts: Eine Textsammlung*. Munich: Wilhelm Fink.

Gadamer, Hans Georg. 1965. *Wahrheit und Methode: Grundzüge einer philosophischen Hermeneutik*. 2nd ed. Tübingen: Mohr.

Galinsky, Hans. 1968. *Wegbereiter moderner amerikanischer Lyrik: Interpretations- und Rezeptionsstudien zu Emily Dickinson und William Carlos Williams*. Heidelberg: Carl Winter.

———. 1972. *Amerikanisch-deutsche Sprach- und Literaturbeziehungen: Systematische Übersicht und Forschungsbericht 1945–1970*. Frankfurt am Main: Athenäum.

Gehring, Hansjörg. 1977. "Literatur im Dienst der Politik: Zum Re-education Programm der amerikanischen Militärregierung in Deutschland." In *Literaturmagazin 7: Nachkriegsliteratur*. Ed. Nicholas Born and Jürgen Mauthey, 252–70. Hamburg: Rowohlt.

Geist, Peter. 1993. "Voices from No Man's Land: Recent German Poetry." In *Cultural Transformations in the New Germany: American and German Perspectives*. Ed. Friederike Eigler and Peter C. Pfeiffer. Trans. Friederike Eigler, 132–53. Columbia: Camden House.

Gerhardt, Rainer M. 1965/66. "Valse triste et sentimentale." Trans. Anselm Hollo. *Work* 3:24–26.

Gleick, James. 1987. *Chaos: Making a New Science*. New York: Viking Penguin.

Gnüg, Hiltrud. 1979. "A.v.H. (1769–1859)." In *Geschichte im Gedicht: Texte und*

Interpretationen. Protestlied, Bänkelsang, Ballade, Chronik. Ed. Walter Hinck, 292–301. Frankfurt am Main: Suhrkamp.

Goethe, Johann Wolfgang von. 1970. *Theory of Colours.* Translated by Charles Lock Eastlake. Cambridge, Mass.: MIT Press.

———. 1974. "An den Mond." In *Goethe Gedichte.* Ed. Erich Trunz, 129–30. Munich: Beck.

———. 1994. "Selige Sehnsucht." In *West-Östlicher Divan: Teil 1.* Ed. Hendrik Birus, 24–25. Frankfurt am Main: Deutscher Klassiker.

Goetz, Müller. 1981. "*Der Untergang der Titanic:* Bemerkungen zu Enzensbergers Gedicht." *Zeitschrift für deutsche Philologie* 2:254–74.

Golding, Alan. 1995. *From Outlaw to Classic: Canons in American Poetry.* Madison: University of Wisconsin Press.

Goodbody, Axel. 1990. "Enzensberger, the German Question and the West German Left." In *Lektüre: Ein Anarchischer Akt: A Nottingham Symposium with Hans Magnus Enzensberger.* Ed. Hinrich Siefkin and J. H. Reid, 37–55. Nottingham: University of Nottingham.

———. 1991. "*Deutsche Ökolyrik:* Comparative Observations on the Emergence and Expression of Environmental Consciousness in West and East German Poetry." In *German Literature at a Time of Change, 1989–1990.* Ed. Arthur Williams, Stuart Parkes, and Roland Smith, 373–412. Bern: Peter Lang.

Grimm, Erk. 1997. "Mediamania? Contemporary German Poetry in the Age of New Information Technologies: Thomas Kling and Durs Grünbein." *Studies in Twentieth Century Literature* 21, no. 1 (winter): 275–301.

Grimm, Reinhold. 1967. "Die problematischen 'Probleme der Lyrik.'" In *Festschrift Gottfried Weber.* Ed. Heinz Otto Burger and Klaus von See, 299–328. Bad Homburg: Gehlen.

———. 1984. *Texturen: Essays und anderes zu Hans Magnus Enzensberger.* New York: Peter Lang.

———. 1998a. "'Once upon a Time': Some Fleeting Sidelights on Contemporary Western Poetry." *Manusya* 1, no. 1 (March): 25–46.

———. 1998b. "Von Katzen und Translatzen." *Neue Rundschau* 109, no. 1:101–19.

———, ed. 1984. *Hans Magnus Enzensberger.* Frankfurt am Main: Suhrkamp.

Gryphius, Andreas. 1962. *Andreas Gryphius: Gedichte.* Ed. H. M. Enzensberger. Frankfurt am Main: Insel.

———. 1980. "Abend." In *Gedichte des Barock.* Ed. Ulrich Maché and Volker Meid, 118. Stuttgart: Philipp Reclam Jun.

Guillory, John. 1993. *Cultural Capital: The Problem of Literary Canon Formation.* Chicago: University of Chicago Press.

Gültig, Heinz, ed. 1959. *Baemu suti oder Das ibolithische Vermächtnis: Ein literarisches Gesellschaftsspiel,* by Hans Magnus Enzensberger. Zurich: Diogenes.

Gumpel, Liselotte. 1976. *"Concrete" Poetry from East and West Germany: The Language of Exemplarism and Experimentalism.* New Haven, Conn.: Yale University Press.

Gutmann, Helmut. 1970. "Die Utopie der reinen Negation: Zur Lyrik H. M. Enzensbergers." *German Quarterly* 43, no. 3:435–52.

Gutzat, Bärbel. 1977. *Bewußtseinsinhalte kritischer Lyrik: Eine Analyse der ersten drei Gedichtbände von Hans Magnus Enzensberger.* Wiesbaden: Akademischer Verlagsgesellschaft Athenaion.

Habermas, Jürgen. 1968a. *Technik und Wissenschaft als "Ideologie."* Frankfurt am Main: Suhrkamp.

———. 1968b. "Technik und Wissenschaft als 'Ideologie.'" Parts 1 and 2. *Merkur* 243 (July): 591–610; 244 (August): 682–93.

———. 1975. *Legitimation Crisis.* Trans. Thomas McCarthy. Boston: Beacon Hill.

Hacks, Peter. 1977. "Der Sarah-Sound." In *Maßgaben der Kunst: Gesammelte Aufsätze,* 267–84. Düsseldorf: Classen.

Hage, Volker. 1980. *Lyrik für Leser: Deutsche Gedichte der siebziger Jahre.* Stuttgart: Reclam.

Hahn, Ulla. 1978. *Literatur in der Aktion: Zur Entwicklung operativer Literaturformen in der Bundesrepublik.* Wiesbaden: Akademische Verlagsgesellschaft Athenaion.

———. 1988. *Unerhörte Nähe: Gedichte, mit einem Anhang für den, der fragt.* Stuttgart: Deutsche Verlags-Anstalt.

Hamburger, Michael. 1976. "Erfahrung eines Übersetzers." *Neue Rundschau* 87:602–10.

Haney, David P. 1999. "Aesthetics and Ethics in Gadamer, Levinas, and Romanticism: Problems of Phronesis and Techne." *PMLA* 114, no. 1:32–45.

Hans Magnus Enzensberger. 1976. Special issue of *Text + Kritik* 49 (reprint 1985).

Hans Magnus Enzensberger: Der Raum des Intellektuellen. 1999. Special issue of *Du* 699, no. 9.

Hansen, Kurt Heinrich. 1979. "Die Sinnlichkeit des Übersetzens." *Der Monat* 32, no. 2:110–16.

Hartung, Harald. 1985. "Warten auf das lange Gedicht." In *Deutsche Lyrik seit 1965: Tendenzen, Beispiele, Porträts,* 66–82. Munich: Piper.

———. 1994. *Poesie im Prozeß: Überlegungen zur internationalen Lyrik.* Mainz: Akademie der Wissenschaften und der Literatur.

———. 1999. "Die Sache der Hände." *Lyrik: Über Lyrik.* Special issue of *Merkur* 53, nos. 3–4:324–31.

———, ed. 1991. *Luftfracht: Internationale Poesie 1940 bis 1990.* Frankfurt am Main: Eichborn.

Hartung, Rudolf. 1960. "Zorn als Landessprache." *Neue Deutsche Hefte* 77:826–29.

Hauptmann, Christoph. 1997. "Medientheoretische Konzepte und Strategien im Werk von Hans Magnus Enzensberger." Ph.D. diss., New York University.

Hayles, N. Katherine. 1990. *Chaos Bound: Orderly Disorder in Contemporary Literature and Science*. Ithaca, N.Y.: Cornell University Press.

———. 1991. *Chaos and Order: Complex Dynamics in Literature and Science*. Chicago: University of Chicago Press.

Heidegger, Martin. 1927. *Sein und Zeit*. Halle an der Saale: Max Niemeyer.

Herzog, Dagmar. 1998. " 'Pleasure, Sex, and Politics Belong Together': Post-Holocaust Memory and the Sexual Revolution in West Germany." *Critical Inquiry* 24 (winter): 393–444.

Hesse, Eva. 1968. "Das rechte Wort zu finden für den stimmlosen Laut des Herzens." *Deutsche Akademie für Sprache und Dichtung Jahrbuch 1968*, 25–31. Darmstadt: Deutsche Akademie für Sprache und Dichtung.

Heuss, Theodor. 1957. "German Character and History." Trans. Richard Winston and Clara Winston. *Perspectives of Germany*. Special issue of *Atlantic Monthly* (March): 103–9.

Hielscher, Martin. 1995. "Literatur in Deutschland-Avantgarde und pädagogischer Purismus." *Neue Rundschau* 106, no. 4:53–68.

Hinderer, Walter. 1984. "Ecce poeta rhetor: Vorgreifliche Bemerkungen über H. M. Enzensbergers Poesie und Prosa." In *Hans Magnus Enzensberger*. Ed. Reinhold Grimm, 189–203. Frankfurt am Main: Suhrkamp.

Hoffman, Daniel. 1979. *Harvard Guide to Contemporary American Writing*. Cambridge, Mass.: Harvard University Press, Belknap Press.

Hohendahl, Peter Uwe. 1995. *Prismatic Thought: Theodor W. Adorno*. Lincoln: University of Nebraska Press.

Holbeche, Brian. 1981. *Die Lyrik Gottfried Benns im westdeutschen literarischen Leben der 50er Jahren: Rezeption und Einfluß*. Heidelberg: Carl Winter.

Holden, Jonathan. 1986. *Style and Authenticity in Postmodern Poetry*. Columbia: University of Missouri Press.

Höllerer, Walter. 1959. "Junge Amerikanische Lyrik." *Akzente* 6, no. 2:29–43.

———. 1959. "Deutsche Lyrik in der Mitte des 20. Jahrhunderts und einige Verbindungslinien zur französichen und englischen Lyrik." In *Comparative Literature: Proceedings of the Second Congress on the ICLA,* 707–24. Chapel Hill: University of North Carolina Press.

———. 1966. "Gedichte in den sechziger Jahren." *Akzente* 13, no. 4:375–83.

Holmes, James S., ed. 1978. *Literature and Translation: New Perspectives in Literary Studies*. Leuvain, Belgium: Acco.

Holmes, James S., Frans de Haan and Anton Popovic, eds. 1970. *The Nature of Translation: Essays on the Theory and Practice of Literary Translation*. The Hague: Mouton.

Holthusen, Hans Egon. 1967. "Die Welt in sechzehn Sprachen." In *Plädoyer für den Einzelnen,* 186–99. Munich: Piper.

———. 1970. "Die Zornigen, die Gesellschaft und das Glück: Lyrik von H. M. Enzensberger." In *Über Hans Magnus Enzensberger*. Ed. Joachim Schickel, 40–67. Frankfurt am Main: Suhrkamp.

———. 1976. "Bruder Niccolo." In *Kreiselkompaß*, 84–98, 230–31. Munich: Piper.

———. 1980a. "Chorführer der Neuen Aufklärung: Über den Lyriker Hans Magnus Enzensberger." *Merkur* 26, no. 9:896–912.

———. 1980b. "Der Dichter im Eisernen Käfig, Versuch über Ezra Pound." In *Der unbehauste Mensch*, 104–34. Munich: Piper.

———. 1980c. "Ruhe auf der Flucht: Versuch einer kritischen Orientierung über die deutsche Literatur seit 1945." In *Ensemble 11*, 99–133. Munich: Deutscher Taschenbuch Verlag.

———. 1982. "Utopie und Katastrophe: Der Lyriker Hans Magnus Enzensberger 1957–1978." In *Sartre in Stammheim*, 5–97. Stuttgart: Klett-Cotta.

Hölzer, Max. 1967. "Zur Übersetzung von Gedichten," *Sprache im Technischen Zeitalter* 21:59–64.

Honig, Edwin. 1985. *The Poet's Other Voice*. Amherst: University of Massachusetts Press.

Horst, Eberhard. 1961. "Zornige Landessprache." *Rheinische Post*, 11 March.

Huyssen, Andreas. 1986. *After the Great Divide: Modernism, Mass Culture, Postmodernism*. Bloomington: Indiana University Press.

———. 1993. "The Search for Tradition: Avant-Garde and Post-Modernism in the 1970s." In *Postmodernism: A Reader*. Ed. Thomas Docherty, 220–36. New York: Columbia University Press.

———. 1995. *Twilight Memories*. New York: Routledge.

Innerhofer, Roland. 1980. "Hans Magnus Enzensbergers *Mausoleum*: Zur 'dokumentarischen' Lyrik in Deutschland." Ph.D. diss., University of Vienna.

Jahn, Janheiz. 1970. "Eine Kunst zwischen den Stühlen." *Deutsche Akademie für Sprache und Dichtung Jahrbuch 1970*, 41–48. Darmstadt: Deutsche Akademie für Sprache und Dichtung.

Jähnichen, Manfred, et al. 1973. "Über die Kunst des Nachdichtens." *Weimarer Beiträge* 19, no. 8:34–74.

Jameson, Fredric. 1992. "Aesthetics and Politics." In *Art in Modern Culture: An Anthology of Critical Texts*. Ed. Francis Franscina and Jonathan Harris, 64–73. London: Phaidon.

———. 1999. "Cognitive Mapping." In *Poetics/Politics: Radical Aesthetics for the Classroom*. Ed. Amitava Kumar, 155–67. New York: St. Martin's.

Jameson, Fredric, and Masao Miyoshi. 1998. *The Cultures of Globalization*. Durham, N.C.: Duke University Press.

Janson, H. W. 1991. *History of Art*. New York: Harry N. Abrams.

Jens, Walter. 1974. "Probleme einer modernen Bibelübersetzung." *Reutlinger Drucke* 9, no. 2 [no pagination].

Jordan, Lothar. 1984. "Eine Dichtung unter Einfluß: Zur amerikanischen Wirkung auf westdeutsche Lyrik seit 1965." In *Lyrik: Blick über die Grenzen.* Ed. Lothar Jordan, Axel Marquardt, and Winfried Woesler, 139–58. Frankfurt am Main: Fischer.

Kafka, Franz. 1974. "Die Sorge des Hausvaters." In *Sämtliche Erzählungen.* Ed. Paul Raabe, 139–40. Frankfurt am Main: Fischer.

Kaiser, Joachim. 1999. "Spannende Wandlungen eines Poeten." In *Der Zorn altert, die Ironie ist unsterblich: Über Hans Magnus Enzensberger.* Ed. Rainer Wieland, 159–68. Frankfurt am Main: Suhrkamp.

Kapur, Geeta. 1998. "Globalization and Culture: Navigating the Void." In *The Cultures of Globalization.* Ed. Fredric Jameson and Masao Miyoshi, 191–217. Durham, N.C.: Duke University Press.

Kaschnitz, Marie Luise. 1950. *Zukunftsmusik.* Hamburg: Claassen.

Kayser, Wolfgang. 1946. *Kleine deutsche Versschule.* Bern: Francke.

Kenner, Hugh. 1968. *The Counterfeiters.* Bloomington: Indiana University Press.

Kesting, Hanjo. 1984. "Gespräch mit Hans Magnus Enzensberger." In *Hans Magnus Enzensberger.* Ed. Reinhold Grimm, 116–35. Frankfurt am Main: Suhrkamp.

Kiermeier-Debre, Joseph. 1986. " 'Diese Geschichte vom untergehenden Schiff, das ein Schiff und kein Schiff ist': H. M. Enzensbergers Komödie vom Untergang des *Untergangs der Titanic.*" In *Apokalypse: Weltuntergangsvisionen in der Literatur des 20. Jahrhunderts,* 222–45. Frankfurt am Main: Suhrkamp.

Kirsch, Rainer. 1976. *Das Wort und seine Strahlung: Über Poesie und ihre Übersetzung.* Berlin: Aufbau.

———. 1979. "Das Wort und seine Strahlung: Über Poesie und ihre Übersetzung." *Neue Deutsche Literatur* 23, no. 12:124–43.

Kloepfer, Rolf. 1967. *Die Theorie der literarischen Übersetzung: Romanisch-deutscher Sprachbereich.* Munich: Wilhelm Fink.

Knape, Franz Josef. 1995. *. . . zugeritten in manchen sprachen . . . Über Werk und Wirkung des Dichters und Vermittlers Rainer Maria Gerhardt.* Würzburg: Königshausen und Neumann.

Knörrich, Otto. 1978. *Die deutsche Lyrik seit 1945.* Stuttgart: Alfred Kröner.

Koepke, Wulf. 1971. "Mehrdeutigkeit in Hans Magnus Enzensbergers 'Bösen Gedichten.' " *German Quarterly* 44, no. 3:341–59.

———. 1980. "Enzensberger and the Possibility of Political Poetry." In *Bertolt Brecht: Political Theory and Literary Practice.* Ed. Betty Nance Weber and Herbert Heinen, 179–89. Athens: University of Georgia Press.

Kolb, Marina. 1993. "Im Namen der Sprache: Benn, Sachs, Bachmann und Enzensberger Zusammengedacht." Ph.D. diss., University of Oregon.

Korte, Hermann. 1989. *Geschichte der deutschen Lyrik seit 1945.* Stuttgart: Metzler.

————. 1997. "Hans Magnus Enzensberger." In *Kritisches Lexikon zur deutschsprachigen Gegenwartsliteratur*. Munich: Text + Kritik.

Kristeva, Julia. 1984. *Revolution in Poetic Language*. Trans. Margaret Waller. New York: Columbia University Press.

Krolow, Karl. 1954. "Wesenszüge deutscher Lyrik in diesen Jahren." *Deutsche Rundschau* 80, no. 5:475–79.

————. 1958. "Kampagne gegen die Welt." *Neue Deutsche Hefte* 52:741–42.

————. 1960. "Zorniges Dichten." *Der Tagesspiegel*, 11 September, 35.

————. 1961. *Aspekte zeitgenössischer deutscher Lyrik*. Berlin: Gütersloher Verlagshaus Gerd Mohn.

————. 1963. "Der Lyriker als Übersetzer zeitgenössischer Lyrik." *Jahrbuch Gestalt und Gedanke* 8:109–34.

————. 1966. "Das Problem des langen und kurzen Gedichts heute." *Akzente* 13, no. 3:271–87.

Kruntorad, Paul. 1969. "Persönliches Credo zum Problem der Lyrik-Übersetzung." *Literatur und Kritik* 35:258–59.

Kumar, Amitava. 1997. "The Poet's Corpse in the Capitalist's Fish Tank" *Critical Inquiry* (summer): 894–909.

Künzel, Horst. 1980. "Vom Vergnügen in der Kunst." *Die horen* 25, no. 4:57–63.

Lamping, Dieter. 1987. "Die Komödie des Weltuntergangs: Eine Anmerkung zu H. M. Enzensbergers Der Untergang der Titanic." *Germanisch-Romanische Monatsschrift* 2:229–31.

————. 1991. *Moderne Lyrik: Eine Einführung*. Göttingen: Vandenhoeck and Ruprecht.

————. 1994. "Williams Carlos Williams, deutsch: Zur Rezeption moderner amerikanischer Lyrik in Deutschland." *Arcadia* 29, no. 1:43–57.

Lau, Jörg. 1999. *Hans Magnus Enzensberger: Ein öffentliches Leben*. Berlin: Alexander Fest.

Lawrence, Tim. 1997. "Edward Said, Late Style and the Aesthetic of Exile." *Third Text* 38:15–24.

Ledanff, Susanne. 1981. *Die Augenblicksmetapher: Über Bildlichkeit und Spontaneität in der Lyrik*. Munich: Hanser.

Leeder, Karen. 1996. *Breaking Boundaries: A New Generation of Poets in the GDR*. Oxford: Clarendon.

Lefevere, André. 1992. *Translating Literature: Practice and Theory in a Comparative Literature Context*. New York: MLA.

Lehmann, Hans-Thies. 1984. "Eisberg und Spiegelkunst: Notizen zu Hans Magnus Enzensbergers Lust am Untergang der Titanic." In *Hans Magnus Enzensberger*. Ed. Reinhold Grimm, 312–34. Frankfurt am Main: Suhrkamp.

Lepenies, Wolf. 1999. "Der Zorn altert, die Ironie ist unsterblich." In *Der Zorn altert, die Ironie ist unsterblich: Über Hans Magnus Enzensberger*. Ed. Rainer Wieland, 23–32. Frankfurt am Main: Suhrkamp.

Lettau, Reinhard. 1967. *Die Gruppe 47: Bericht, Kritik, Polemik: Ein Handbuch.* Neuwied: Luchterhand.

Levenston, Edward A. 1992. *The Stuff of Literature: Physical Aspects of Texts and Their Relation to Literary Meaning.* Albany: State University of New York Press.

Levy, Jirí. 1969. *Die literarische Übersetzung: Theorie einer Kunstgattung.* Trans. Walter Schamschula. Frankfurt: Athenäum.

Linder, Christian. 1975. "Der lange Sommer der Romantik: Über Hans Magnus Enzensberger." In *Literaturmagazin 4. Die Literatur nach dem Tod der Literatur: Bilanz der Politizierung.* Ed. Hans Christoph Buch, 85–106. Rowohlt: Hamburg.

Lohner, Edgar. 1973. "Hans Magnus Enzensberger." In *Deutsche Dichter der Gegenwart.* Ed. Benno von Wiese, 531–44. Berlin: E. Schmidt.

Lyotard, Jean-François.1984. *The Postmodern Condition: A Report on Knowledge.* Trans. Geoff Bennington and Brian Massumi. Minneapolis: University of Minnesota Press.

Mandelbrot, Benoit B. 1975. *Les Objets Fractals.* Paris: Flammarion.

Maurina, Zenta. 1973. "Übersetzung als Umdichtung." In *Deutung und Bedeutung.* Ed. Brigitte Schludermann et al., 376–78. The Hague: Mouton.

Mayer, Hans. 1969. *Das Geschehen und das Schweigen: Aspekte der Literatur.* Frankfurt am Main: Suhrkamp.

McFarlane, James. 1953. "Modes of Translation." *Durham University Journal* 14:77–93.

Melin, Charlotte. 1983. "Hans Magnus Enzensberger and America: A Study of his Activities as a Poet, Translator and Editor." Ph.D. diss., University of Michigan.

———. 1987. "Enzensberger—A Self-Taught Lesson." *Germanic Notes* 18, nos. 1–2:4–5.

———. 1989. "A Look at Enzensberger's America Before and After 'On Leaving America.'" In *Amerika! New Images in German Literature.* Ed. Heinz D. Osterle, 293–313. New York: Peter Lang.

———. 1990. "A Proletarian Portrait?—Williams in East Germany." *William Carlos Williams Review* 16, no. 1:26–29.

———. 1991. "Autobiography and Epic in *Der Untergang der Titanic.*" *Germanic Notes* 22, nos. 1–2:14–16.

———. 1992. "Williams, Enzensberger, and Recent German Poetry." *Comparative Literature Studies* 29, no. 1:77–93.

Meyer-Clason, Curt. 1966. "Aus der Schule des Übersetzens. Persönliche Anmerkungen zu einem unpersönlichen Thema." In *Null und Zwanzig: Almanach der Nymphenburger Verlagshandlung 1946–1966,* 166–92. Munich: Nymphenburger.

Michel, Karl Markus. 1999. "Der eigensinnige Charakter: Sieben Variationen über ein Thema." In *Der Zorn altert, die Ironie ist unsterblich: Über Hans Magnus Enzensberger.* Ed. Rainer Wieland, 148–55. Frankfurt am Main: Suhrkamp.

Mignolo, Walter D. 1998. "Globalization, Civilization Process, and the Relocation of Languages and Cultures." In *The Cultures of Globalization.* Ed. Fredric Jameson and Masao Miyoshi, 32–53. Durham, N.C.: Duke University Press.

Monroe, Jonathan. 1987. *A Poverty of Objects: The Prose Poem and the Politics of Genre.* Ithaca, N.Y.: Cornell University Press.

———. 1997. "Between Ideologies and a Hard Place: Hans Magnus Enzensberger's Utopian Pragmatist Poetics." *Studies in Twentieth Century Literature* 21, no. 1:41–77.

Moretti, Nanni. 1994. *Caro Diario.* Video, 98 min. Milan: RCS Films.

Mueller, Agnes C. 1997. "Brücken zur Neuen Welt: Rezeption und Wirkung zeitgenössischer Amerikanischer Lyrik in der Bundesrepublik." Ph.D. diss., Vanderbilt University.

———. 1999. *Lyrik "made in USA": Vermittlung und Rezeption in der Bundesrepublik.* Amsterdam: Rodopi.

Muhr, Adelbert. 1960. "Glanz und Elend der Übersetzungen." *Wort in der Zeit* 6, no. 8:36–41.

Müller, Volker Ulrich. 1977. "Cuba, Machiavelli und Bakunin." In *Literatur und Studentenbewegung: Eine Zwischenbilanz.* Ed. W. Martin Lüdke, 90–123. Opladen: Westdeutscher.

Murphy, Robert John. 1992. "The Continuity and Consistency of Hans Magnus Enzensberger's Political Development in His Poetry and Essays." Ph.D. diss., University of Alberta.

Nägele, Rainer. 1984. "Das Werden im Vergehen oder Das untergehende Vaterland: Zu Enzensbergers Poetik und poetischer Verfahrensweise." In *Hans Magnus Enzensberger.* Ed. Reinhold Grimm, 204–31. Frankfurt am Main: Suhrkamp.

———. 1997. *Echoes of Translation: Reading between Texts.* Baltimore: Johns Hopkins University Press.

Nietzsche, Friedrich. 1982. *Also sprach Zarathustra.* Munich: Carl Hanser.

Nossack, Hans Erich. 1965. "Übersetzen und übersetzt werden." In *Übersetzen: Vorträge und Beiträge vom Internationalen Kongreß literarischer Übersetzer in Hamburg 1965.* Ed. Rolf Italiaander, 9–18. Frankfurt am Main: Athenäum.

Novak, Helga M. 1975. "Der Fortschritt des Grauens." *Der Spiegel* 29, no. 41:178–79.

Nussbaum, Martha C. 1995. *Poetic Justice: The Literary Imagination and Public Life.* Boston: Beacon.

Øhrgaard, Per. 1978. "Carceri d'invenzione: Über Enzensbergers *Mausoleum.*" *Text und Kontext* 6, nos. 1–2:416–28.

Oleschinski, Brigitte. 1999. "Sturmzwitter." *Lyrik: Über Lyrik*. Special issue of *Merkur* 53, nos. 3–4:389–95.

Pabisch, Peter. 1993. "Hans Magnus Enzensberger: 'landessprache.'" In *luslustigtig: Phänomene deutschsprachiger Lyrik 1945 bis 1980*, 48–60. Vienna: Böhlau.

Parkes, K. Stuart. 1986. "Hans Magnus Enzensberger: The Will o' the Wisp." In *Writers and Politics in West Germany*, 182–204. New York: St. Martin's.

Pastior, Oskar. 1975. "Prosatexte: Was aber ist die Übersetzbarkeit?" *Literatur und Kritik* 91:1.

Paulson, William R. 1988. *The Noise of Culture: Literary Texts in a World of Information*. Ithaca, N.Y.: Cornell University Press.

Peitgen, Heinz-Otto and Peter H. Richter. 1986. *The Beauty of Fractals: Images of Complex Dynamical Systems*. Berlin: Springer.

Perelman, Bob. 1996. *The Marginalization of Poetry: Language Writing and Literary History*. Princeton, N.J.: Princeton University Press.

Perloff, Marjorie. 1990. *Poetic License: Essays on Modernist and Postmodernist Lyric*. Evanston, Ill.: Northwestern University Press.

———. 1991. *Radical Artifice: Writing Poetry in the Age of Media*. Chicago: University of Chicago Press.

———. 1998. *Poetry on and off the Page: Essays for Emergent Occasions*. Evanston, Ill.: Northwestern University Press.

Peters, Robert. 1981. "Meeting Mick Jagger." In *The Brand-X Anthology of Poetry: Burnt Norton Edition*, 296–97. Cambridge: Apple-Wood.

Petersdorff, Dirk von. 1996. "Im Nachhall der Systeme: Literatur und Anthropologie. Wieland, Henscheid, Enzensberger." *Neue Rundschau* 107, no. 2:35–49.

———. 1997. "Neue Medien." *Neue Rundschau* 108, no. 1:168–72.

Pinsky, Robert. 1976. *The Situation of Poetry: Contemporary Poetry and Its Traditions*. Princeton, N.J.: Princeton University Press.

Poe, Edgar Allan. 1965. "The Philosophy of Composition." In *Literary Criticism of Edgar Allan Poe*. Ed. Robert L. Hough, 20–32. Lincoln: University of Nebraska Press.

Porush, David. 1991. "Fictions as Dissipative Structures: Prigogine's Theory and Postmodernism's Roadshow." In *Chaos and Order: Complex Dynamics in Literature and Science*. Ed. N. Katherine Hayles, 54–84. Chicago: University of Chicago Press.

Pound, Ezra. 1953. *Dichtung und Prosa: Mit einem Geleitwort von T. S. Eliot*. Trans. Eva Hesse. Zurich: Arche.

———. 1956. *Selected Poems of Ezra Pound*. New York: New Directions.

———. 1968. "How to Read." In *Literary Essays of Ezra Pound*, 15–40. New York: New Directions.

Price, Derek de Solla. 1975. "Celestial Clockwork in Greece and China." In *Science since Babylon,* 25–48. New Haven, Conn.: Yale University Press.

Price, Lawrence Marsden. 1966. *The Reception of United States Literature in Germany.* Chapel Hill: University of North Carolina Press.

Rabassa, Gregory. 1987. Preface to *The World of Translation.* Conference on Literary Translation, New York, 1970. New York: PEN American Center.

Ransom, John Crowe. 1968. "Criticism, Inc." In *The World's Body,* 327–50. Kingsport: Louisiana State University Press.

Reichert, Klaus. 1967. "Zur Technik des Übersetzens amerikanischer Gedichte." *Sprache im Technischen Zeitalter* 21:1–16.

Reinhold, Ursula. 1971. "Literatur und Politik bei Enzensberger." *Weimarer Beiträge* 17, no. 5:94–113.

———. 1981. "Geschichtliche Konfrontation und poetische Produktivität: Zu H. M. Enzensberger in den siebziger Jahren." *Weimarer Beiträge* 27, no. 1:104–27.

Riebling, Barbara. 1993. "Remodeling Truth, Power and Society: Implications of Chaos Theory, Nonequilibrium Dynamics and Systems Science for the Study of Politics and Literature." In *After Poststructuralism.* Ed. Nancy Easterlin and Barbara Riebling, 177–201. Evanston, Ill.: Northwestern University Press.

Rilke, Rainer Maria. 1996. "Rose, oh reiner Widerspruch." In *Rainer Maria Rilke: Werke.* Vol 2. *Gedichte 1910–1926.* Ed. Manfred Engel et al., 394. Frankfurt am Main: Insel.

Rimmon-Kenan, Shlomith. 1983. *Narrative Fiction: Contemporary Poetics.* London: Methuen.

Ritter-Santini, Lea. 1984. "Ein Paar geflügelter Schuhe." In *Hans Magnus Enzensberger.* Ed. Reinhold Grimm, 232–36. Frankfurt am Main: Suhrkamp.

Roberts, David. 1996. Introduction to *Debating Enzensberger: Great Migration and Civil War.* Ed. Gerhard Fischer, ix–xvi. Tübingen: Stauffenburg.

Rodiek, Christoph. 1990. "Lyrische Weltsprache als Intertext: Zum anthologischen Verfahren in H. M. Enzensbergers *Museum der modernen Poesie.*" *Germanisch-Romanische Monatsschrift* 40, no. 2:190–205.

Rohn, Matthew. 1987. *Visual Dynamics in Jackson Pollock's Abstractions.* Ann Arbor, Mich.: UMI Research Press.

Rolleston, James. 1981. "Der Drang nach Synthese: Benn, Brecht und die Poetik der fünfziger Jahren." In *Die deutsche Lyrik 1945–1975.* Ed. Klaus Weissenberger, 78–94. Düsseldorf: August Bagel.

———. 1987. "Double Time, Double Language: Benn, Celan, Enzensberger." In *Narratives of Ecstasy,* 133–74. Detroit: Wayne State University Press.

———. 1997. Introduction to *Contemporary German Poetry.* Special issue of *Studies in Twentieth Century Literature* 21, no. 1:7–8.

Rorty, Richard. 1989. *Contingency, Irony, and Solidarity.* Cambridge: Cambridge University Press.

Rowohlt, Ernst. 1950. "Befruchtung oder Überschwemmung?" *Das literarische Deutschland* 1, no. 1:9.

Rühmkorf, Peter. 1962. "Das lyrische Weltbild der Nachkriegsdeutschen." In *Bestandsaufnahme: Eine deutsche Bilanz 1962.* Ed. Hans Werner Richter, 447–76. Munich: Kurt Desch.

———. 1999. "Der Sänger und sein Widergänger," In *Der Zorn altert, die Ironie ist unsterblich: Über Hans Magnus Enzensberger.* Ed. Rainer Wieland, 169–81. Frankfurt am Main: Suhrkamp.

Rutschky, Michael. 1998. "Was ist Lyrik heute?" *Neue Deutsche Literatur* 4:169–84.

Ryan, Judith. 1980. "Ezra Pound und Gottfried Benn: Avantgarde, Faschismus und ästhetische Autonomie." In *Faschismus und Avantgarde.* Ed. Reinhold Grimm and Jost Hermand, 20–34. Konigstein: Athenäum.

———. 1982. " 'Your life jacket is under your skin': Reflections on German Poetry of the Seventies." *German Quarterly* 60, no. 3:296–308.

———. 1992. "Dead Poets' Voices: Rilke's 'Lost from the Outset' and the Originality Effect." *Modern Language Quarterly* 53, no. 2 (June): 227–45.

———. 1997. " 'Deckname Lyrik': Poetry after 1945 and 1989." In *Wendezeiten, Zeitenwenden: Positionsbestimmungen zur deutschsprachigen Literatur 1945–1995.* Ed. Robert Weninger and Brigitte Rossbacher, 37–54. Tübingen: Stauffenburg.

Sadji, Amadou Booker. 1984. "Hans Magnus Enzensberger und die 'Dritte Welt.' " In *Hans Magnus Enzensberger.* Ed. Reinhold Grimm, 258–75. Frankfurt am Main: Suhrkamp.

Sartorius, Joachim, ed. 1996. *Atlas der neuen Poesie.* Hamburg: Rowohlt.

———. 1998. " 'Language, Foreign: Saying You and Being Heard': On Poetry in German, 1986–1996." Trans. Melanie Richter-Bernburg. *Contemporary German Poetry.* Special issue of *Poetry* 173, no. 1:121–28.

———. 1999. "Schmuggler, Torwächter, Virtuose: Hans Magnus Enzensberger als Vermittler." In *Der Zorn altert, die Ironie ist unsterblich: Über Hans Magnus Enzensberger.* Ed. Rainer Wieland, 204–9. Frankfurt am Main: Suhrkamp.

———, ed. 1991. *William Carlos Williams: Der Harte Kern der Schönheit.* Munich: Hanser.

Saunders, Frances Stonor. 1999. *The Cultural Cold War: The CIA and the World of Arts and Letters.* New York: New Press.

Schadewaldt, Wolfgang. 1970. "Das Problem des Übersetzens." In *Hellas und Hesperien,* 608–22. Zurich: Artemis.

Schäfer, Hans Dieter. 1977. "Zur Periodisierung der deutschen Literatur seit 1930." In *Literaturmagazin 7: Nachkriegsliteratur.* Ed. Nicolas Born and Jürgen Mauthey, 95–115. Hamburg: Rowohlt.

———. 1981. "Zusammenhänge der deutschen Gegenwartslyrik." In *Deutsche*

Gegenwartsliteratur: Ausgangspositionen und aktuelle Entwicklungen. Ed.
Manfred Durzak, 166–203. Stuttgart: Reclam.

Schickel, Joachim, ed. 1970. *Über Hans Magnus Enzensberger.* Frankfurt am
Main: Suhrkamp.

Schimmel, Annemarie. 1980. ". . . und singe sie für die Welt." *Deutsche Akademie
für Sprache und Dichtung Jahrbuch 1980,* 98–101. Darmstadt: Deutsche
Akademie für Sprache und Dichtung.

Schirmer, Walter F. 1954. *Geschichte der englischen und amerikanischen Literatur
von Anfängen bis zur Gegenwart.* Tübingen: Niemeyer.

Schmied, Wieland. 1961. "Wolfslyrik—Nicht Schafslyrik." *Wort in der Zeit*
3:4–6.

Schmitt-Kaufhold, Angelika. 1977. *Nordamerikanische Literatur im deutschen
Sprachraum nach 1945.* Frankfurt am Main: Peter Lang.

Schnell, Ralf. 1993. *Geschichte der deutschsprachigen Literatur seit 1945.* Stuttgart:
Metzler.

Schödlbauer, Ulrich. 1995. "Die Modernitätsfalle der Lyrik." *Merkur* 49, no. 2
(February): 171–77.

Schonauer, Franz. 1969. "Literaturkritik und Restauration." In
Bestandsaufnahme: Eine deutsche Bilanz 1962. Ed. Hans Werner Richter,
477–93. Munich: Kurt Desch.

Schrott, Raoul, ed. 1998. *Die Erfindung der Poesie: Gedichte aus den ersten
viertausend Jahren.* Frankfurt am Main: Eichborn.

Schulte, Rainer, and John Biguenet, eds. 1992. *Theories of Translation: An
Anthology of Essays from Dryden to Derrida.* Chicago: University of Chicago
Press.

Schultz, Karla Lydia. 1984. "Ex negativo: Enzensberger mit und gegen Adorno."
In *Hans Magnus Enzensberger.* Ed. Reinhold Grimm, 237–57. Frankfurt am
Main: Suhrkamp.

———. 1986. "Writing as Disappearing: Enzensberger's Negative Utopian
Move." *Monatshefte* 78, no. 2:195–202.

———. 1993. "Lyrik und Engagement: Enzensberger contra Friedrich."
Monatshefte 85, no. 4:430–37.

Schumacher, Horst. 1981a. "Entwicklungsphasen der modernen
deutschsprachigen Lyrik." In *Weltliteratur im 20. Jahrhundert.* Ed. Manfred
Brauneck, 56–68. Reinbek: Rowohlt.

———. 1981b. "Entwicklungsphasen moderner deutscher Lyrik seit 1945."
Universitas 36, no. 7:927–34.

Schürenberg, Walter. 1956. "Über einige Verschiedenheiten des Englischen und
Deutschen." *Akzente* 5:420–25.

Schwab-Felisch, Hans. 1963. "Hans Magnus Enzensberger." In *Schriftsteller der
Gegenwart.* Ed. Klaus Nonnemann, 102–8. Freiburg: Olten.

Schwedhelm, Karl. 1947. "Übersetzung Übertragung Nachdichtung: Möglichkeiten der Verdeutschung von Gedichten." *Aussaat* 1, nos. 10–11:14–15.

Schwenk, Theodor. 1976. *Sensitive Chaos*. London: Rudolf Steiner.

Seeba, Hinrich C. 1981. "Der Untergang der Utopie: Ein Schiffbruch in der Gegenwartsliteratur." *German Studies Review* 2:281–98.

Sewell, William S. 1979. "Hans Magnus Enzensberger and William Carlos Williams: Economy, Detail and Suspicion of Doctrine." *German Life and Letters* 32:153–65.

Sieburth, Richard. 1989. "Benjamin the Scrivner." In *Benjamin: Philosophy, History, Aesthetics*. Ed. Gary Smith, 13–37. Chicago: University of Chicago Press.

Silens, Peter. 1959. "Zorn in dieser Zeit: Zu den Gedichten von Hans Magnus Enzensbergers *Verteidigung der Wölfe*." *Telegraf*, 13 April.

Simic, Charles. 1999. "Das Leben der Alchimisten." In *Der Zorn altert, die Ironie ist unsterblich: Über Hans Magnus Enzensberger*. Ed. Rainer Wieland, 128. Frankfurt am Main: Suhrkamp.

Sontag, Susan. 1976. "Against Interpretation." In *Against Interpretation and Other Essays*, 3–14. New York: Farrar, Straus and Giroux, 1966. Reprint, New York: Schocken (page references are to reprint edition).

Sorg, Bernhard. 1985. "Komödie und Rechenschaftsbericht: Zu H. M. Enzensbergers *Der Untergang der Titanic*." *Hans Magnus Enzensberger*. Special issue of *Text + Kritik* 49 (1976; reprint, 1985): 44–51 (page references are to reprint edition).

Spengler, Oswald. 1940. *Today and Destiny: Vital Excerpts from* The Decline of the West *of Oswald Spengler*. Ed. Edwin Franden Dakin. Trans. Charles Francis Atkinson. New York: Knopf.

Staiger, Emil. 1946. *Grundbegriffe der Poetik*. Zurich: Atlantis.

———. 1991. *Basic Concepts of Poetry*. Ed. Marianne Burkhard and Luanne T. Frank. Trans. Janette C. Hudson and Luanne T. Frank. University Park, Pa.: Penn State University Press.

Stavropoulos, Pam. 1996. "Eliding Politics: Enzensberger and the Aesthetics of Evasion." In *Debating Enzensberger: Great Migration and Civil War*. Ed. Gerhard Fischer, 73–91. Tübingen: Stauffenburg.

Stein, Kevin. 1996. " 'The Hour Farthest from God': Ethical Matters in Carolyn Forché's Poetry." In *Private Poets, Worldly Acts*, 144–65. Athens: Ohio University Press.

Steiner, George. 1981. *After Babel: Aspects of Language and Translation*. London: Oxford University Press.

Stephan, Jakob. 1998. "Lyrische Visite (10)." *Neue Rundschau* 109, no. 4:153–61.

Stevens, Wallace. 1972. "Sad Strains of a Gay Waltz." In *The Palm at the End of the Mind: Selected Poems and a Play*, 116–17. New York: Vintage.

————. 1995. *The Man with the Blue Guitar/Der Mann mit der blauen Gitarre.* Trans. Karin Graf and H. M. Enzensberger. Munich: Schirmer, Mosel.

Stoffer-Heibel, Cornelia. 1981. *Metapherstudien: Versuch einer Typologie der Text- und Themafunktionen der Metaphorik in der Lyrik Ingeborg Bachmanns, Peter Huchels und Hans Magnus Enzensbergers.* Stuttgart: Akademischer Verlag Hans-Dieter Heinz.

Stoicheff, Peter. 1991. "The Chaos of Metafiction." In *Chaos and Order: Complex Dynamics in Literature and Science.* Ed. N. Katherine Hayles, 85–99. Chicago: University of Chicago Press.

Suhrkamp, Peter. 1956. "Der Verleger—und die Übersetzung." *Akzente* 6:561–66.

Sulzer, Dieter, Hildegard Dieke, and Ingrid Kußmaul. 1987. "Hans Magnus Enzensberger 1963." In *Der Georg-Büchner-Preis 1951–1987,* 153–64. Munich: Piper.

Teraoka, Arlene A. 1996. " 'World Theater' vs. 'European Periphery': Third World Paradigms in Peter Weiss and Hans Magnus Enzensberger." In *East, West, and Others: The Third World in Postwar German Literature,* 27–78. Lincoln: University of Nebraska Press.

Theobaldy, Jürgen, and Gustav Züricher. 1976. *Veränderung der Lyrik: Über westdeutsche Gedichte seit 1965.* Munich: Edition Text + Kritik.

Thomasberger, Andreas. 1994. *Verwandlungen in Hofmannsthals Lyrik.* Tübingen: Niemeyer.

Tranter, John. 1995. "Three Poems & amp: An Interview." Interview by John Kinsella. Available on-line from epc.buffalo.edu/authors/tranter/jtiv.html.

Treichel, Hans-Ulrich. 1999. " 'Von mir selber würde ich nie und nimmer reden.' " *Zur Lyrik Hans Magnus Enzensbergers.* Special issue of *Merkur* 53:367–73.

Trommler, Frank. 1970. "Der 'Nullpunkt 1945' und seine Verbindlichkeit für die Literaturgeschichte." *Basis: Jahrbuch für deutsche Gegenwartsliteratur* 1:9–25.

————. 1971. "Der zögernde Nachwuchs: Entwicklungsprobleme der Nachkriegsliteratur in Ost und West." In *Tendenzen der deutschen Literatur seit 1945.* Ed. Thomas Koebner, 1–116. Stuttgart: Kröner.

————. 1977. "Nachkriegsliteratur—eine neue deutsche Literatur?" In *Literaturmagazin 7: Nachkriegsliteratur.* Ed. Nicolas Born and Jürgen Mauthey, 167–86. Hamburg: Rowohlt.

Urban, Peter. 1972. "Čechov übersetzen." *Theater heute* 13, no. 5:29–33.

————. 1981. "Neugier und Leidenschaft auch." *Theater heute* 22, no. 1:50–52.

Volckmann, Silvia. 1979. "Gottfried Benn und H. M. Enzensberger: Chopin-Gedichte," In *Geschichte im Gedicht: Texte und Interpretationen. Protestlied, Bänkelsang, Ballade, Chronik.* Ed. Walter Hinck, 280–91. Frankfurt am Main: Suhrkamp.

Vormweg, Heinrich. 1981. "Deutsche Literatur 1945–1960: Keine Stunde Null."

In *Deutsche Gegenwartsliteratur: Ausgangspositionen und aktuelle Entwicklungen*. Ed. Manfred Durzak, 14–31. Stuttgart: Reclam.

Walser, Martin. 1999. "Einer der auszog, das Fürchten zu verlernen." In *Der Zorn altert, die Ironie ist unsterblich: Über Hans Magnus Enzensberger*. Ed. Rainer Wieland, 18–22. Frankfurt am Main: Suhrkamp.

Weaver, Mike. 1971. *William Carlos Williams: The American Background*. Cambridge: Cambridge University Press.

Weissbort, Daniel, ed. 1989. *Translating Poetry: The Double Labyrinth*. Houndmills, Eng.: Macmillan.

Weissenberger, Klaus, ed. 1981. *Die deutsche Lyrik 1945–1975*. Düsseldorf: August Bagel.

Wellershoff, Dieter. 1997. "Alle Dinge sprechen." *Neue Rundschau* 108, no. 4:123–38.

Werner, Klaus. 1968. "Zur Brecht-Rezeption bei Günther Kunert und Hans Magnus Enzensberger." In *Brecht-Sonderheft*. Special issue of *Weimarer Beiträge*. Berlin: Aufbau, 61–73.

West, Paul. 1981. "Drowning as One of the Fine Arts." *Parnassus* (spring/summer): 91–109.

Weyrauch, Wolfgang, ed. 1949. *Tausend Gramm: Sammlung neuer deutscher Geschichten*. Hamburg: Rowohlt.

Widmer, Urs. 1966. *1945 oder die "Neue Sprache."* Düsseldorf: Pädagogischer Verlag Schwann.

Wieland, Christoph Martin. 1984. "Die Aeronauten." In *Sämtliche Werke*. Vol. 10. Ed. Hamburger Stiftung zur Förderung von Wissenschaft und Kultur, Wieland Archiv, and Hans Radspieler, 40–136. Hamburg: Hamburger Stiftung zur Förderung von Wissenschaft und Kultur.

Wieland, Rainer, ed. 1999. *Der Zorn altert, die Ironie ist unsterblich: Über Hans Magnus Enzensberger*. Frankfurt am Main: Suhrkamp.

Williams, Eric B. 1993. *The Mirror and the Word: Modernism, Literary Theory and Georg Trakl*. Lincoln: University of Nebraska Press.

Williams, William Carlos. 1951. "the r r bums." Trans. Rainer M. Gerhardt. *Fragmente* 1:17–18.

———. 1963. *Paterson*. New York: New Directions.

———. 1967a. *The Autobiography of William Carlos Williams*. New York: New Directions.

———. 1967b. *Pictures from Brueghel*. New York: New Directions.

———. 1969. *Selected Essays*. New York: New Directions.

Wilpert, Gero von. 1969. *Sachwörterbuch der Literatur*. Stuttgart: Kröner.

Witting, Gunther. 1981. "Übernahme und Opposition: Zu H. M. Enzensbergers Gattungsinnovationen." *Germanisch-Romanische Monatsschrift* 62:432–61.

Wittstock, Uwe. 1989. *Von der Stalinallee zum Prenzlauer Berg: Wege der DDR-Literatur 1949–1989*. Munich: Piper.

Wittstock, Uwe, and Hubert Winkels. 1992. "Wieviel Literatur im Leben, wieviel Politik in der Poesie? Eine Umtrage unter deutschsprachigen Schriftstellern der Jahrgänge 1950–1966." *Neue Rundschau* 103, no. 2:95–136.

Wodtke, Friedrich Wilhelm. 1968. "Die Entwicklung der deutschen Lyrik seit 1945." *Wissenschaftliches Jahrbuch der Philosophischen Fakultät der Universität Athen,* 267–338. Athens: University of Athens.

Wollschläger, Hans. 1976. "Am Ende eines 'Welt-Alltags.'" *Ensemble* 7:156–68.

Wunberg, Gotthard. 1964. "Die Funktion des Zitats In den politischen Gedichten von H. M. Enzensberger." *Neue Sammlung* 4, no. 3:274–82.

Wuthenow, Ralph-Rainer. 1969. *Das fremde Kunstwerk: Aspekte der literarischen Übersetzung.* Göttingen: Vandenhoeck and Ruprecht.

Ziebritzski, Henning. 1997. "Vielen Dank für mein sonderbares Gehirn: Bemerkungen zur religiösen Thematik in H. M. Enzensbergers Gedichtband *Kiosk.*" *Neue Rundschau* 4:53–66.

Zimmer, Bernhard. 1988. "Literary Criticism from 1933 to the Present." In *A History of German Literary Criticism, 1730–1980.* Ed. Peter Uwe Hohendahl. Trans. Franz Blaha et al., 359–437. Lincoln: University of Nebraska Press.

Zimmermann, Arthur. 1977. *Hans Magnus Enzensberger: Die Gedichte und ihre literaturkritische Rezeption.* Bonn: Bouvier.

Zuidervaart, Lambert. 1991. *Adorno's Aesthetic Theory: The Redemption of Illusion.* Cambridge, Mass.: MIT Press.

Zuther, Gerhard H. W. 1965. *Eine Bibliographie der Aufnahme amerikanischer Literatur in deutschen Zeitschriften 1945–1960.* Munich: Dissertations Druck Franz Frank.

Index

Adenauer, Konrad, 165

Adorno, Theodor W., x, 10, 102, 127, 217n12, 218n26; influence of, 49–50, 101, 129; and poetry after Auschwitz, 6, 33, 120, 178, 181. WORKS: *Ästhetische Theorie,* 132–33; on Beethoven, 187; "Commitment," 178, 182; *Minima Moralia,* 32; "Rede über Lyrik und Gesellschaft (On Lyric Poetry and Society)," 32, 33; "Retour à l'expéditeur (Addressee Unknown)," 32–33; "Valéry Proust Museum," 48, 203n13

African-American folk songs, 143

Agitprop verse. *See* Politics

Akzente (literary journal), 17, 18, 96

Altieri, Charles, 84, 90, 97

American Association of Teachers of German, 126

American New Criticism, 47

American poetry, 49, 202n5, 215n60; Anglo-American, 47, 63, 206–7n47; anthologized, 39, 51, 86; compared to French, 101; compared to German, 160, 162, 186; German connection, 11, 203n15, 206–7n47; German interest in, 39, 46, (wanes) 40; imagist, 11–12, 53, 56, 203n15; modern, 72, 79, 212n41, (discussed) 53–55, 207n1, (parodied) 62–63; Poetry Month, 202n4; prose poems, 87, 101; readership of, 28, 29; translated, 18–19

American Poetry Review, 178, 179, 180

Andersch, Alfred, 75; *Deutsche Literatur in der Entscheidung (German Literature at the Decision Point),* 38

Anderson, Sascha, 160

Anderson, Sherwood, 52; *Winesburg, Ohio,* 53

Anthologies, x, xiii, xv, 10, 15, 30, 40, 206n41; of American poetry, 39, 51, 86; function of, 211–12n36. *See also* Enzensberger, Hans Magnus: ANTHOLOGIES/TRANSLATIONS

Aragon, Louis, 15

Arendt, Erich, 85, 205n28

Arendt, Hannah, 169–70

257

Darwin, Charles, 117, 119

"Death of literature," 27, 37, 97–100, 103, 202n3, 206n38

De' Dondi, Giovanni, 104, 110–13, 116; ballad about, 107, 108–13

Demetz, Peter, 206n37

Derrida, Jacques, 14, 128, 221n19

Deschner, Karlheinz, 214n53

Deutsche Universitätszeitung (literary journal), 215n59

Dickinson, Emily, 46, 220n9

Diego, Gerardo, 47

Dietschreit, Frank, 84, 97, 153

Discursive style, 69–82, 83, 121, 148, 150; of American poetry, 19; defined, 207–8n1

Domin, Hilde, 21, 205n28

Donne, John, 219n38

Döring, Stefan, 226n34

Dove, Rita, 207n47

Drawert, Kurt, 27

Drews, Jörg, 206n37; *Das bleibt: Deutsche Gedichte 1945–1995 (That Remains: German Poetry 1945–1995)*, 29–30

Du (cultural magazine), 225n27

Dylan, Bob, 221–22n20

Dystopian literature, 105, 153, 186

Easthope, Anthony, 63. WORKS: *Contemporary Poetry Meets Modern Theory* (co-editor), xi; *Poetry as Discourse*, xi

Eich, Günter, 23, 181, 196, 201n1, 214n53; Enzensberger dedicates poem to, 55. WORKS: "Inventur (Inventory)," 38, 77; *Zu den Akten*, 201n1

Eichendorff, Joseph, 6

Einstein, Albert, 144

Electronic media, xi, 100, 173, 183, 196; effects of, 27, 178, 191; Internet sites,

31, 178, 202n4, 225n25; print and audio CD, 22; radio plays, 80, 124, 221n13; skepticism toward, 31, 50, 197

Eliot, T. S., 39, 45, 47, 53, 67, 213n43, 221–22n20. WORKS: "A Coronal," 65; "The Hollow Men," 65, 66–67, 137, 139; "The Love Song of J. Alfred Prufrock," 173, 176; "Preludes," 64–65, 66; "Rhapsody on a Windy Night," 66; translated, 62, 63, 65–66; "Triumphal March," 66

Emmerich, Wolfgang, 206n37

Encounter (journal), 163

Enigma code, German, 171

Enlightenment, the, 112, 117, 164

Entstellung technique, 9, 121, 203n11

Enzensberger, Hans Magnus: and American poetry, 39–40; conversations and interviews with, 12, 187, 209n7, 222n20, 225n25; lectures at University of Frankfurt, 102; as parodist, 43, 62–63, 68–69, 72; political views, xiii, 9–10, 162, 165–69; pseudonyms used by, 145, 146, 205n34; recognition and awards, ix, 81–82; speaks at Nobel Symposium, 25; translations of works of, ix, 23, 207n47, 225n28; as translator, ix, xiii, 15, 18–25, 44, 62–66, 148–49, 178; travels, 63, 90, 124, 135, 136, 162, 167, 206n42, 223n8, 226n29. ANTHOLOGIES/TRANSLATIONS: *Die Andere Bibliothek*, x, 145; *Ein Buch von Göttern und Teufeln*, 178; *César Vallejo*, 19; *David Rokeah*, 205n27; *Edward Lears kompletter Nonsens (Edward Lear's Complete Nonsense)*, 22, 132, 208n2; *Franco Fortini*, 19; *Geisterstimmen (Phantom Voices)*, 24; *Eine literarische Landkarte (A Liter-*

Eurocentrism, xiv, 166, 171, 210n19
Evans, Oliver, 118
Even-Zohar, Itamar, 17
Evergreen Review, 178

Falkner, Gerhard, 30, 31; *Über den Unwert des Gedichts (On the Worthlessness of the Poem),* 29
The Family of Man (photographic exhibition), 11
Fascism, 4, 41, 210n25; antifascist criticism, 8; avoided as topic, 5; rhetoric of, 43, 169–70, 180; rise of, 39
Faulkner, William, 50, 52
Federal Republic of Germany, 63, 164, 209n15
Feigenbaum, Mitchel, 220n3
Ferber, Christian, 40
Fischer, Gerhard, 216n5
Fleischmann, Wolfgang B., 18–19
Fluxus artists, 207n47
Forché, Carolyn, xiv, 162, 179. WORKS: *Against Forgetting,* 181–83; "El Salvador," 180
Foucault, Michel, x, xiii, 101, 132, 219n36. WORKS: *The Archaeology of Knowledge,* 105, 219n36; *Madness and Civilization,* 133; *The Order of Things,* 219n36
Fourier, Charles, 118
Fractals, 125, 128, 156, 157, 172, 220n8
Frank, Armin Paul, 212n36
Frankfurt school, xii, 102
Franz, Michael, 218n26
Fredman, Stephen, 86–87, 101
Freiburg circle, 43
French poetry: compared to American, 101; symbolist, 47, 120
French Revolution, 117
Freud, Sigmund, 14
Frey, John R., 39, 40
Fried, Erich, 80, 86, 141, 164, 182,

214n53; as translator, 18, 21, 45, 68, 205n28
Friedrich, Caspar David: "The Sea of Ice," 147
Friedrich, Hugo, 47–48, 49; influence of, x, xii, 21, 45, 206n39; *Die Struktur der modernen Lyrik (The Structure of Modern Poetry),* 46, 47
Frischmuth, Barbara, 21
Fritz, Walter Helmut: *Bemerkungen zu einer Gegend,* 104
Fulbright Foundation, 214n52

Gadamer, Hans Georg, 20, 47, 211n29
Galinsky, Hans, 208n7, 212n40, 213n48
Gehring, Hansjörg, 39
Genocide, 107–8, 114–15, 120, 171
George, Stefan, 47
Gerhardt, Rainer Maria, 40, 43, 149, 207nn47,51, 208n7; Enzensberger dedicates poem to, 62; radio broadcasts, 216n68
German Democratic Republic (GDR), 27, 85, 164
German expressionism, 45, 47, 104
German postwar verse, xi–xii, 3–13, 98, 198; Allied occupation and, 39; American compared to, 160, 162, 186; American influence on/knowledge of, 37, 179–80, 203n15; Auschwitz and, 40–41, 81; authorial presence and, 160; ballads, 104; bleak prognosis for, 26–31; cold war politics and, 63; debates about, 13, 25, 38, 160–61; East German, 160; electronic media and, 178; Enzensberger's influence on, 141, 212n40; evolution of/changes in, 41, 85, 149, 186, (traditional form returns) 153; expectations for, 156; literary interpretation of, 47; nature

poetry, 41–42, 126, 153, (parodied) 43; 1960s–1980s, 85, 128, 153; translation and, 13–25

Ginsberg, Allen, 214n53, 220n1

Gleick, James, 134, 144, 220n3; *Chaos: Making a New Science,* 127

Gödel, Kurt, 130–31, 133, 173, 222n21

Goethe, Johann Wolfgang von, 6, 7–8, 43, 154, 175, 190, 196. WORKS: "An den Mond," 197; *Faust,* 139, 192; "Selige Sehnsucht," 193

Golding, Alan, 202n5, 211n36, 216n8

Gomringer, Eugen, 85

Goodbody, Axel, 153

Gottsched, Johann Christoph, 14, 15

Gramsci, Antonio, 223n5

Grass, Günter, 54, 81, 129, 182

Great Depression, 169

Green movement, 153

Grimm, Erik, 178

Grimm, Jakob and Wilhelm: "Von dem Machandelboom (The Juniper Tree)," 56

Grimm, Reinhold, 22, 48, 56, 133, 153. WORKS: "Bildnis Hans Magnus Enzensberger," 162; "Montierte Lyrik (Montaged Poetry)," 45, 57

Grünbein, Durs, 27, 31

Gruppe 47 (Princeton, N.J.), 85, 135

Gryphius, Andreas, 196; "Abend," 197

Guevara de la Serna, Ernesto "Che," 168, 172; ballad about, 104, 107, 120, 117, 119

Guillory, John, 202n5, 218n29

Guillotin, Joseph Ignac, 117, 172, 218n28

Gültig, Hans, 23

Gumpel, Liselotte, 56

Gustafsson, Lars, x

Gutenberg, Johann, 31, 114

Habermas, Jürgen, x, xiii, 101, 139, 211n27, 218nn25,30; on learning, 217n21, 219n41. WORKS: *Legitimation Crisis,* 102, 103, 117, 130; *Technik und Wissenschaft (Technology and Science),* 102

Hacks, Peter, 161

Hage, Volker: *Lyrik für Leser,* 99

Hagelstange, Rudolf (poet-translator), 205n28

Hahn, Ulla, 161, 207nn48,51

Haller, Albrecht von, 172

Hamburger, Michael, 22, 216n6

Haney, David P., 211n29

Hansen, Kurt Heinrich, 19, 45

Hardy, Thomas: "The Convergence of the Twain," 133

Harnhardt video collection, 225n25

Harper's magazine, ix, 178

Hartung, Harald, 28, 96; *Luftfracht,* 206n41

Haussmann, Baron Georg Eugène, 119

Hayles, N. Katharine, 140, 141, 158; *Chaos and Order: Complex Dynamics in Literature and Science,* 127–28

Heidegger, Martin, 7, 154; *Sein und Zeit,* 202n7

Heine, Heinrich, 172

Heinrich Heine Prize, 81

Heinze-Dietschreit, Barbara, 84, 97, 153

Heissenbüttel, Helmut, 45, 94, 205n28

Hensel, Georg, 161

Henze, Hans Werner, 222n22

Hermetic verse, 42, 85, 91, 118

Hermlin, Stephan, 45, 160, 205n28

Hesse, Eva, 18, 19, 21–22, 45, 212n43, 215n59

Heuss, Theodor, 209n15, 212n37

Heym, Georg, 104

Hielscher, Martin, 29

Hilbig, Wolfgang, 27

Hildesheimer, Wolfgang, 23

Hiroshima, 40, 41

Hitler, Adolf, 42, 69, 72; rhetoric of, 203n11

Hoffmann, E. T. A., 172

Hofmannsthal, Hugo von, 47, 223n30

Holden, Jonathan, 79, 80

Hölderlin, Friedrich, 6, 63

Höllerer, Walter, 18, 95–96, 203n15, 208n7, 209n8; Enzensberger paro dies, 43

Hollo, Anselm (poet), 222n27

Holocaust, the, 115, 164, 182; poetry after, 80, 181; as subject, 41, 108, 160

Holthusen, Hans Egon, 19, 47, 216n5

Hölzer, Max, 20–21

Homer, 6, 57

Hopkins, Gerard Manley, 46

Huchel, Peter, 85, 182

Hulme, T. E., 203n15

Hulse, Michael, 213n47

Humboldt, Alexander von, 116, 118, 171

Huyssen, Andreas, 31, 105, 220n4

Ignatow, David: "How Come," 74

Imagist poetry, 88–89; American origins of, 11–12, 53, 56, 203n15

Industrial Revolution, 100, 117

Inquisition, the, 115

Internet, the. *See* Electronic media

Irigary, Luce, 128

Jahn, Janheinz, 21

Jahrbuch für Amerikastudien (annual), 18

Jameson, Fredric, 128, 211n27, 224n17; "Aesthetics and Politics," 179

Jandl, Ernst, 31, 85

Janson, H. W., 222n24

Jens, Walter, 21

Johnson, Uwe: *Mutmassungen über Jakob (Speculations about Jacob)*, 165

Joyce, James, 11, 53, 133

Kafka, Franz, 50. WORKS: "Josefine, die Sängerin oder Das Volk der Mäuse (Josephine the Singer, or the Mouse Folk)," 97; "Die Sorge des Hausvaters (The Cares of a Family Man)," 188–89

Kahlschlag (a clear-cutting), 38

Kaiser, Joachim, 161

Kapur, Geeta, 163

Karsunke, Yaak, 81, 86

Kaschnitz, Marie Luise, 45, 47; *Zukunftsmusik*, 155–56, 189

Kayser, Wolfgang, 104; *Kleine deutsche Versschule (Little German Verse School)*, 6, 8

Kenner, Hugh, x, 139; *The Counterfeiters*, 106, 118

Kepler, Johannes, 171

Kerouac, Jack, 51; *On the Road*, 51

Kirsch, Rainer: *Das Wort und seine Strahlung (The Word and Its Radiance)*, 21

Kirsch, Sarah, 27, 81, 85, 161, 182, 203n14

Kiwus, Karin, 27

Kling, Thomas, 31, 226n34

Kluge, Alexander, 226n36

Knape, Franz Josef, 209–10n16, 213n48

Knörrich, Otto, 206n37

Koepke, Wulf, 45

Köhler, Barbara, 31

Kolbe, Uwe, 27, 226n34

Koller, Christine, 68

Kolmar, Gertrud, 182

Korte, Hermann, 26, 38, 81, 85, 153

Krechel, Ursula, 27, 217n15

Kristeva, Julia: *Revolution in Poetic Language*, xi

Krolow, Karl, 40, 41, 47, 95–96, 207n51; as translator, 16, 17, 18, 45

Kruntorad, Paul, 205n27

Kußmaul, Ingrid, 161